# Double Vision

# Double Vision

## Ben H. Bagdikian

*Reflections on My Heritage, Life, and Profession*

BEACON PRESS Boston

Beacon Press
25 Beacon Street
Boston, Massachusetts 02108-2892
www.beacon.org

Beacon Press books
are published under the auspices of
the Unitarian Universalist Association of Congregations.

First digital-print edition 2001

*Library of Congress Cataloging-in-Publication Data*
Bagdikian, Ben H.
Double vision : reflections on my heritage, life, and profession / Ben H. Bagdikian.
p.    cm.
ISBN 0-8070-7066-1 (cloth)
ISBN 0-8070-7067-X (pbk.)
1. Bagdikian, Ben H.  2. Journalists—United States—Biography.  I. Title.
PN4874.B227A3   1995
070´.92—dc20    [B]    90-22592

FOR MARLENE

# Contents

# Acknowledgments

This book contains recollections about my family and my own early life. I am indebted to my late sister, Lydia Bagdikian. Years ago, Lydia compiled a series of typed memoirs in two large loose-leafed notebooks, each page, typically, neatly typed. These notebooks are a remarkable document about memories of a young Armenian girl born in Turkey and then growing up as a new American citizen. It is the best coherent history of our family and of my own infancy. It was Lydia, as family historian, who saved the notebooks with my mother's poems.

I have also been the beneficiary of conversations over the years with older members of my family, and have read books about episodes involving my family in that distant city where I was born.

For some specific dates and other material about my earlier days as a journalist, I am indebted to staff members of the *Providence Journal* and *Evening Bulletin*, especially its former librarian, Joseph Mehr, and its editor, James Wyman, who made facilities of my old paper pleasantly available. The files of a favorite haunt during my Providence days, the Providence Public Library, were helpful, thanks to Shirley Long and John Santos of the library's staff. They confirm my lifelong devotion to that extraordinary tribe in our culture, librarians.

Anita Mintz, of Washington, D.C., did useful research on aspects of Washington, D.C., bureaucracies. Vincent Valvano, at the time a graduate student in economics at the University of California at Berkeley, was responsible for some extensive research on taxes and other economic data. Nadav Savio provided detailed research on news handling of an important national strike. Peter Leonard collected most of the newspapers' before-and-after treatment of the Proposition 13 issue in California.

I am particularly grateful to the bright intelligence of a young reference librarian, Michael Levy, who solved endless research problems by coming to the rescue with his uncanny skill in finding data needles inside informational haystacks.

I had many occasions to be grateful for the informal culture of mutual help among journalists and ex-journalists, to mention only one, Paul McAuliffe, Executive Editor of the Evansville, Indiana, *Courier*, who helped confirm an old memory about a plane crash from World War II Air Corps days.

David Eisen, research director of The Newspaper Guild, AFL-CIO, was, as always, ready to help with data and updates on developments not just in unions of reporters but in legislation affecting them. Pamela Wilson, of the Department for Professional Employees, AFL-CIO, provided me with authoritative information on wages and other characteristics of American workers.

I bow in gratitude to an old inanimate friend. Throughout my reportorial and writing career I have been the constant beneficiary of that remarkable compendium, *The Statistical Abstract of the United States*. As it has been many times in the past, the *Abstract* was a constant source for me in this book.

To my editor, Wendy Strothman, the director of Beacon Press, I owe gratitude for her faith in the possibility of bringing off this work. She provided the kind of editorial support and advice about which authors fantasize but seldom receive.

The tradition of writers includes an almost obligatory verbal bouquet to their spouses. In this case, that is hardly enough. My wife, Marlene Griffith, though simultaneously working on her own book, was

x »  DOUBLE VISION

an unfailing rescue worker and supporter of the idea of this book. She has an unerring eye for error and logical lapses. At special times, she had more confidence in the book than I did.

Despite all the help I have received from others, there probably are lapses and errors in this book for which I can take undiluted credit.

# Preface

Now that I am removed from the hurly-burly of daily excitements and look back, I am struck at how much my work as a journalist was shaped by my heritage, my early life and those who most influenced me. I am just as amazed at the radical transformation in the country's journalism and what this has meant, both good and bad, for our country. In this book I write about some of my own life, and some of the profound changes in all American journalism since World War II.

If I write about myself, there are reasons beyond the egocentric compulsion of every writer. I have no illusion that my life and experience are exemplary; I know my own sins and omissions too well. But my life in journalism was during these years of change, from the start as a bumbling cub reporter to years as a reporter, Washington correspondent, foreign correspondent, and an assistant managing editor of a major daily. Almost from the start, while I worked as a reporter I also took time to look at the news process through research and media criticism.

I write, of course, with that marvel of all vision, hindsight, but also with a complex of double visions. The world looks divided when you grow up in a traumatized immigrant family devoted to becoming total Americans. As with everyone else, my early life experiences remained the subjective undercurrent beneath disciplines I learned in order to do "objective" reporting.

In a real sense, all of journalism is a double vision. The news system likes to think it sees the world impersonally, but, of course, it doesn't. The longer I was a journalist, the more I realized that what the country sees on its living room television screens every night and on its front pages every morning reflects the personal experience, values and social views of every man and woman in the news process, from the media investors on Wall Street to the lowest cub reporter alone with notebook at the scene of an intersection accident. These very human hands, one way or another, shape something central to democratic life—the public image of what is important in society and what is not, of what is good and what is bad, of what should be changed and what should stay the same.

With the exception of one prewar year, my time in journalism was the years of the country's great changes since the end of what my generation thinks of as *the* war. Right out of college in 1941, I spent a bizarre year in a newsroom that still used a telegraph key, on a paper owned by a coldhearted eccentric. I spent three and a half years in the wartime Air Corps, but though I was never fired at in anger, the war changed how I saw life and how I felt about journalism. Afterward, my real career started, and for the next forty-five years I both reported the news and criticized how news was reported in a role that eventually became a cottage industry and was given a new name, "media critic."

It was during my time in daily journalism that a new household machine, television, forever changed American journalism, including those of us who once called ourselves "the press," serenely certain that it included everyone and everything in the business of news.

In my generation, the world of American journalism has been transformed and, not surprisingly, having lived and loved my time in it I, too, have changed.

## CHAPTER I

# A Not-So-Secret Mission

One hot June night in 1971, I found myself in the dismal room of a rundown motel in Boston. The air conditioner wasn't working. The room was stifling. It was 2:00 A.M. but the twin beds were still unused. Both beds were covered with thousands of pages of the top-secret Pentagon Papers.

All over the country, the White House and FBI were trying to keep the papers from falling into outside hands and at the moment the outside hands were mine. If I succeeded in what I was contemplating, the documents would end up on the front pages of the *Washington Post* where I was Assistant Managing Editor for National News.

Already, the Pentagon Papers were creating startling news. For years, the secret history of American involvement in Vietnam had been locked in government safes. Now the papers had escaped and started to appear in the *New York Times*. In cold public print, the cables and secret orders began to prove years of official lying and fantasy about the continuing tragedy of the Vietnam War.

Similarly alarming, two days earlier the White House had obtained a federal court order in New York with a perilous precedent: the court had censored the *Times*. It stopped the *Times*'s presses from further printing of what I assumed were pretty much the same documents I was looking at on the twin beds.

Even as I sorted through the stacks of paper in the motel

room, the war continued to kill Americans and Vietnamese in numbers ever more appalling. Masses of citizens, frustrated by the government's self-delusion, duplicity, and arrogance, were taking to the streets.

The papers on the bed could confirm the suspicion of millions of citizens that for years their government had been obsessed with a failing policy and was systematically lying about it. Publishing the historical proof could dissuade later leaders from the same kind of errors and deceptions. Besides, if the *Post* resumed printing the papers, it would make it more clear that official censorship is not only unconstitutional—it is unwise and won't work.

Days before the *Times's* publication, the Pentagon Papers had created tension in the *Post* newsroom. For a week, we at the *Post* had known that the *Times* had "something big," that the *Times* had created an unprecedented secret editorial shop so secure that most *Times* reporters also were in the dark. Probably the *Times* feared what I now feared in my dingy motel room, that a government-tapped telephone or an informer within the newspaper plant would bring a knock on the door by FBI agents bearing a search and seizure warrant before the truth could come out.

The *Post* was not the only paper aware of something extraordinary going on at the *New York Times*. The same week, I received a call from a former Washington correspondent I knew, David Kraslow, then with the *Los Angeles Times*, who had heard the same rumors we had and that it had something to do with an exclusive report from Rand, the research organization in Santa Monica, California. Kraslow knew I had spent some time at Rand.

I called Henry Rowen, the president of Rand. He said he knew nothing of the sort.

It all came clear a few nights later when I was having dinner in the Watergate apartment of Congressman and Mrs. William Anderson and a few of their close friends. Anderson, former captain of the nuclear submarine *Nautilus*, had become one of the growing number of congressional members opposed to the continuation of American military involvement in the Asian war, then in its seventeenth year.

At 11:30, as I did every night wherever I was, I excused myself momentarily for my regular late-night call to the *Post*'s National Desk. I always checked with the night editor for late developments or problems before the paper's main edition. And I always asked the routine question, "Any surprises in the *Times*?"

In Washington, the *Times* and the *Post* were the principal competitors for serious national news in the capital, with the *Times* the traditional paper of record, and the *Post* more enterprising than its rival and in recent years more authoritative than it had been in the past. Besides, the *Post*'s executive editor, Benjamin Bradlee, was a fierce competitor.

Each night, the *Times* had a wire service send them a photocopy of our front page, picked up by a special courier who took one of the first papers of our first edition at the *Post* plant on 15th Street in Washington, hot off the presses, or at least still warm. We had a similar arrangement with someone outside the *Times* pressroom on 43rd Street in New York. Often at about eleven o'clock each night, I smiled inwardly at the knowledge that my counterpart in New York was scanning the facsimile of our front page exactly as I was scanning his in Washington.

That night, standing in a small alcove off the Andersons' living room, I wasn't smiling. The country was about to be jolted out of its national nightmare. A banner headline of the next day's *Times* announced stories from a secret history of the Vietnam War, a mass of primary documents that would thereafter be known as "The Pentagon Papers."

Hectic days followed at the *Post*. Publication of the papers by the *Times* and their suppression by the government created tidal waves of official and public reaction, which had to be reported. The day after the *Times* presses were censored, as I left the afternoon daily conference in which editors made final decisions on the next day's national news, my deputy, Peter Silberman, a man of calm and inscrutable demeanor, quietly handed me a note. "Maybe you ought to look at this."

Editors frequently hear from callers who insist they have urgent news. It is seldom news and rarely urgent. I glanced impatiently at the note as I laid it on my desk. The message said, "Call Mr. Boston from a secure phone." The only Mr. Boston I knew was a media scholar but he was at the University of Cardiff in Great Britain, and the area code on the message was 617. Then it hit me: 617 was the area code for Boston. Call Mr. Boston in Boston. Probably a false name. And worried about a tapped phone. At that moment, I suspected that the note had something to do with the Pentagon Papers.

I quickly walked across the street to the Statler Hilton Hotel where the outer lobby had a bank of public phones. In Richard Nixon's paranoid Washington, the disease spread and we assumed, not unwisely, that some of the *Post* phones might be tapped.

At the Boston number, a voice said an old friend had an important message for me, but I had to give the number of a public phone where the friend could call me in a few minutes. I gave the number of the phone next to mine. Before long my hunch was confirmed. It was someone I knew.

If I were able to get "the papers," would the *Post* print them? I said it would.

"Can you commit the *Post?*"

This was too grave a story to decide by ordinary standards. I paused.

"I'll have to call you back."

He gave me another phone number with an answering machine. If I had assurance the *Post* would publish "the material," I should leave a cryptic message on the machine. It would be, "Mr. Medford from Providence will wait for you at the hotel." I once worked on the *Providence Journal*. Medford is a suburb of Boston where I used to hike with my Boy Scout troop to the Tufts College museum. He said my message should name the hotel where we would meet and warned me to make a reservation quickly because most hotels and motels were full. This was commencement week for the many colleges and universities in the Boston area.

Back in the newsroom, I went into the office of Managing Editor Eugene Patterson. I didn't close the door because editors at the *Post* live in glass-walled offices where visible activities are studied and interpreted by the full staff of imaginative reporters. I wanted no assumptions about something secret. We sat close to each other on his office divan.

"Gene, if I can get some documents that haven't been published yet, will we print them?"

He knew what I meant and his eyes widened. He thought a moment.

Gene is one of the most likeable men I have ever met—honest, humane, and not given to the game-playing relationships so characteristic of Washington and all too common among newsroom executives. But he was also an old-fashioned patriot from the South, a decorated tank commander in World War II. I liked and respected him, but recently I, along with some of my fellow assistant managing editors, had been having uncharacteristically bad-tempered meetings with him because he seemed determined to turn down any story critical of the Pentagon and the Vietnam war effort.

His jaw stiffened and he tapped me on the knee.

"Ben, as far as I'm concerned, you get them and we'll print them."

We knew Bradlee would have to agree. Bradlee would be back in the city in less than an hour.

I asked Silberman to take over for the night.

Later, I called Bradlee from the airport.

He was excited and enthusiastic.

"Is that a commitment?"

"Pal, if you get the goods and they aren't in the next day's paper, that night the *Washington Post* will have a new executive editor."

Bradlee, who finds it intolerable not to be in on anything hot, took a stab: "Say hello to California." He obviously thought I was on my way to someone at Rand in Santa Monica. I said nothing. Waiting for the next plane to Boston, I grabbed two hot dogs and a glass of milk. It was going to be a long night.

In Boston when I checked into the motel under the name "Medford," I was dismayed when the young man behind the desk said, "I got a message for a 'Mr. Bagdikian' who's expected tonight. Is that anything to do with you?"

I hated to break my cover, but I said it was. He asked for some identification and when I took out my wallet he saw my *Post* press pass. I told him I wrote under the name of "Medford."

"Oh," he said brightly. "Do you know Mr. Coe?"

Richard Coe was the paper's drama critic. The young man, apparently a frustrated playwright, said he did occasional Boston reviews for Coe. I agreed with the clerk that Dick Coe was an excellent man and I cursed the gods of coincidence.

I was in for more surprises. I had decided to push ahead that night, ignoring government demands, because I knew from experience the widespread abuse of the official claim of "national security secret." But with all my skepticism, I was not prepared for the new levels of irrationality that lay ahead.

My night in the motel room was just the opening step in a series of events that were not without low comedy, but the subsequent bitter battles inside the paper and beyond were only part of the long drift toward fantasy and fanaticism in mainstream American politics during our peculiar American version of the Cold War, which carried much of our journalism along with it.

Practically everyone in the journalistic process, from owner to reporter, claims that personal values do not influence the news, but I think that is clearly untrue. Otherwise I would not have been in the motel room that night. Some reporters would consider it unpatriotic or too risky. Nor would my paper have approved the project. After it became public, more than one newspaper condemned the *Post*.

But that night in 1971, these were not the thoughts that came to mind as I looked at the formidable pile of Pentagon documents on the twin beds.

At that moment, I was not even concerned whether I was right or wrong in doing what my government had said publicly would cause my country "grave and irreparable harm." I had already decided about that earlier.

What concerned me at that moment was something more absurd. I was afraid that the attempt to smuggle the papers undetected into Washington would fail because trying to carry the weight of more than ten thousand pieces of paper might throw out my vulnerable back.

## CHAPTER 2

## And 5,400 Pages of Not-So-Secret "Secrets"

T he moment I stepped into my third-floor motel room, the phone rang. It was a familiar male voice. I was to go to an address in Cambridge to pick up the "material." And tell the clerk to let in some friends while I'm out.

"Do you have back trouble? This stuff is very heavy."

"I'm not worried," I lied. I have a rebellious back.

On a dark, tree-lined street of modest cottages in Cambridge, the cab driver had to walk up to unlit porches and peer at street numbers by striking matches. In between houses, the driver told me about his divorce lawyer's "awful" bill of $150. All I said was, "You're lucky." I did not tell him that I, too, was in the midst of divorce proceedings and it cost me $150 simply to inquire into the health of my fashionable attorney.

We found the right house. In the cellar I was shown two large boxes with covers, each two feet long and a foot square. One box had heavy twine around the middle. I picked that one because the cord as a handle would make it less treacherous to carry.

As I dragged the box off the motel elevator into the third-floor corridor, there was Daniel Ellsberg, a plastic bucket in hand, returning from the motel ice machine.

I had first met Ellsberg in 1967 at Rand, the research institute in Santa Monica, California. Most Rand work has been secret analysis for the Department of Defense.

Through a quirk, I found myself at Rand writing an ordinary open book that had nothing to do with the government, government money, secrecy, or defense. At Rand, most of that special Cold War elite, "the defense intellectuals," were engaged in classified work, but some of them found it interesting, or perhaps merely quaint, to have lunch with their resident curiosity, a journalist writing a book totally unrelated to their work. My book was about the coming transformation of the mass media by modern communications.

Dan Ellsberg was one of the special elite. A few of my friends at Rand were analysts who had worked on Vietnam data for years and, despite their careful avoidance of talk about their classified work, when we went across the street for lunch on the Santa Monica pier, it emerged that they saw overwhelming evidence against continuing American action in the war. They were also exercised about the government's misuse of their research in justifying escalation in Vietnam.

Six of these men, one of them Dan, were agonizing over a step that is normal and even personally advantageous for most intellectuals and academics as well as other concerned citizens—writing a letter to the *New York Times* mildly demurring from government policy. But traditionally at Rand even that thought was heresy. Hearing of their plans some of their colleagues stopped speaking to them. The six letter writers asked Henry Rowen, the more relaxed president of Rand, who said he would not stop them if they made it clear that they spoke only for themselves and not Rand. From time to time, writers of the joint letter stopped by my office or to have lunch, wanting to know how best to approach which newspaper.

Ellsberg, whom I had met at parties, had a reputation for flaming romances and an equally compulsive pursuit of intricate analysis. From childhood through college and government service the adjective that usually struck his colleagues was "brilliant," followed by "relentless." Once a passionate supporter of the war, his access to secret records and observations in Vietnam itself led him first to doubt the possibility of a military solution and finally to a passionate determination to expose the data that might end the war.

Dan spent a lot of time in my office asking about the press and its dynamics. I assumed that his intense queries were solely because of the letter he and the others were writing. I was wrong, of course. By the fall of 1969, Ellsberg, unknown to me or anyone else at Rand, had rented a copying machine and was secretly reproducing the 7,400 pages of the top-secret Pentagon Papers.

Ellsberg had taken part in compiling the original documents. Fifteen sets of the papers were in existence, one copy assigned to Rand in Santa Monica and that one assigned to Ellsberg's office safe. That was the set that ended up clandestinely being run through his rented Xerox machine. It was his unauthorized copies that created the furor of the Pentagon Papers and had brought me to the dingy motel in Boston.

When I saw him in the third-floor corridor of the motel, Dan Ellsberg did not look brilliant or relentless. He was haggard and complained of a terrible headache.

We entered my room and to my surprise there was Dan's wife, Patricia, and another man. I had met and liked Pat at Santa Monica parties. In contrast to Dan, she was quiet and modest in manner. The other man was introduced as a lawyer-friend. He seemed to be intensely monitoring all the conversation and activity in the motel room. He made me uneasy. I called Dan into the bathroom where he assured me the lawyer could be trusted.

Dan looked at the box I had just lifted onto the bed.

"Where's the other box?"

"I thought this one had all the material."

"It does, but I wanted you to bring the other box, too."

Dan made a phone call and in due course a young man knocked at the door. Dan opened the door just wide enough to drag the second box into the room and quickly shut the door to hide the messy scene inside.

As he began taking the cover off the second box, he said he had some conditions he wanted me to accept before we got going. At that point, the lawyer said to Pat, "I think this is when we should leave." The lawyer seemed to be a friend of Pat's there to protect her from any later legal action over handling secret papers.

After Patricia and the lawyer left, Dan laid down his conditions.

He wanted me to promise that any handwritten notes on the margins of the papers would be cut out. That was no problem.

He also wanted a promise that if the paper printed any literal text of any cable, it would not print the time codes and message numbers, because theoretically it could compromise the secret code.

Dan said, "This could be the difference between a ten-year sentence and a life sentence." I had no trouble with cutting out the code groups because they had no pertinent value to the public.

Dan demanded that I not reveal his identity. I had taken that for granted. Afterward, I refused to confirm or deny Dan as my source even after news stories and books insisted that he was. That night Dan revealed, with unexpected bitterness, that he was the source of the *Times*'s documents but that once they had the documents they had refused to talk to him, answer his phone calls, or in any other way let him know what the paper planned to do. The *Times*'s publication a few days earlier had surprised him as much as it did us at the *Post*.

My real trouble was with his last demand. I was to deliver "the second box" secretly to a member of Congress. That, I did not like. I had always felt that a journalist and an official working too closely in concert tempted both to change their behavior for the benefit of the other. For the journalist that means only one thing, to alter news to favor or avoid criticizing the politician. I knew that some other journalists, prominent ones, made such deals, and I knew their stories had the predictable flavor of promotional bias. I had always avoided it.

Merely accepting the papers for publication already was taking risks for me and my paper, but this was asking me to be a party in some unknown enterprise by some unknown government official.

I argued, but in the end, agreed. It in no way tied my journalistic hands. Nevertheless, it still disturbs me, and until now I have never told anyone except my wife about the private transaction. It would have been an even tougher dilemma if I had known in the motel room what I would discover many days later: my delivery of "the second box" would become the basis for one of the most bizarre scenes in the history of the United States Senate.

Dan and I worked, cutting and sorting until the early hours, when he left.

I called American Airlines and made a reservation on the first plane to Washington. The ticket was for two first-class seats on flight 287 for "Mr. Medford and package" on June 17, 1971.

(I would learn later that June 17 was the anniversary of the birth of the Pentagon Papers four years before, when Leslie Gelb, then a young policy analyst in the Pentagon, was assigned by Secretary of Defense Robert McNamara to head the task force that compiled and wrote the full Pentagon Papers. Gelb became a columnist for the *New York Times*, and then head of the private Council on Foreign Relations.)

As the sky began to lighten outside the motel window, I began plans for the trip back. I was stuck with two boxes, a total of more than ten thousand sheets of paper. Any experienced back sufferer knows that carrying that weight in two ungainly boxes is an invitation to spinal paralysis.

I had enough trouble carrying the first box. At least it had heavy twine around its middle. The second box had nothing for a handhold or to keep its cover on. I foresaw walking into Logan Airport in Boston, dropping the second box and seeing the lobby floor strewn with documents marked, "Top-Secret Sensitive."

I went down to the motel lobby. The young dramatist had been replaced by a sleepy older man who had just set up an urn of hot water with styrofoam cups and instant coffee. As I sipped some acidic coffee, I asked the clerk if he would look around for some rope I needed. He opened drawers and looked under counters and returned shrugging his shoulders hopelessly.

Trying to be helpful, he said that sometimes guests tied their dogs to the chain link fence around the swimming pool.

I walked out into the blessed coolness of predawn Boston. At least it was not going to rain. I carefully patrolled the fence in the semidarkness until I came upon a beautiful sight: six feet of stout rope dangling onto the ground from the fence.

In the room, I tied the boxes as tightly as I could and, after lying down for about an hour, called a cab. With the help of the driver, I loaded the boxes, and once in the cab, realized that I would not be able to put both boxes in the airplane seat beside me.

I hated to check one of those boxes into baggage. In my mind's eye I saw a version of my earlier nightmare: some husky airline baggage handler cavalierly tossing the box onto the luggage cart, the box bursting open and secret documents scattering on the tarmac. I would be met at Washington National Airport by a crew of expressionless men in dark suits, with snap brim hats and bulges under their armpits, raising shiny badges in my face. But it seemed the lesser risk compared to trying to juggle two big boxes inside the passenger compartment. As I hoisted the second box onto the airline counter scale, I looked down to make sure that my Boy Scout square knot was properly made and tight, mentally thanked the unknown owner of the unknown dog, and hoped for the best.

Carrying my box, I went to a phone to call Bradlee. He said, "Where are you?"

"I'm calling from an airport you're very familiar with and I've got the whole thing." Benjamin Crowninshield Bradlee grew up in Boston and went to Harvard. He exploded with excitement. He said to bring "it" directly to his house on N Street in Georgetown.

I went to the American Airlines gate. There, to my dismay, smiling at me from the gate, were Stanley Karnow and his wife, Annette.

Stanley was the *Post*'s China expert. He had just returned from years as our correspondent in Hong Kong. Stanley had agreed to give some seminars at Harvard before reporting to the paper for the domestic assignment with the *Post* in Washington, where I would be his editor. Newspapers usually want their foreign correspondents to return periodically to the home office in order to get reacquainted with the United States and their own paper.

But returning foreign correspondents are a problem for all editors, the more distinguished the correspondent, the bigger the headache. In their foreign bureaus the chiefs are powerful viceroys, far from the influence of their editors. They have high status among heads of state and prime ministers, and, in Stanley's case, genuine respect as an extraordinary journalist in his field. Furthermore, the correspondents often live royally, as Stanley had in Hong Kong, in a mansion with inexpensive chauffeurs, maids, and other amenities no domestic newspaper editor can offer in the United States.

The problem for their editors is that few such returning stars wish to do routine home duty, like chasing fire engines or hijinks in City Hall. At the least, they want to be on the paper's most prestigious staff, preferably as senior diplomatic correspondents covering foreign affairs and national security policy.

At the *Post*, the most prestigious staff was my National Staff, where we already had our top reporters covering the State Department and national security issues at the White House. Each considered himself "senior."

I was delighted to have Stanley on the National Staff, but it required delicate diplomacy among senior staff members who were intensely jealous about their assignments and their status. I had visited Stanley earlier at Harvard where we conducted friendly negotiations in which, as they say in the trade, "we had a frank exchange of views," and, as usual in the diplomatic trade, the most sensitive points were deliberately left unresolved until a more propitious moment. Now on his way for final home assignment, Stanley found himself on the same plane with the editor who had told him we would get specific about his work after he came to Washington. Expectedly, Stan said, "Great. Let's sit together."

Then he noticed the big box beside me. Stanley was not a highly respected journalist for nothing. He stared at the box and then stared at me. A slow, sly grin spread over his face. Looking me straight in the eye, he said:

"I hoped he would give them to me."

I hoped he was faking, an old journalistic trick to make your source think you know it all anyway. I smiled as vaguely as possible. I was grateful that we were asked to board the plane and that the first box occupied the seat beside me.

After landing I left the plane before Stanley did. Once I had retrieved the (still tied) second box, I took a cab and carried both boxes into the Idaho Avenue Washington apartment where I had moved after my separation. My younger son was staying with me while he was home from college for the summer. I was relieved that Eric was still asleep. I put the second box in a closet and quietly left to re-enter the cab for Bradlee's house on N Street.

Bradlee's house was on one of the more fashionable streets in what is usually described as "fashionable Georgetown," and as I arrived, I saw the Bradlees' charming daughter Marina selling lemonade on the front steps. It was the last charming moment I would have for the next several days.

Bradlee came to the door, shook my hand warmly, and led me to his living room, where I joined Chalmers Roberts, Murrey Marder, and Don Oberdorfer, three of the National Staff reporters who had been covering Vietnam affairs for years, and two secretaries, Donna Crouch, Bradlee's personal secretary, and Kitty Kelly, who some years later would write best-sellers about the private lives of celebrities.

Bradlee led us to the far end of the living room, where a few steps led upward to his book-lined library. There we talked about the monumental task of sorting 5,400 documents in ways that would make them quickly coherent and usable for a story by the first deadline early that same evening. (There were 7,400 documents in each full set, but Ellsberg never released four volumes that in his opinion would truly have jeopardized national security.)

We decided to sort the documents chronologically, make a rough index, and let the first story be written by Roberts, the fastest writer in the group. Oberdorfer had just finished a book on the Tet offensive in Vietnam, and Marder would do stories two and three. All three knew the published—and not a little of the unpublished—information about the war and government policy.

By the time Bradlee and I returned to the living room, there were more arrivals, Philip Geyelin, editor of the editorial page and a close friend of Bradlee's, and Meg Greenfield, assistant editorial page editor. There was an excited, congratulatory atmosphere.

The doorbell rang again and we were joined by the two lawyers who always dealt with *Post* stories that could have legal problems. The senior of the two, Roger Clark, was a tall, youngish, polished lawyer; a younger and less formal lawyer, Anthony Essaye, also came from the same firm, Royall, Koegell, and Wells. The firm earlier had been called

Royall, Koegell, Rogers and Wells, but senior partner William Rogers, once counsel for the *Washington Post*, had left the firm to become Richard Nixon's Secretary of State.

I had always been happy with the advice of Clark and Essaye. They had often been in my office to look at stories that might have legal complications. Unlike some newspaper libel lawyers, they were clear on legalities and the need for documentation, but gave their opinion and left it to the editor to weigh their advice against the degree of risk and the urgency of the story. They had always done their best to make it possible to publish a serious story, making sensible changes that did not alter the basic thrust and did not fill the story with incomprehensible legalistic language.

There were greetings all around and I retired to the library to help with decisions in the frantic work already in progress.

The library began to look like a model skyline with piles of documents in various shapes and heights. As the content of each story began to take shape, the reporters shuttled between their typewriters, the piles of documents, and our periodic huddles over a document or episode.

I called the office to have John Reistrup, a National Desk editor, come to the Bradlees' house where, from a small desk at the foot of the library steps, he would process each typed sheet of the story as Roberts wrote it. Once edited, it was given sheet by sheet to the newsroom's chief copy aide, who drove his motorcycle the mile and a half to a special, isolated corner of the *Post* composing room on 15th Street.

The copy deadline for our first edition was 4:00 P.M. and as it became clear that Roberts's story would easily be completed in time and things were going smoothly in the library, I relaxed and joined the group in the living room.

As I walked toward the gathered sofa and chairs at the other end of the room, I knew something was wrong. Excitement was gone. No one was smiling. Conversation was not genial. No one asked about progress inside the library. Glumly, Bradlee told me that the lawyers were adamantly against publication.

I was shocked. As I listened, it seemed to me that this was not just a disinterested legal opinion. It was ferocious opposition. In my past experience, Roger Clark, who did all the talking, had never been so hard and angry.

This was no ordinary story, of course, and it would have no ordinary consequences. It would be natural and necessary for the lawyers to press us for answers to every possible tough question. But as I tuned into the argument, it seemed to me that the lawyer was not playing devil's advocate or issuing advice but making a nonnegotiable demand.

What alarmed me was a sense of the exhaustion on our side from what had clearly been a long and tense argument. People seemed spent, or even numb, from hours of bitter interchanges while I had been in the library. I had to be introduced to the arguments that had been exchanged. Later I realized that when one side of a negotiation is rigid and immovable, it's useful for the losing side to gain a new person, full of innocent alarm at the prospect of defeat.

Roger Clark told me that the matter was already before the court in the *Times* case and we should await the decision. Otherwise, he said, it would appear that we were flouting the courts.

But the *Times* was under a court order, not the *Post*.

Yes, but even so it would appear to the courts and the public that we were being arrogant and irresponsible in the face of the danger raised by the government and a court order that already agreed with the government.

It seemed to me that it would be disastrous to establish the precedent that if the government could get a single court order against one paper in another jurisdiction automatically all other papers in the country would be silenced before they were ordered to.

Clark said we were acting in haste, that the *Times* had three months to read and write their stories with great care and we would be seen as acting out of irresponsible impulse. I argued that we had reporters and editors who had been handling precisely this kind of material for ten or fifteen years and knew what was relevant and reasonable, and what was genuinely dangerous to print.

Clark argued that there would be no harm in our holding off until the courts had decided the *Times* case—the stories would still be there and, once clear, we could do what we wanted. If we published with "unseemly haste" it would go badly for us if we got into legal trouble.

But if we did what he advised, it would be unilateral self-censorship we did not think justified. Besides, we had no way of knowing what the appellate courts would decide in the New York case or when.

Geyelin and Greenfield, who had initially been enthusiastic about publishing, did not seem to be arguing for it any longer. Even Bradlee had been silent while I argued. It was not like him to take a back seat. I leaned over and whispered:

"Ben, you're committed to print it."

He restated his strong support for publication.

At this point, Frederick Beebe, chairman of the board of the *Post* company, arrived from New York. Everyone called him "Fritz," and liked him, probably because he was a warm and open man who took journalists and journalism seriously. I had liked him in our informal meetings and I knew that our publisher, Katharine Graham, had enormous confidence in his advice.

He listened to a resume of the pros and cons, and announced that he was against publication. The angry debate started all over again. This time he was the fresh soldier for the other side. And he was chairman of the board of the whole company.

Bradlee and I continued to argue against the lawyers and Beebe.

I argued that we had always handled such material responsibly without automatically accepting government's objections at face value. And in addition, if we held back now we would be pulling the rug out from under the *Times* and the whole tradition of an independent press. Under the circumstances, we had a positive obligation to print.

Beebe sighed and said:

"Ben, you're a journalist and you may believe you have an obligation to publish and I respect that. But I have other obligations, too. I'm obligated to protect the interests of The Washington Post Company. We own broadcasting stations and under the law a convicted felon may not hold a license to broadcast. If we're indicted and convicted of a crime, we lose valuable parts of our company. Furthermore, the company at this moment is issuing its first public offering of stock and, under the contract with its underwriters, a catastrophic event to the corporation can be the basis for the underwriters to cancel the stock issue. Just a mere indictment, not a conviction, would be a catastrophic event for the corporation. I cannot put the company under that risk."

His arguments were the most pointed and real that I had heard so far. They were not enough to change my mind or Bradlee's but enough to make us respect his worries. He and Katharine Graham had reason to worry. The Nixon White House made no secret of their hatred of the *Post*. It was not abstract hostility. A group of Nixon's Republican friends in Florida were challenging the *Post*'s valuable television licenses. And I knew that two days earlier, the New York investment house of Lazard Freres had offered more than a million shares of *Post* stock on the American Stock Exchange.

I told Beebe I respected his concerns and responsibilities, but in the long run I thought we were suggesting the wiser course for the paper.

At this impasse, the arena for the argument shifted as the lawyers, Beebe, and Bradlee retired to the kitchen, where they obviously were talking on the phone to Katharine Graham at her mansion on R Street in Georgetown. I knew things were going badly when, after a few trips to the kitchen telephone, they no longer invited Bradlee to join them.

Bradlee was grey. He had dark circles under his eyes. I had never seen him so depressed.

The three men returned from the kitchen phone with "a compromise." The *Post* would not publish any story the next day but would run a front page box announcing that they had the stories and planned to start them the next day.

I was thunderstruck. It was ridiculous and dangerous. Geyelin and Greenfield seemed to make no objection. Bradlee was as stunned as I was.

"That's inviting the attorney general to stop us," he said. "It's begging him to stop us."

Roger Clark shot back, "No, it's a way to assert the right to publish through the courts."

I said, "No, Roger. The way to assert the right to publish is to publish."

Bradlee said the announcement was asking for an injunction, but his words, like mine, seemed to be brushed aside without even a response. The tide had definitely gone against us. I leaned over to Bradlee.

"Ben, if we do something like this, we're going to have a full-scale rebellion from the staff of the *Washington Post*."

Bradlee nodded grimly. He whispered back, "This is the toughest one I've ever had."

What happened next was one of those strange psychological events that seem superficial compared to any logic, law, or finely fashioned rationale. The library crew had been under extreme pressure for about six hours. I had gone into the library from time to time but been careful to give no hint of the bitter argument raging in the living room. It would have demoralized the reporters as they struggled in total concentration to meet the deadline.

With the bulk of Roberts's story written, they trooped into the living room for a drink and cold cuts, happy and satisfied.

Roger Clark announced to them the decision that instead of a story there would be the "compromise" front-page box. The three reporters and two secretaries froze. Oberdorfer gasped, wide-eyed, and exploded:

"That's the shittiest idea I have ever heard."

It was not a phrase that will echo down the corridors of history, but it was a spontaneous splash of cold water in the face of inflexible victors. That moment blew away all the exhaustion and defeat.

Chalmers Roberts, who sometimes spoke in the tones of the diplomats he covered, announced that he was planning to retire anyway and "tomorrow I will put my name to a public statement that I disassociate myself from this decision."

The argument began again from square one, once more uncertain. But the lawyers, Beebe, Bradlee, Geyelin, and Greenfield were overdue at Katharine Graham's mansion for a banquet honoring a retiring *Post* executive. They left with the issue still tentative.

The first edition passed without a decision, but it was a small edition for outlying areas. Deadlines for the next two editions went without approval or definite disapproval. The deadline for the main edition was approaching, when, as I was reading over Roberts's last paragraphs, the phone rang. Katharine had agreed to go ahead with Roberts's story for the Late City, the main edition circulated within the capital.

I was jubilant. Standing beside me, waiting to run the last piece of the story to the paper, was Paul McCarthy, the chief copy aide. I said, "Let's go, Paul. I'll ride with you on the bike."

Paul was worried that I had no helmet, but we roared off on his Triumph motorcycle, I clinging on back. On Pennsylvania Avenue as we weaved through traffic we kept crossing the old trolley tracks, ideal for making motorcycles spin out. I didn't want the last twenty-four hours to end in a skid within a few blocks of the goal, but luckily Paul McCarthy was an expert cyclist.

In the newsroom Gene Patterson greeted me with a curse on all lawyers. Silberman said I was wanted down in the composing room for last-minute approval of headlines, captions, and layout. The special story had circumvented the editing and proofreading routines that normally screen important stories between the editing desk and the composing room. The front page, unseen up in the newsroom, already was in metal form. The last thing we wanted was an unwitting mechanical misstep.

It was comforting to be in the third-floor composing room. It was filled with the clanking sounds of massive linotype machines transposing typed letters on paper to the certitude of metal. There was the smell of hot metal castings making the semicircular plates that would be bolted to the presses. These uncensored plates would replace the plates for the earlier editions that had been self-censored. It was a relief from the endless threads of convoluted argument leading to nothing proven or disproven. It was now about to be established in unarguable metal.

The four-column headline read, "Documents Reveal U.S. Effort to Delay Viet Election."

I was still looking over the printing forms when a composing-room foreman told me I had a telephone call from the desk upstairs: "Go to Bradlee's house right away. The lawyers want to see you."

Bradlee's house looked dark. I found the two lawyers, Clark and Essaye, alone in the kitchen. I greeted Tony Essaye but Clark was on the telephone, alternately with Beebe at the Graham mansion on R Street and with a senior partner of the law firm in New York. The senior lawyer in New York was William Glendon, who happened to be a classmate of mine in the graduating class of 1937 at Stoneham High School in Massachusetts.

It was hard for me to believe what I heard. The side of the conversation I heard sounded like the afternoon argument all over again.

Clark had his back to me as he hunched over the phone. I walked around to face him as he talked and asked loudly, "Roger, are we on the verge of not publishing?" Essaye, standing behind Clark, nodded yes.

Clark stopped talking and placed his hand over the mouthpiece. He told me we could not print because there was a danger that the court would find collusion between the *Times* and the *Post*. I said there was no collusion.

He insisted that the *Times* court order forbade them or—and here he bit off the words—"*or any agent of the Times*"—to act to circumvent the restraining order. I told him I had not dealt with anyone from the *Times* or any agent of the *Times*.

"Then I have to know your source."

"I can't tell you because I promised confidentiality."

"As *Washington Post* attorney, I must know."

"Roger, if I tell you, are we in a lawyer-client relationship? Nothing I tell you will become known to anyone else? Literally?"

"Yes."

"Then, please come over to the corner."

I turned to Essaye, "I hope you understand, Tony."

I told Clark my source was Daniel Ellsberg.

Clark returned to the phone with Glendon waiting at the other end in New York. Clark said to Glendon: "I can't tell you. He told me in confidence."

Clark was silent while Glendon said something, to which Clark replied, "Yes."

Clark then called the Graham mansion and talked to Beebe. To my amazement, he said with the certitude of a man with new and absolute evidence, that the *Post* cannot publish the papers because it would be collusion with the *Times*. "We can't be in contempt of the New York court."

I demanded to speak to Beebe or Bradlee to correct the misstatement. But Clark would not relinquish the phone. As I spoke more and more insistently, he excused himself from Beebe momentarily, his hand over the phone, and turned to me.

I told him that my getting the papers had nothing to do with anyone from the *Times* or an agent of the *Times*. I told him the only contact with anyone from the *Times* had been the day after they were stopped by the New York court and had nothing to do with my later getting the papers. I told him the full background details, as I always had in the past when he raised legal questions about stories.

Jack Rosenthal of the *Times*, whom I had known from his years in Washington, was now collecting historical details of secrecy cases for the *Times*'s defense in the New York court. He had left a message for me asking if we would let the *Times* know what the government had done to the *Post* when many years ago the *Post* had published the "secret" Gaither Report, and how the paper had replied to government objections. (I put "secret" in quotation marks because though stamped "Secret" it is now known that the Gaither Report was deliberately leaked to build public support for its recommendations.)

I had given our library Rosenthal's message and asked them to call him when they found the old *Post* stories on the case. I had not spoken to Rosenthal personally (I had been on my way to Boston). It was the only contact with the *Times* since the start of the *Times*'s stories on the Pentagon Papers. It did not occur to me at that moment, but Jack Rosenthal had once worked for the attorney general in the Department of Justice and he would not have done anything so stupid as to jeopardize the *Times*'s case by violating the judge's order.

I told all of this to Clark and repeated that at no time in obtaining the *Post*'s documents had I dealt with anyone connected with the *Times* or anyone who could even remotely be seen as an agent of that paper.

"But you had the same source as the *Times* and that makes him an agent."

By that time, the wire services had carried a bulletin reporting that a former reporter for the *Times* had, for reasons of his own, held a press conference to say that he knew for a fact that Ellsberg was the *Times*'s source.

I told Clark that even if Ellsberg had been the source, he in no way acted as an agent for the *Times* because he had not been in touch with the paper since long before the court order and was bitter about being frozen out after the *Times* obtained the documents months earlier.

Clark turned back to the phone and again insisted to Beebe that we would be charged with collusion and both the *Times* and the *Post* held in contempt.

I was outraged that he did not at least pass on the gist of my statement. I stared at the red brick pattern on the kitchen floor, angry and helpless as I listened to what sounded to me like last-minute desperate moves by a lawyer to stretch any point any distance to prevent publication.

By this time, he and I had abandoned all decorum and were shouting at each other. "Roger," I said over his conversation with Beebe, "you're trying to find any excuse you can to keep this out of the paper."

I held out my hand for the phone. "Let me speak to Fritz or Bradlee," I shouted.

He glared at me, held onto the phone, and defensively turned his back to me.

I said loudly enough to penetrate to the phone, "Roger, if we don't publish, there'll be a new National Editor of the *Post* tomorrow."

I had always felt that a threat to quit in high dudgeon during an argument was melodramatic and pretentious. But that night in the kitchen, I was enraged at what struck me as Clark's last-minute attempt to scuttle the agreement and his refusal to let Beebe know my answer to his claim that I had conspired with the *Times*. I felt it was an unprofessional double-cross by the paper's lawyer and I meant it about resigning.

Clark's former senior partner was now secretary of state, probably part of the government's pulling of all available strings to block the *Post*. The *New York Times*'s regular law firm, headed by a former attorney general of the United States, had refused even to touch the

*Times*'s case. I had bitter thoughts about lawyers in private practice with close personal connections with high government officials.

It was clear I would not be given the phone. I looked at my watch. It was 12:30, the last moment before the presses rolled for the main edition. The fight was just about over.

I waited in the kitchen just long enough for the evil moment of the passed deadline. Suddenly, Clark turned from the phone and said, "Kay has just said go ahead and publish."

Katharine Graham's last-minute decision took courage. Leadership of the Washington Post Company empire had descended on her after the traumatic death of her husband eight years earlier when she was forty-six years old. Between that bewildering passage of power and the Pentagon Papers, she had been forced to learn from scratch the intricacies of shepherding a growing media conglomerate through treacherous waters. And now she gambled losses to her empire against the advice of her chairman of the board and in the face of predictions of disaster from her law firm. She did it knowing that her decision would enrage a ruthless White House that already hated her and her paper. She also must have been aware that at the time she was still openly patronized or sneered at privately by most of her male peers among newspaper publishers. I had heard some of their little jokes about a *liberal* paper run by a *woman*. A lot of those same contemptuous publishers would have run from this decision as they did from most important challenges to established power.

I walked out of Bradlee's house and took a cab home. In the apartment, I called the National Desk to ask if the Late City had come up to the newsroom. The night man said it had and the story was in. By now I was exhausted and almost paranoid. I asked him to read me the headline and first paragraph. The story seemed to be intact and I went to sleep for the first time in forty-eight hours.

≫

The next morning there was a celebratory atmosphere in the newsroom. Someone, probably Reistrup, had put in large letters on the National Desk, "The way to assert the right to publish is to publish."

I was called to a meeting in Bradlee's office. As I approached it, Katharine Graham paused and turned toward me before she entered, her face grim, "Well, what trouble did you get us into today?" She was not joking. There was no celebration inside Bradlee's office. The meeting was tense and unpleasant, with the certainty of impending White House retaliation—a warning call from the Department of Justice followed by an accusation made in court—all with unknowable consequences. I also assumed that Katharine had been hearing from some of her close friends, including Robert McNamara, the former secretary of defense.

When I returned to my office, I called in Silberman and told him about the meeting and Mrs. Graham's response. "If there has to be a goat in all this, I'll be it. I'll keep you clued in so you can take over if you have to."

By the next day, Katharine Graham had changed. There had been congratulations from papers and editors she respected, like James Reston of the *Times*, and Tom Winship of the *Boston Globe*. It was now a historic fight for freedom of the press, and perhaps that put a new light on it all. Later, she told Sanford Ungar, author of a book on the case, that the fear of demoralizing the entire *Post* staff weighed heavily on her last-minute decision to go ahead.

In days that followed, the *Post* also was stopped by a court order. Life became increasingly hectic. In the *Post* case, the trial judge, Gerhard Gesell, faced with thousands of pages of documents and the need for a quick decision, asked the government lawyers to give him the "ten worst" cases of "grave and irreparable harm" if censorship were to be lifted. It was my job to spend the night directing research into what was publicly known in our library and elsewhere about the real level of secrecy of the "ten worst" cases. It had to be completed in time for the lawyers' arguments the next day.

The results surprised even me. Like any experienced Washington correspondent, I knew the degree of mindless compulsion with which secrecy stamps were used. Like others, I had been handed classified documents by high officials who made the "secrets" public when it suited their political purposes.

Furthermore, violations of genuine national security by either officialdom or newspeople were rare. Even when truly dangerous information has become known, there is a record of self-restraint in the news. During the Cuba missile crisis, for example, dozens of correspondents knew the gist of secret negotiations under way to prepare for but avoid an immediate nuclear war. No one used the knowledge.

But even I was surprised at the way the Pentagon selected their "ten worst" cases. They were probably confident that anything that they told a judge was a national security threat would be accepted at face value. Judges, publishers, and editors who do not deal with national security people day in and day out usually are innocent of the wide circle of known "secrets" and are intimidated by the awesome word, accompanied by the phrase, "will jeopardize the lives of American soldiers and sailors." Most working reporters in the field have more realistic experience with which to judge when the words refer to something real and when they are public relations catechisms of security agencies.

The "ten worst" cases soon evaporated. They were not secret at all. They had been publicly disclosed earlier by the government itself, or by former officials writing published memoirs or giving public testimony. Some of the "Top-Secret Sensitive" cases had been printed first by trade magazines like *Aviation Week and Space Technology*, available on newsstands around the world and studied assiduously by every major embassy and military attaché in Washington. There were published *New York Times* and *Washington Post* stories clipped by the government and now marked "Top-Secret."

The case quickly reached the Federal District Court of Appeals in the District of Columbia, the most influential in the country except for the Supreme Court. Here, the government said they really had a story so secret, so irreversibly damaging to the security of the United States, that the intelligence agencies could show it only to the chief judge himself, David Bazelon. The judge insisted that lawyers for the parties had to be present. But the lawyers, once admitted, initially agreed that no reporters would be allowed.

Luckily, Bradlee, who was not admitted himself, won the fight to have George Wilson present for the secret session in Judge Bazelon's chambers. Wilson was on the National Staff and the best Pentagon correspondent I knew in Washington. What he later described to me was the quintessential story of fantasy in the national cult of secrecy.

On the appointed day, a select group formed around the judge's desk in the federal courthouse. Contrary to constitutional guarantees, the legal hearing was closed to the public. Present were the solicitor general of the United States, Erwin Griswold, former dean of Harvard Law School, now the government's chief lawyer; J. Fred Buzhardt, general counsel for the Department of Defense; Glendon and Beebe representing the *Post*; and George Wilson.

The lawyers wore their standard black suits, black shoes, black socks, and each one carried a leather attaché case. Wilson, a tall, balding, laconic man, wore a somewhat rumpled suit with Wallabee shoes and carried a bulging vinyl zipper case of the kind offered at discount in unfashionable stationery stores.

A knock on the door introduced an official courier carrying a brief-case latched by special combination locks. Only the courier knew the codes to open the container. He had come directly from Admiral Noel Gayler, chief of the National Security Agency, the most secret of all secret federal agencies. Concerned with codes and worldwide eaves-dropping, it is more secure even than the CIA or the FBI.

From the open briefcase, the courier handed a large manila envelope to Judge Bazelon.

From the manila envelope the judge drew a white envelope. From that envelope, the judge pulled out yet another envelope, this one tied with a red ribbon sealed with wax. The judge, no stranger to court-room dramatics, laid the ribboned and sealed envelope on his desk, gazed quizzically over his half-glasses at his audience, sighed, and broke the seal.

It was a decoded message from North Vietnamese naval vessels in the Gulf of Tonkin on a crucial night of August 1964. President John-son had used (and distorted) the incident there as his reason for esca-lating the war. If this cable were printed by the *Post*, the government said, it would be a disastrous revelation of our ability to eavesdrop on enemy communications and to decode their most secure battle messages. Once the ability was disclosed, our defenses would be blinded to enemy intentions and it would jeopardize the lives of soldiers and sailors in the war zone.

The *Post* officials were stunned. Glendon leaned down to Wilson and said hopelessly, "What do we do now?"

Wilson whispered back that he thought he had seen that message somewhere before.

Glendon whispered back fiercely: "Jesus Christ, George, don't fake it here."

Wilson said firmly: "Stall for time. Do something. But stall for time."

Glendon straightened and asked the judge if he could read the cable once more.

Wilson opened his green vinyl bag. It was filled with thick green paperbound volumes of printed congressional hearing reports from the Government Printing Office.

He was sure it would have been from Senator Fulbright's 1968 hearings on the origins of the Vietnam War. For Wilson and all conscientious correspondents following government policy, these thick volumes were regular required reading. Flipping pages rapidly while Glendon became more nervous, Wilson finally stopped, took time briefly to read a page, and handed one of the green-bound books to Glendon. Glendon read the indicated passage and handed it to the judge.

It was a public document. It had been issued three years earlier and was available to anyone who had a few dollars to buy the report.

It was a crucial incident in the case that would eventually go from Judge Bazelon's chambers to the Supreme Court, where the *Times* and *Post* ultimately would win the case for continuing to publish.

At the very moment the judge was breaking the melodramatic seal in the coded briefcase, the Soviet Embassy—which clearly would have bought the document three years earlier—or anyone, U.S. citizen or not, could have seen it in a number of public libraries.

How can one explain this incident? How could the highest level of

American intelligence leadership, desperate to prove that the *Post* publication of this document would cause "grave and irreparable harm" to our country and risk the lives of our service people, send over in sealed solemnity a document that had been on public sale to anyone, American or foreign, for more than three years?

The government has cadres of skilled people who could be called on to dig up a more frightening document. Yet, in the "ten worst" cases and this supposedly "supremely worst" case, they seemed to have acted with incredible carelessness and stupidity. But the people who run our intelligence agencies are not stupid.

I think the explanation is that in the twenty-three years of the American mutation of the Cold War, the whole country had become conditioned to secret government in high places. Over the years, through political trials and spy scares and melodramatic hearings, the public came to accept the idea that in order to save the country, the public is best kept ignorant about the most critical operations of their government.

A religious aura developed around the word "Secret" and its escalating permutations like "Top-Secret" and "Top-Secret Sensitive" and ultimately classifications so secret that their existence is a secret. Taking these at face value gradually came to be seen as synonymous with ensuring the nation's survival.

After a prolonged period of being protected from public accountability, even the most intelligent and sensitive of leaders come to feel it is justified and necessary to be insulated from the judgments of outsiders. Inevitably, conscious assumptions of unquestioned power develop unconscious arrogance. Held in awe, and protected from being held to account, such leaders stop worrying about how they look to the ignorant outside world. Like all human beings given godlike powers, they become capable of acting carelessly and behave in ways that, when exposed to the ordinary light of day, seem stupid but really betray the expectation of unquestioned authority.

Inevitably, the whole process also leads to the ultimate trap in a democracy, to lie "for good purposes."

The newspapers would win the Supreme Court decision 6 to 3, but the problem of progressive secrecy would continue to grow. Ten years later, Ronald Reagan would order increased secrecy.

But, simultaneous with that Supreme Court decision, there was a strange final chapter to the case in which I played a role and about which I am still ambivalent.

If it had not been for the Supreme Court decision issued in time for the news on Wednesday, June 30, 1971, national attention would have been focused instead on a bizarre event in the United States Senate.

The melodrama, extraordinary even for congressional excess, occurred in the small morning hours of Monday, June 28, too late for Tuesday's news, but ready for the national news on Wednesday. But by Wednesday the news was massively concerned with the Supreme Court decision on the Pentagon Papers, relegating the spectacle in the Senate to a tiny item in the back pages. Many news outlets did not report it at all. I was not unhappy with that.

The largely unreported incident in the Senate involved my "second box" from the Boston motel. It had been sitting inside my apartment closet, forgotten even by me during the frantic days and night before the court decision.

Ellsberg had arranged for the box to be delivered to a young Democratic senator from Alaska, Mike Gravel. Gravel had taken a strong position against the Vietnam War. He agreed to accept a copy of Ellsberg's copied documents after J. William Fulbright, chairman of the Senate Foreign Relations Committee, had declined Ellsberg's offer, because Fulbright was already politically under fire because of his open opposition to the war. I had never met Gravel before and neither had Ellsberg.

When I had breathing space I called Gravel's office and asked for an appointment to meet him in a room in the East front of the Senate Building. As we strolled in the marble chamber overlooking the plaza beyond, to my dismay Senator Robert Dole walked up to us as though he wanted to talk. I did not relish being identified with this particular mission. But Gravel and Dole exchanged only passing small talk.

A few nights later, together with Betty Medsger, I loaded the second box into a car. I was waiting for a divorce and would later marry Betty, a reporter at the *Post*, so she had known most of what had transpired. We drove to the Mayflower Hotel and, as agreed, there was the senator with two of his aides waiting on the sidewalk.

When Gravel came to our car, I told him the box was heavy and perhaps his two aides should take it out of the car. He said he did not want them to touch it since only he had congressional immunity. Once the box was in the trunk of Gravel's car, we all retired to the Mayflower bar for drinks and unrelated small talk. That was the last I heard until I saw something brief in the back pages of the papers the day the Supreme Court decision hit the front pages. The small item did not tell much of the events that followed our drink at the Mayflower. I learned the details only long afterward.

Gravel had planned to read the entire 5,400 pages of the Pentagon Papers on the floor of the Senate. At the time, the papers were still censored. There was a real possibility they would remain censored. Gravel planned to read all 5,400 pages in what he planned to be the longest filibuster in Senate history. If a senator has gone through the parliamentary steps and has no opposition from his party, once the senator has the floor no one can stop him—as long as he does not stop talking or sit down. The successful senator can do this until the Senate, desperate to complete other urgent business, agrees to grant the desire of the filibustering senator.

A successful filibuster demands elaborate preparations, including hours of a salt-free diet, a hidden urine bag tied inside the senator's trousers, medication to stay awake, special compounds to assuage battered vocal cords, and steel braces to keep legs from collapsing with exhaustion. It is a technique that was sharpened by conservative Southern senators who had used it for decades to defeat civil rights legislation. In Gravel's case, success would mean that in the end, when the Senate would be empty, he would order all the documents to be entered into the Congressional Record, and thereby make the Pentagon Papers publicly available. He could not depend on any other senator to take up a relay of his filibuster. He had to do it alone.

Gravel made all these preparations, but at the last minute an uncooperative fellow Democrat and a breach of normal bipartisan courtesy by a hostile Republican blocked his filibuster. Frustrated and enraged, he chose the only forum remaining to him. There no one could stop him, he could still be protected from arrest because of his congressional immunity, and he would still have the power to order the papers publicly printed.

In desperation, he announced an "executive session" of the Senate committee that he chaired, the obscure Senate Subcommittee on Buildings and Grounds.

As chairman, his "executive session" consisted of him alone. He took the whole apparatus to a small nearby hearing room where he began his reading. Word quickly got around Washington, and the small room was soon crowded with reporters and TV cameras.

Gravel droned on for some time but there was a point when he reached detailed official battle reports. The reports described horribly dismembered American soldiers in Vietnam. Gravel was exhausted and at descriptions of the battle wounds began to weep as he read. He had to pause to regain a reading voice and before long, as the descriptions of maiming and death went on, he wept uncontrollably and had to stop. With tears still on his face, he repeated the congressional term of art, "by unanimous consent" the proceedings and accompanying documents would be printed for the public as a committee report. He, of course, constituted the unanimity.

Had the Supreme Court voted to sustain censorship, Gravel's act would have guaranteed that the Pentagon Papers would be publicized.

But I was pleased that news of the Supreme Court decision obscured news of the extraordinary Senate scene—and with it possible disclosure of my unjournalistic role in it. I had violated my own rule of not becoming a secret actor in something I would report as a supposedly outside reporter. It embarrassed me then and does still.

The coincidences that touched me, however, did not end. Gravel's Buildings and Grounds Subcommittee did not have to bring out the papers. Instead, months later, after careful editing and annotation by scholars, the documents were published as *The Senator Gravel Edition of the Pentagon Papers.*

The volumes were brought out by Beacon Press, the nonprofit publishing arm of the Unitarian Universalist Association. Perhaps because Beacon had published my first book eighteen years earlier and I had been active for many years in Unitarian affairs, Beacon sent me a routine courtesy invitation to the Washington news media reception they held to publicize their issuing the Gravel Edition of the Pentagon Papers. They may have assumed that as a newsperson, I might be interested in a chance to actually see a set of the famous documents.

The reception was held in the Statler Hilton Hotel, across the street from the *Post*, where, that night on the way to the Beacon Press affair, I strolled as casually as possible past the bank of public phones from which, months earlier, I had first called "Mr. Boston" in Boston.

CHAPTER 3

## *The Good Old Days Weren't*

If I were inclined toward warm nostalgia about past American journalism, which I am not, I could get romantic about the newsroom where I first worked on the *Springfield Morning Union* in Massachusetts. Alongside the desks of older reporters were big brass spittoons that might or might not catch their spit from chewing tobacco and loose ends of cigars. The oak desks and hardwood floors were mottled with cigarette burns. Late sports scores and stock market quotations came to a telegrapher named Sam whose key was mounted on an empty Prince Albert tobacco tin to amplify the rapid-fire dits and dahs. While part of Sam's brain automatically translated the Morse code into notes he wrote to the copy desk, another part of Sam's brain simultaneously told a stream of dirty jokes to anyone in hearing distance. Most outside news came from banks of teletype machines, their endless chugging combined with the clatter of old manual typewriters and the shouted curses of reporters, many of whom wore green eyeshades. A permanent cloud of cigar and cigarette smoke hung over the place. Whenever an editor went through the swinging doors to the composing room it added the noise of great clanking linotype machines turning words on paper into letters in metal. To the eye, ear, and nose the newsroom looked, sounded, and smelled like what it really was, a dirty, noisy factory.

Today's newsrooms could be mistaken for a roomful of doctoral candidates working on their dissertations, often complete with file cabinets and shelves of books. The faint clicking of computer keyboards is hushed by carpeting on the floor. Any reportorial curses are discreetly muttered—after all, these usually are university educated men and women, some with graduate degrees. Data banks of vast quantities of regional, national, and world news are quietly accessed by computer, the selected stories issued from all but noiseless machines. Sam the telegrapher is forever gone, as are the sounds of all the other noisy newsroom devices of fifty years ago. There is no cigarette smoke. If a brass spittoon appeared, some resident old geezer would have to explain and the men and women reporters would rebel.

Since the day, right out of college in 1941, that I walked on an impulse into the *Springfield Morning Union* to ask for a job, the world has changed and so has the news. Today, I wouldn't be hired. Editors are fussier than they used to be.

Even the name of the whole news enterprise has changed from the traditional "the press" to that mushy replacement, "the media," which can mean anything from the billboards on Route 66 to materials Cezanne used for canvasses. Like most journalists, I dislike the word but use it reluctantly because no one has come up with anything better to cover both printed news from presses and electronic news from antennas.

But since I started in journalism, more than the vocabulary has changed. The news itself has undergone a radical transformation. The audience for news has changed, reporters are different, and those who own and control the news are a new breed. Much of it is simply slicker and more frenzied in money-making, but many of the changes have been an improvement over the widespread crudities and limited agendas of prewar news.

For one thing, the modern American audience needs a different kind of news and knows it. World War II ended the country's cultural isolation and made sixteen million veterans eligible for free college educations. Sobered war veterans forever changed American campuses from part-time playgrounds to places of full-time purposeful study. Sales of books quadrupled after the war. Demands of the modern world became more complex than ever. Nuclear weapons and rapid air travel and then television brought much of the once-unseen world into living rooms, making foreign news seem as real as a house fire in the next block.

Wars, international trade, and travel have made foreign policy serious items in the news. Grim experience has convinced the American public that events in distant countries—once only bizarre footnotes in most local news outlets—can take away their sons and daughters, their incomes, their gasoline, and with the spread of nuclear weapons, all life on earth.

Today, more Americans work at jobs that require serious information about the political and economic world. To cope, children are expected to be better academically and learn more complex subjects than their parents did. Newspapers are no longer the main source of information about the outside world. For the first time since town criers spread the news in tiny villages three hundred years ago, practically everyone, even those who fail modern literacy standards, has access to major news through broadcast pictures and spoken words.

A new kind of journalist responded to the new audience.

Before the war a common source for the reporter was an energetic kid who ran newsroom errands for a few years before he was permitted to accompany the most glamorous character on the staff, the rough-tough, seen-it-all, blood-and-guts police reporter. Or else, as in my case, on a paper with low standards, reporters started off as merely warm bodies that could type and would accept $18 a week with no benefits.

Prewar journalists had their talents and occasional brilliance, but the initial demand on me and my peers was the ability to walk fast, talk fast, type fast, never break a deadline. And to be a male of the species. Some of us on that long-ago paper had college educations but we learned to keep quiet about it; there was a suspicion that a degree turned men into sissies. Only after the war did the U.S. Labor Department's annual summary of job possibilities in journalism state that a college degree is "sometimes preferred."

Reporting and editing was a men's club that lasted even longer than newsroom suspicions about college boys. There have always been women in American journalism, but they tended to be widows who took over their husbands' small papers or held jobs sequestered in the genteel ghetto where they wrote respectful accounts of local tea parties. As late as the 1960s when I attended the National Press Club luncheons where prime ministers and Cabinet members delivered their speeches to the Washington press corps, the only correspondents on the main ballroom floor were men; women Washington correspondents were permitted only in an upstairs side balcony, like an Orthodox synagogue or the seating "upstairs for colored" in old Southern movie houses. Only in the 1970s and 1980s did women appear in numbers in regular reporting assignments and on important editing desks.

Black reporters on white newspapers were almost nonexistent. In 1957, four years after the Supreme Court ended legal school segregation, Jim Rhea, my colleague on the Providence papers, may have been the only African-American reporter besides Carl Rowan at the *Minneapolis Tribune*.

Racial stereotypes were prolonged by the wire services that served papers and radio stations all over the country, including in the South where segregation was still the norm. Even after the Supreme Court desegregation decision, wire stories about race relations were written in ways to least offend the Southern papers that denigrated blacks and upheld segregation. Jim Rhea had to argue bitterly with the copy desk that just because an Associated Press story was written to satisfy a segregationist editor in Jackson, Mississippi, didn't mean it should be acceptable in Providence, Rhode Island. For me, his battles provided an insight into just one advantage of having members of different ethnic groups and women on news staffs.

To this day, neither women nor members of minorities hold responsible positions in journalism in anything close to their numbers in society, though they now appear more often than in the past.

Today, it is no longer seen as egghead eccentricity or high-brow pretension to write daily on subjects like education and science, or to report the personality and background of influential men and women. Today, being streetwise about crime and police or a drinking pal of politicians is no longer enough for a reporter.

In the early 1950s, Leo Sonderegger, City Editor of the *Providence*

*Evening Bulletin*, asked a senior legislative reporter to write a profile of the Speaker of the Rhode Island General Assembly who for years had appeared in the paper only as a voice and vote. The political reporter exploded with indignation, "Goddammit, Leo, this is a newspaper, not *The New Yorker!*"

Before World War II, most papers around the country concentrated on highly stereotyped versions of crime, courts, and city hall politics. Reporting about medicine was often dangerous to health. News of science was wildly unscientific. Investigative reporting consisted mostly of undocumented police tips about gangsters. In most papers, the only foreign report of the day was apt to be something like a freak suicide in Budapest.

When I first began reporting, most printed and broadcast stories were clumps of clichés. Journalism writing was understandably sneered at in the past as "journalese" (dictionary: "The slick, superficial style of writing often held to be characteristic of newspapers and magazines"). Stories were written by deadly formula and only sports reporters were permitted to write humanoid prose. In my early years on newspapers, the copy desks that "corrected" reporters' stories and prepared them for the printers often deleted straightforward phrases and substituted the clichés. Both reporters and copy desks were overly proud of their knowledge of specialized jargon. In accident stories if I wrote that victims suffered cuts and bruises, the desk might change it to police jargon, "contusions and abrasions." A court story in which a judge sent the case back to a lower court became "the court issued a write of mandamus." All three-alarm fires were "conflagrations."

» 

Any look at the average newspaper fifty years ago makes clear that in many respects the daily news today, even with its flaws, looks out at a larger world and does it with greater expertise.

In my early reporting years, there was no hesitation in routinely beginning stories of police arrests with something like "John Jones, a Negro . . . ," while arrest accounts never mentioned race if the detained person was white. Any working-class man arrested with even a slight previous offense might be referred to as a "hoodlum." Libel suits by aggrieved citizens and groups, despite the excesses and exploitation of libel suits, have helped eliminate some of the thoughtlessness of the past. The civil rights movement and hiring of minority journalists and women has helped raise institutional sensitivities.

Only forty years ago it was sometimes difficult to separate any news about a woman from the male reporter's description of her appearance ("Shapely Blonde Wins Lottery . . ." or "Mary Smith, an attractive brunette, declared her candidacy for county school board today . . .").

In every newspaper newsroom of the past that I knew, the photo editor had in his bottom drawer a pile of titillating pictures for the boys and regularly sneaked one into the paper on some pretense. Press agents knew how to get press attention with photographs of plunging necklines or backlighting on transparent dresses ("Starlet Jennifer Lust, above, is one of 200 trying for a role in the upcoming epic film version of the Johnstown flood."). A major wire service machine sending national and international photographs to newspaper clients had a daily capacity for only twenty-six photographs and, along with the usual train wrecks, presidential appearances, and floods, one of the twenty-six was likely to be a photograph of a young woman displaying enough flesh to give the boys in the newsroom their daily fix. Stories about raped or murdered women frequently listed irrelevant detail about the victim's lingerie. The phrase "bra-burning feminists" was used to describe a crucial early demonstration for women's rights even though on that occasion no bras were burned. Its inaccuracy has not prevented the phrase from becoming a mythic male news symbol of feminism in the 1970s.

I'm sure I was not immune from stereotypes as the standard way of "reporting the news." It took closer contacts with the stereotyped men and women to realize the "standard news" was not just socially destructive but simply inaccurate. When ethnic Americans and women began to have regular jobs on news staffs they began confronting their editors, who in the past had heard no complaints and had seen nothing wrong in the old practices.

Another jolt came from journalism reviews that started in the 1960s and often embarrassed editors and news organizations by exposing the use of stereotypes. The new reviews also made criticism more respectable in the trade. For years, before media criticism became popular, I was referred to in the trade weekly of newspaper publishing, *Editor & Publisher*, as "Ben H. Bagdikian, a so-called media critic" or, on other occasions, "a self-appointed critic."

Before the war, famous journalists were proud of their fictional "news" stories. Damon Runyon, whose short stories I enjoy, practiced his fictional art as a reporter writing "news" accounts in the *Denver Post*. H. L. Mencken, an icon to some newspeople (but, for a number of reasons including his antisemitism, not to me), liked to boast about the phony stories he wrote as a reporter for the otherwise sober *Baltimore Sun*. An imaginative rewrite man (always a man) was a valued person on any staff, able to turn a simple police arrest into a highly imaginative but largely embroidered drama.

For all their hard-boiled manner and language, newspeople are romantics and some still insist that the news was better in "the old days." It wasn't.

Today, the gap between the quality of news in large papers and small ones has disappeared. Before 1940 readers of small dailies and many large ones seldom got a view beyond the county line. While some small papers were extraordinary, like William Allen White's legendary *Emporia Gazette* in Kansas, most were full of amateur journalism written by people whose chief skill was typing.

Today in small towns as well as in major cities, reporting staffs consist of trained journalists, and smaller papers often surpass some big city dailies in enterprise and in-depth reporting of community issues. In 1989, when I studied one day of the 120 daily papers of California, the *Hemet News*, a small paper of 14,000 circulation in a town with a population of 30,000, had more of all the important national and international news than some of the state's dailies ten times its size.

Postwar journalism has produced admirable reporting, and in cities around the country there have been investigative reports, some printed and some broadcast, that created positive community growth, exposed dangerous conditions, and unseated corrupt officials.

There is good news and bad in the changes. To say that in real ways our journalism is better than before and at the same time is seriously flawed is not as paradoxical as it may seem. The American journalism enterprise is unique. It is huge, with the world's largest number of daily papers. Most industrialized countries have national newspapers and broadcast networks in the central city and only minor ones of little importance outside the capital. But unlike any other developed country, the United States leaves some central governmental functions to local communities—like schooling, police, land use, most taxation, and local transportation and streets. No American community can govern itself intelligently with only national news. Consequently, in the United States there is only a tiny number of national newspapers, but approximately 75,000 professional print and broadcast journalists spread throughout the country in 1,600 local daily papers, more than 8,000 weeklies, 11,000 broadcast stations, and 11,000 cable channels.

Yet, even though neither the organizations nor the individuals who work in our extraordinary mass of news outlets and newspeople are homogeneous, they produce a daily product of surprising uniformity. Too many of the old flaws and some new ones keep American journalism from meeting the public's need for serious news.

》

Beginning in the 1960s, one of the best-kept secrets in the American newspaper world escaped. And the most shocked beneficiaries were the experts on Wall Street, who, despite all their shrewd and cynical authority, had been fooled for decades by the heart-rending phony performance by owners of American newspapers.

The secret was the fabulous money-making ability of newspapers. The admission of high profits rose out of a quirk in the country's tax laws that would transform the structure of the news industry.

Most of the country's current daily papers began in the nineteenth century as small local and family enterprises, usually started by some strong-willed ancestor with only a small nest egg. Adolph Ochs, for example, bought the foundering *New York Times* in 1896 with only $75,000 of his own money. But by the 1960s, most of these family enterprises, including the *Times*, had reached the third-generation limit of family trusts that postpone inheritance taxes. By then, their newspapers had become worth multiples of millions and the postponed taxes were huge.

It had been no secret that the country's most prominent paper, the *New York Times*, thanks to the owning family's sense that they operated a national institution, had low profits (other subsidiaries made the company more profitable). And millions of Americans had seen the movie *Citizen Kane* in which a thinly disguised William Randolph Hearst lost money on his papers but poured in millions from the family gold mines and other enterprises to promote his insatiable ego and political hobbyhorses. But the *Times* and a few others were exceptions.

As competing papers slowly disappeared during this century, local monopolies grew and so did the survivors' profits. But each time a competing paper fell by the wayside, lamentations were heard in the land about the sad fate of the disappearing American newspaper. (I still receive calls from writers asking if it is not true that newspapers are about to disappear.) Newspaper owners didn't discourage the impression that daily papers nobly endured meager or even nonexistent profits in sacrificial devotion to the First Amendment. It was an illusion useful to silence advertisers' complaints about high advertising rates and news employees' protests about low pay. No privately owned paper ever showed outsiders its books.

But in the 1960s some papers decided to trade shares of their companies on the open stock market by way of letting public stockholders share the new estate taxes. The Securities and Exchange Commission laws require open financial statements for prospective buyers of shares. Now the newspapers not only wanted to stop their cries of poverty, but boast—privately to Wall Street—that they really made a lot of money. That is when Wall Street discovered that most newspapers are among the biggest profit-makers in American industry. Newspapers became attractive properties to acquire, often in large numbers by a single national corporation. Some papers, like the ones in Providence, or the Newhouse and Hearst chains, remained privately owned with closed books, but they are more the exception than rule.

Even publicly traded companies still conceal the profits of their individual newspapers and broadcast stations. News outlets usually are only one set of subsidiaries owned by the large national and multinational media conglomerates, and because only their combined corporate finances must be disclosed—their magazine and book divisions, cable systems, billboards, and firms unrelated to any medium—the profit margins of each paper remain largely private.

Before I did some studies that let me see a cross-section of newspaper books, I had my own naivete about the subject of profits in the news. One day in Washington, for example, I was having a neighborly drink with the irreverent heir of a chain of medium-sized daily papers in the Midwest. He had just been appointed as one of the bright whiz kids in the administration of John Kennedy. I asked something about the low profits of papers like the ones his family owned. He laughed at me.

"Are you kidding? Papers like ours are gold mines. We wouldn't accept a pretax margin lower than forty percent and we wouldn't buy a paper if we couldn't get back our total investment in less than five years."

»

The old local owners were a mixed lot. A few understood good journalism and strived for it. The majority ran somewhat useful but uninspired daily bulletin boards. Many were greedy and narrow-minded, like the owner of the *Morning Union* where I worked before the war. At that time, Sherman Bowles controlled all four daily papers in Springfield. He was a long, lean Yankee with rosy cheeks, a fixed smile, and calculating eyes. One day on one of his periodic rapid walks through the newsroom, a reporter friend of mine who had been waiting a year on his request for a raise timidly stopped Bowles and asked about his raise. Mr. Bowles smiled his secret smile, said, "Come with me," and took my friend to the cashier's office where he said, "Mr. Cook, give this man his pay. He doesn't want to work for us anymore."

A more common type of older owner was paternalistic and would occasionally give financial help to an approved employee with financial problems. It was both a warm gesture toward a valued employee and a hedge against unions that might want outlandish luxuries like guaranteed health and pension benefits.

But some of the old owners understood good journalism. They made the long-range investment always needed to produce higher quality news and in the process established the best standards that influence the country's serious journalists. They included the Ochs-Sulzberger family of the *New York Times*, the Knights in Miami and elsewhere, the Binghams in Louisville, the Sharpes and Metcalfs in Providence, the Pulitzers in St. Louis, and, by the time of World War II, the Meyers and Grahams in Washington. These families and a few others created standards that persisted when they were absorbed into the new corporate conglomerates.

If the old owners were a wild mixture of the terrible, the mediocre, and the inspired, the new owners are a more uniform lot. They are money institutions—a complex of Wall Street brokers, law firms, banks, insurance companies, and pension fund managers that finance the mergers and acquisitions that build the growing media empires. They ride herd on quarterly earnings of their media investments, which they call "profit centers" and to which they look for ever-rising results every three months.

The news business traditionally had been backward in technology—a nineteenth-century reporter or linotype operator would have felt at home on a 1960s newspaper. Most papers also were backward in accounting, only faintly changed from the time cashiers on high stools kept books with pen and ink. Beginning in the 1960s, new owners introduced advanced technology and modern business practices. But they also brought something else—less interest in serious news. If quarterly earnings do not rise steadily, or if mergers are accomplished by loading the captured company with huge debt requiring huge profits, the new owners and investors have been unsentimental in demanding shrinkage of serious news, substituting inexpensive syndicated features and entertainment to attract more ads.

The national wire service machines produce endless quantities of national features, entertainment, and distant news at negligible cost per paragraph. The machines do not ask for health benefits, pensions, or a reasonable work week. But men and women reporters on local staffs do.

Scaling back real news and local news slowly but steadily is easy in most daily papers. Readers don't notice it at once and when eventually they do both readers and local advertisers have little choice, since in ninety-eight percent of American cities with their own daily papers there is a local monopoly.

In broadcasting, comparable changes were imposed by new owners. In the 1980s, when large corporate investors took over all three major networks, their first moves were to close most foreign bureaus, get rid of the experienced news staff, and eliminate the documentary units that had done some of the most memorable work in television.

Not all the new corporate owners are so ruthless. Some of the country's better family-owned papers formed corporate empires but retained control by reserving voting stock for a family trust, as with the *New York Times* and the *Washington Post*. But they, too, must now respond to the demands of the stock market.

》

Something else happened during my years in daily reporting. Television would transform all news.

While still in junior high school I used to accompany my father to Boston where, as in many other cities, the papers still had large blackboards in their downtown street floor windows on which they wrote late bulletins for office workers and shoppers who gathered on the sidewalk to watch for the chalked-in news breaks and ball scores.

On really major local or national news breaks, papers issued an unscheduled edition, an Extra, devoted to that one spectacular item, with small armies of schoolboys running through the streets yelling "Extra!" to people who ran out of shops and homes to buy a copy.

It was on a Sunday off from my first reporting job in December of 1941 that I heard an announcer interrupt the live broadcast of the New York Philharmonic Orchestra to say the ominous words, "We interrupt this broadcast . . ." I knew what would happen and rushed to the *Morning Union* office where the staff automatically gathered knowing that there would be an Extra on the Japanese attack on Pearl Harbor. My job was to interview people in the street, and the answer of one young man remains with me: "Why, it's ridiculous. We'll whip the dirty little Japs and it will be all over in two weeks." Within an hour boys were running through the streets of Springfield waving the huge headlines and yelling, "Extra! Extra! Read all about it! Japs bomb Pearl Harbor!"

Television changed all that. It not only took away the function of first announcement from newspapers but it kept people watching their sets all evening, which helped kill big-city afternoon dailies. Television changed the functions of the daily newspaper from mere announcer of news to provider of confirmation, detail, and background for major news that radio and television has already announced in brief. I was the first national editor of the *Washington Post* who had to watch all three network evening newscasts merely to know what would be on the country's mind when people picked up our paper the next morning.

The vividness, technical excellence, and creativity of which television is capable has served high purposes. The improvement in Deep South civil rights after World War II would not have happened without television's vivid pictures of racial brutality that generations of printed accounts had not ended. Network documentaries of the 1950s, 1960s, and 1970s led to reforms of national policies and politics, like Edward R. Murrow's documentaries on Senator Joseph McCarthy and on hunger in America. In the 1980s, Bill Moyers's documentaries on public television raised national consciousness of long-ignored social problems.

Television overrode some parochial mores. The whole country saw the same television network national news, unlike what they read in their local papers that reflected each community's own standards. In the early 1960s, the front page of the leading paper in Jackson, Mississippi denounced Northern reporters as "radical journalist race mixers" and referred to me as a writer for the "pinko *Saturday Evening Post*." Now for the first time people in Jackson, Mississippi saw the same national and world news as people in Nashua, New Hampshire or Los Angeles.

Symbolic chapters in our history since World War II live vividly in the nation's memory as television images with lasting power and influence—civil rights confrontations, the 1960s' assassinations that wiped out the country's liberal leaders, scenes from Vietnam which, like scenes of racial brutality in the Deep South, helped change history.

In the past, many white Southern journalists wanting to escape inflexible racism became regional refugees in Northern newspapers and magazines. In the 1950s and 1960s, Southerners were a dramatic fixture in national publishing; the expatriates headed the two largest magazines of the period, *Look* and the *Saturday Evening Post*, and a number of important newspapers, including the *New York Times*. I became used to discussing stories with New York editors who had Georgia, Mississippi, and Carolina accents. When I worked at the *Saturday Evening Post* in the 1960s, I often flew to New York to talk about stories on the magazine. Bill Emerson, the editor, was a native Carolinian, who hid shrewd instincts behind a manic personality. He shouted welcomes into his office with either "Miscreant!" or "Hey, Tiger!" or, in my case, "Come in, you crazy Armenian." With subeditors Otto Friedrich, Don McKinney, and Tom Congdon, the magazine was a lively and adventurous magazine, full of the high morale that always adds poignancy to a ship doomed to sink.

Television was about to catch up with magazines like the *Saturday Evening Post* despite its aggressive journalism (and some of my happiest free-lance years). These full-color national magazines designed for a general audience were once the monarchs of national advertising. Unlike newspapers, they could run ads in glossy color and unlike newspapers they had a national audience. But by the mid-1960s enough American households had bought color television sets. The coaxial cable reached every city. The new living room appliance took the lion's share of full-color national ads, and before the end of the decade all the big, general interest national magazines were dead.

Television eventually brought something else with it. Its constantly moving images are so seductive and its audience so huge that commercials and entertainment soon intruded into the news. Because visible men and women deliver news and announcements, "personality" and "celebrity" have become highly profitable commodities, worsening the confusion of commercial television's news with a mixture of advertising and personality projection.

» 

Through all of postwar American journalism, in the midst of its accomplishments, there is a limitation that has persisted so long it has become our flawed definition of news. Despite conservatives' perpetual complaint of a "liberal bias in the news," all of broadcast and printed news is pulled by a dominant current into a continuous flow of business conservatism. It has a sufficiently powerful effect to shrink other ideas and news of tax-supported social needs necessary in any self-correcting democracy.

The conservative emphasis in the news does not announce itself in the flamboyant style of old William Randolph Hearst. It is done in the selection of unflamboyant, carefully worded news compiled under rules with the presumed goal of being "fair to both sides." But most often "both sides" merely represent nuances of differences among those who wield public and private power. The main news mostly ignores or obscures the true "other side," the social and economic realities that most Americans live with.

American reporting is governed by a doctrine we like to call "objectivity." It ordains that reporters stick to the facts and leave out their own opinions and judgments. It is a useful discipline. A truly objective account is an unbiased recording of all significant elements in an event. But the daily news tends to limit itself to the views of the movers and shakers of society. Lost is the impact of the movers and shakers on the ordinary, unaffluent Americans who are the moved and the shaken. Objective reality can become dim, distorted, or lost.

The result is that American news is overwhelmingly the world as seen from the top down and negligibly the world as seen from the bottom up. It concentrates on the views of institutions, not the effect of those institutions on the largest groups of flesh-and-blood people.

Typical was reportage in 1993 when President Clinton proposed a major social change, universal health coverage, that would affect every man, woman, and child in the country. During a crucial period of decisions on the proposals, a Kaiser Foundation study reported: "The story of health care reform, as reported in five of the country's major daily newspapers over a four month period, was largely about its likely impact on institutions rather than individuals. Far more attention was given to politics than to patients."

The news likes to think that it weighs public information on the scales of objectivity and fairness, but there are prejudicial thumbs on the scales. Advertisers weigh more than consumers, upper-income more than lower-income families, corporations more than unions, the private sector more than the public sector, and in political controversy the rhetorical slogans of contenders weigh more than the substance of their arguments. It is why the 1980s Reaganite years were mostly in the news as economic "miracles" or "reforms" even as the evidence mounted that the "miracles" would cripple the American economy into the next century.

Even our foreign reporting has favored the centers of power over observable realities. During the Cold War, the news signed up like an obedient soldier, and when official foreign policy sanctified or lied about brutal dictatorships, the news followed either by nonreporting or false reporting, as would later be documented in Central and South America and places like Cambodia and Indonesia. Nations seen in Washington as too leftist or hostile were certain to be depicted as possessing no redeeming qualities, like Allende's Chile, Sandanista Nicaragua, and Castro's Cuba.

When the United States invaded Grenada, Panama, and the Persian Gulf, "both sides" in the news tended to be limited to high military people who differed only over the tactics to be used in the invasion. Voices raising the question of whether the country had sufficient reason to conduct the invasions at all were excluded.

If the public remains confused on many issues, unable to follow the evolution of a particular issue, news commentators tell us that "the audience has a short memory."

I do not blame the audience. It is subjected to an hourly and daily barrage of wildly confusing noise in the news, isolated items of the gravest matters immediately followed by a morass of murder and sex, life-jolting changes in work life cheek-by-jowl with the latest scandal among celebrities. Most ordinary people do not have a short memory about matters that affect the central needs in their own lives. It is our news institutions that have short memories.

If our news is, in Walter Lippmann's image, like a searchlight focused now here and now there on a darkened stage of public affairs, it shines its light with periods of outstanding dedication on matters of civil rights and individual suffering. But when it comes to basic errors and injustices caused by corporate economics, the flashlight may turn to the subject for a figurative strobelike second, after which it lingers lovingly on highly illuminated slapstick, strip-tease, and the latest murders, natural disasters, and excitements on Wall Street.

I do not blame reporters. Given the chance and the time, most modern American reporters can put their stories of surface events into a real context. I would like to change some things in our news and I want to suggest a few in this book. But I would not change what American journalists do best.

Something else strikes me as important in our view of news as "objective." I learned and respect the discipline of fairness and balance, but, as I believe owners of the papers for whom I worked did on their part, the news I was most moved to report and that struck me as most vivid had as much to do with my own perspectives and background as with the theoretical objectivity of the organizations I worked for. Both are part of all reporting. These perspectives are exercised with even greater power over the news by those who own newspapers and broadcast stations. If I write so much in this book about my own life, it is because—speaking objectively—I know more about that subject.

CHAPTER 4

## *Seeing Double*

The American journalist" as an individual has an indispens-
able double vision that looks at the world as both insider
and outsider. But fortunately, "the American journalist"
collectively is even more complicated. In the mass, "the
journalist" looks out through seventy-five thousand different sets of eyes conditioned by seventy-five thousand different life experiences, for which the uniquely diverse society of the United States can be thankful. But there are times
when the different perspectives can be personally painful,
as I discovered in a novel assignment from my Providence
editor.

It was in the fall of 1957. National attention was on the
South where federal courts were telling cities that when the
1954 Supreme Court had ordered desegregation of schools
"with all deliberate speed," the court meant the time had
come to obey. All Southern cities were on edge, many torn
by racists shouting at inflamed crowds. Some cities had riots, others teetered on the brink. Even the news from the
South was confused.

That was when Jeff Brown, the editor, and Mike Ogden,
the managing editor, of the *Providence Journal* and *The
Evening Bulletin* decided to send a black reporter and a
white reporter together to report on how the Southern
confusion looked.

My black colleague, Jim Rhea, had been born in Johnson City, Tennessee, gone to the University of Michigan, and been in the Korean War. I had lived in the Deep South for three years during World War II, so I had at least a transplanted white's perspective on the Southern scene. We were good friends, we both liked the assignment, and, I think, neither of us imagined that the trip would put strains on our friendship.

Jim and I started out by dining and rooming in Washington's Mayflower Hotel. Interstate air travel and public facilities in the District of Columbia had already been desegregated, so we filled our first day planning our trip's strategy.

The next morning we headed for the Supreme Court for the final futile appeal by the governor of Arkansas, Orval Faubus, to postpone desegregating Little Rock schools. Our first unplanned event was on our way to the court when our cab ran through a stop sign and almost crashed into another car. As our cab screeched to a stop inches from a collision, we recognized in the back seat of the other car the startled face of Chief Justice Earl Warren, headed for the same building. That was our first bad moment.

The next morning we flew to Memphis where Jim's humiliations began. Greeting us as we walked down the stairs of the American Airlines plane, on the pavement of the municipal airport were two pairs of painted lines directing passengers to the terminal. One pair to the right was painted white and marked "White Only." The other pair to the left was yellow and marked "Colored." Jim and I had decided to report what we saw and try not to become a part of the story. He grimly went left and I went right.

We visited cities where, first, he interviewed black leaders and I white ones and then, not always revealing our partnership, we switched. The same black leader would tell him one thing and me another. We had the same experience with white leaders: public officials try to read the minds of reporters just as much as reporters try to read the minds of officials. It was a good introduction to the confusion and fears of even the most decent people trying to emerge from a malevolent history.

In Little Rock we covered a federal court hearing in which a federal judge issued the final local order to desegregate the city's Central High School. Jim and I had a late dinner assuming that the Little Rock crisis was over and headed for New Orleans.

New Orleans had always been proud to be the most racially relaxed city in the Deep South. When I had visited the city during wartime leaves from Louisiana air bases, I sat in audiences of blacks and whites listening to jazz bands played by blacks and whites together. But now, under segregationist agitation, the city had descended into municipal madness.

If Jim and I stood together hailing a cab, none would stop because there were "white" cabs and "colored" cabs, each forbidden to pick up someone of the "wrong" race. So one of us would stand on the curb alone to hail a cab while the other would hide in a nearby doorway and dash head down into the back seat of the first taxi that stopped. The only way we could eat together was in a black restaurant where a waitress would tell me, "I'm sorry, sir, but I'm not allowed to serve you," and I would say, "I'm colored." That was acceptable because a white-skinned person with 1/64th black blood or one known to "regularly consort with members of the colored race" was legally "colored." Jim, of course, could not use the same technique in a white restaurant.

Jim and I could not legally room in the same hotel and we were in Jim's "colored" hotel room sharing some bourbon when the phone rang. It was Mike Ogden in Providence. There had been a riot in Little Rock where white gangs from outside the city had blocked black students from entering Central High School. While the Arkansas National Guard watched passively, white gangs were beating reporters and any blacks they could find.

President Eisenhower had been assured by Governor Faubus that all would go well, but when the state National Guard, obviously under orders from the governor, refused to stop the riot or help black children enter the school, an angry Eisenhower took command of the state Guard and ordered in the United States Army to control the area around the school and usher the nine black students into their first class.

In Jim's New Orleans hotel room, Mike Ogden filled me in on the latest news, told me to go back at once to Little Rock, but absolutely, under the riotous circumstances Jim was not to go with me. I knew what Jim's reaction would be. I said, "Mike, you speak to Jim." When Ogden ordered Jim not to go with me because the paper didn't want him hurt, Jim argued bitterly on the phone, but Ogden was adamant.

Jim put down the phone, fuming, when the phone rang again. It was Jim's mother calling from Johnson City.

Mrs. Rhea had heard news of the Little Rock riots on the radio. Jim spoke soothingly to her, "It's all right, Mama, I'm safe here. I'm not going back."

When Jim put down the phone he was trembling.

"Do you know what she said? Do you know what she asked me? 'Jim, are you all right?' Do you know how my mother sounded?"

He was glaring at me in accusation.

"That's exactly what she used to say, it's exactly how she sounded when I was in the war. Every time I got a call through to her, she'd say, 'Jim, are you all right? Are you all right?' She said it exactly the same way just now. My mother was worried that I might get killed."

Now he was shouting.

"That was in World War Two, goddamit, a war! I was an American soldier in a goddam war! But I was safer in New Guinea than I am in my own country!" and with all his might he threw his bourbon glass into the bathroom wall where it shattered on the tile with a terrible sound. Tears of rage were streaming down his cheeks.

"My own goddam country!"

I had the feeling I was witnessing the release of a lifetime of repressed rage.

When I flew back to Little Rock, the city was tense. Governor Faubus, playing the ancient Southern political role of a defiant South defending its "way of life," had made a speech denouncing "his" people's oppression under the "nekkid bayonets of the central government." The language could have come out of the South Carolina hotheads who fired on Fort Sumter in 1861. It was still the most reliable trick of every Southern politician needing racial hysteria for reelection.

Few people were on the streets. It was dusk and I went downtown to watch the federal troops arrive. I found Bill Ewald waiting on the same street corner. I had met and liked Bill during my first visit. He was a planner imported earlier from Washington to help the state's industrial development commission. It was clear that Bill was appalled by the events in Little Rock.

From our street corner, we heard sirens and soon saw the first units of the 101st Airborne Infantry, jeeps leading, flying the American flag and a pennant, "327 Recon," followed by six-by-six Army trucks and weapons carriers with five hundred black and white U.S. Army soldiers dressed in full combat gear.

As we watched the first vehicles enter the city over Broadway Street Bridge, Bill said almost to himself, "For the first time in weeks, I feel proud to be an American."

I knew how he felt. I had been in the Army too long to feel any romantic thrill at flag-flying troops on the move, but I felt the same way about a move by my government to restore decency.

But I also remembered how Jim Rhea felt when he shouted, "My own goddam country!" and smashed his glass against the hotel wall.

I was slow in understanding why, from that point on, Jim and I fought with each other on every little point of strategy and over our predictions for the future. It remained a puzzlement to me until afterward, when I visited with a friend in New York, the black psychologist Kenneth Clark. When I told him about our endless arguments on the trip, though in Providence we agreed completely about racial matters, Clark told me what should have been obvious to me but had not been: "Look. He was a black man being humiliated at every step in the South. And you were the only white man handy on which he could safely express his anger at what whites were doing to him."

One of the strengths of American standard journalism, as well as a complicating weakness, was personified by the fact that though Jim and I argued constantly and sometimes bitterly on that trip, we were able to write our joint stories and regain our friendship because Jim began with the same journalistic disciplines that I did. In retrospect, it might have served a more useful long-range public purpose if we had written candidly about the emotional outbursts and my own initial puzzlement about them.

»

Looking behind the comfortable facades of life is the essential difference that distinguishes legitimate news from propaganda, and the majority of reporters know it, just as both Jim Rhea and I knew it.

We reporters deal constantly in abstract, secondhand reconstructions of reality given to us by official sources far from the scene. So most of us have a powerful desire to see primary documents and look at scenes personally—if we are free to do so. Jim Rhea and I could take an unorthodox joint look beneath the surface of Southern racial attitudes, because the Providence papers encouraged us to do it. On the Pentagon Papers story, I could find myself with piles of documents on the motel beds that night in Boston only because the *Washington Post* supported my being there, just as it later approved, somewhat reluctantly, my spending time undercover as a prisoner for "murder" in a maximum security penitentiary. When I wrote about poverty, I spent months reading books, collecting data, and interviewing experts, but I also picked beans with Florida migrant workers and spent time in flophouses because *The Saturday Evening Post* let me take the time to do it.

When I covered a war, something always told me not to go out of my way to avoid the dead bodies. There is nothing revelatory about gore. You don't need to see corpses to know that wars kill. But one trouble with the history of wars is that they can become abstractions. Too much reporting treats war as painless exercises in tactics and strategy, stressing the movements of tanks and planes, all sanitized to make battles more glorious for those who have never witnessed the blood and the terror. Ever since the horrors of our own Civil War receded in the collective American memory, we have been cursed with intellectuals playing war and armchair gunslingers full of keyboard courage.

Plato at one point describes how Leontius approaches dead bodies at a place of execution. He feels simultaneous curiosity and disgust. He freezes and holds a hand over his eyes. But curiosity gets the better of him. Running toward the corpses, with a finger he forces open his eyes, saying, "There you are, curse you, have your fill of the lovely spectacle."

Like most journalists I have known, I have tried to uncover my eyes, though at times it required figurative prying. I did not relish looking at victims of a tornado to see what happens when they are killed by a vacuum, or at the swollen bodies of Sudanese soldiers in the Sinai desert during the 1956 Israeli-Egyptian war to see if they were killed by that special horror of desert warfare, lack of water, or died quickly by rockets from attacking fighter planes.

American journalists, by their trade, are special witnesses at Leontius' places of execution and other corners of life where their fellow citizens would neither try nor be permitted to watch. We are professional voyeurs. At our worst, we are prurient peeping Toms. Or we report scenes that may be real but misrepresent the whole. Or we are lazy and too easily accept the views of those who make our job too easy.

But when permitted to do our best—or being rewarded and not penalized for it—reporters are more than simple voyeurs: we develop a double vision, like theatergoers transfixed by the madness of poor King Lear, but simultaneously able to see the men and women around Lear in ways that poor Lear himself cannot.

Most journalism is an experience in divided perspectives. Journalists are both insiders and outsiders. In the United States, while reporters have privileged access to society's inner workings, something deep in ethical journalism keeps them borderline characters. Journalists move freely in the domains of power, but they are not supposed to take up residence.

Reporters are like the amphibious creatures who live between high and low tide, taking their sustenance from the daily tides but never joining the population that is totally a part of the sea or totally a part of the shore. Good reporters feel at home only in that diurnal shift between two worlds. It may not be accidental that the word "journalism" comes from the Latin that also gives us "diurnal," as in tides.

Our double vision also requires that we be objective in one sense and subjective in another. If we are really doing a good job, we have to be honest in reflecting all the relevant ideas, feelings, characters, and information that play a part in the scenes we describe in our stories. In that, we need to set aside our personal views on the subject. But the news too often ends there, or else forbids using experience to distinguish between what is an official explanation and what is true, what makes money and what makes human misery, what has preventable causes and what is truly random accident.

This distinction between reporting fairly on the observed scene and at the same time reporting the context in which it has happened is not difficult for the majority of experienced journalists.

We journalists need that double vision that assumes every social scene has multiple meanings to be examined, not with cynicism but with a sense of skepticism born of experience. Yet, we have accomplished only one part of our usefulness if we are asked to suppress what we have learned about ourselves and the insights gained from the past.

For me, as with anyone else, being a grown-up person has been part of being a grown-up journalist for whom every experience provides a richer way to see the world.

»

Every morning in Mrs. Hedberg's second-grade class at the old North School in Stoneham, we started the way all classes did in that time and place. There was the Lord's Prayer, a Bible reading—Protestant King James version, of course, ignoring my classmates who were Jewish or Catholic. Then came the Pledge of Allegiance to the Flag, led from the front of the room each morning by a different student.

This particular morning the pledge leader was Walter Hathaway. Walter was big and awkward. He was always the quickest kid to go crying to the teacher about skinning his knee in the schoolyard and he was the butt of our teasing. After the pledge, as he walked by me on the way back to his seat, my foot, governed by a mind of its own, flicked into the aisle and Walter went down like a great oak. He lay there blubbering while the class bathed itself in delight. I had to spend noon recess at my desk in the empty classroom, head down on my arms.

The longer I worked as a journalist, the more I became aware how shamefully easy it is to pick on the world's Walter Hathaways, aiming at easy targets of powerless innocents or people looked down upon socially. We spend endless time pursuing small-fry transgressors like illegal bookies and petty thieves. But only spasmodically do we look with the same daily diligence at misdeeds of the powerful. Both kinds of news are important in keeping society civilized, but only the petty ones dominate our news every day.

Especially at the start, when I hoped to impress my bosses on papers in Springfield and Providence, I was not immune to the too-easy crime story or funny episode at the expense of the weak. I eagerly pursued my assignment to stake out the florist shop in Pawtucket, Rhode Island where a clerk was a miserable little contact for the illegal number lottery. I felt pride when I nailed him. I felt the cheap triumph even though I knew that the florist clerk was a small part-timer for the same illegal national bookie system on which my managing editor placed his afternoon bets—with a privileged "gift shop" two blocks from the newspaper.

Eventually the meaning of Walter Hathaway and my other moral indignities led, slowly, to a growing awareness of how easily an assignment from my editor could make me a self-righteous, mean-minded pursuer of the powerless while being more tolerant of college-educated men in Brooks Brothers suits who boasted about their shady white-collar evasions that cheated thousands. The merciless views of the small fry and more forgiving attitudes about the large sharks in the daily news brings out the mean-mindedness of everyone in the news process. It adds to the sense of false superiority, glamour, and invulnerability common in the journalistic world.

»

Eventually, my memory of incidents like Walter crying on the floor made me wary of my capacity for base impulses. Over time it also helped me appreciate how everyone moves through life not just out of careful rational thought but also out of instinct and impulse.

I certainly did not enter my lifetime occupation as the result of a conscious plan. I graduated from Clark University in 1941 as a pre-medical student who had become editor of the campus paper and no longer wanted to be a doctor. But premedical students are taught more about the periodic table than about people, so in that Depression year my only marketable skill was chemistry. At the appointed hour, I appeared, shoes polished and hair slicked down, in the office of the hiring man at Monsanto Chemical laboratories in Springfield, Massachusetts. The man's secretary said he had been called to a meeting and I would have to come back in two hours.

Walking around downtown Springfield to kill time, I noticed a faded sign that read "Morning Union." My feet, as unbidden as my left foot had been at Hathaway's ankle, took over and propelled me up a set of stairs and I have never looked back.

Of course, on the big decisions—taking new jobs, quitting jobs, moving across the country—I would do all the obligatory rational things. I would pull out that symbol of pure logic, the yellow legal pad, and make two parallel lists. One would be marked "For," the other, "Against." As often as not, my list "Against" was far longer than my list "For." But as I shaved the next morning, I discovered that while I slept during the night I had already chosen the short column marked "For." Life's yellow pads have usually lost out to my unconscious.

There is an irony in the professional discipline that we reporters accept. The majority of journalists are quite properly expected to produce news that is fair, balanced, and objective. But when it comes to matters central to their own personal lives, no two human individuals will agree on what is fair, balanced, and objective. Owners of corporations and leaders of unions, for example, seldom agree on what is fair and proper in labor laws. Like most other human beings, both see the world through eyes focused on their own desires and needs.

Journalism operates by individual professional judgments within a hierarchical system. In most newsrooms the decisions from the top down are usually clothed in surface respect for the reporter, especially when the reporter loses an argument over a story. But collegiality doesn't mask the ultimate authority. The accumulation of editorial decisions by superiors becomes the policy that governs the basic operation of every news organization, that tells reporters what they will look at and what emphasis is to be given to what they see. Those higher editorial decisions become the definition of news, seldom stated in black and white but as definite as a printed doctrine.

Owners of news corporations, their editors, and each of their reporters all have differing ideas on which subjects they prefer to write about, which particular quotes should be chosen from long interviews, which details from the reporter's eyewitness account should be emphasized. But the reality of constant deadlines means that someone has to resolve any differences, do it quickly and beyond appeal. The "five o'clock news" in broadcasting cannot wait until 5:02, and the intricate newspaper machinery of manufacturing, printing, dispatching fleets of trucks and small armies of neighborhood and newsstand deliverers cannot wait more than a few minutes for arguments over what stories should be killed or severely altered. At that point, the executive editor, or for some major stories, the corporate chief, decides. The weight of those basic decisions comes from those who tend to see things from above, and partly because news is so dependent on quick decisions, each decision-maker reacts in ways influenced by inner, often unconscious values.

From the chairman of the board of the corporation that owns the news to the reporter sitting in front of the computer keyboard, each "just happens" to make decisions in reflexes that come from personal experience, inner values, and social goals. For me, one of these reflexes of inheritance and childhood that seems to "just happen" has something to do with the fact that I just happen to be, among other things, an Armenian overlaid by, of all things, the culture of New England Yankees.

»

Double visions and wildly opposing emotions were in the Armenian lore I heard around our dinner table as I grew up at 59 Elm Street in Stoneham, Massachusetts. Almost every weekend, our big dinner table was crowded by our own big family plus relatives and cronies of my father, and they told tales both warm and grim. There was seldom anyone present who had not gone through the genocide. I had been born in the middle of a Turkish massacre of Armenians, yet there we were around the table, all survivors, laughing at favorite old-country stories and eating old-country Armenian food. The exception was on Saturday nights when we had Boston baked beans and brown bread, as regionally traditional as grits in the South.

It's possible that I acquired a divided perspective from absorbing

turbulent Armenian history and stories inside our house and in-
habiting another world outside the house, while going to school, playing, and growing up in a conservative small town dominated by the
values of white Anglo-Saxon Protestant Yankees. Perhaps it was this
childhood experience that gives me the tentative optimism of the survivor within a civilized country, tempered by the knowledge that life
is uncertain, and every happy day a gift.

Throughout history, Armenians became adept at living in divided
circumstances. Once an Armenian monarch ruled unchallenged from
the Caspian to the Mediterranean Sea, but most of the time Armenia was a subkingdom of someone else's empire—the Persians, the
Greeks, the Romans, the Byzantines, the Russians, the Turks, the
Soviets.

Armenians were the first nation to adopt Christianity, but within
Christianity they soon split with Rome, insisting that Jesus Christ was
not God on earth, but human with a divine spirit.

After the fourteenth century, Armenians were a Christian minority
ruled by Turkish Moslems. The divisions among Armenians continued. My family came from Cilicia, known once as "Lesser Armenia,"
in the south of what is now Turkey and much influenced by the Christianity of Europe and America and the nineteenth-century New England Protestant missionaries. But the main body of Armenians was in
the north, in "Greater Armenia," close to the culture of what had been
czarist Russia and the Soviet Union.

Cilician Armenian ties to the Christianity of Europe created another ineradicable influence. Red-bearded Norman Crusaders of the
eleventh century were welcomed by Armenians in the city of my birth,
Marash. In two hundred years of using Marash as a staging area for
assaults on Palestine, the Crusaders and their Marash Armenian Christian hosts were such enthusiastic allies that nine hundred years later,
the mustache I grew came out a repellent pink, and my younger son,
Eric, has bright red hair.

My own life started in divided circumstances. I was four months old
when we reached America. Three weeks later my mother became ill
and spent the next three years until her death in Massachusetts sanitar-
iums for tuberculosis. I spent most of those first three years in the

homes of generous American WASP families in Massachusetts and New Hampshire who took in the infant at the request of the Congregational Church Board of Missions.

At the same time, I was visited most weekends by my four older sisters who attended school during the week while my father, thanks to the same Board of Missions, studied at Harvard Divinity School and served his new church.

Those first three years in the homes of kindly, affluent, middle-class WASPs must have had some unconscious influence. So born an Armenian with all that means, in emotional Mediterranean culture with a tragic history, I also inherit an unlikely early infusion of democratic hope and New England emotional stiffness and rectitude.

Compared to most immigrants, once settled in Stoneham, we had easy entrée to American middle-class life. My father was a professional man, everyone in the family spoke English before we arrived, and we lived in an acceptable part of town. Like most immigrants, I grew up a super American, as did every member of the family. My father used to say things like, "Sometimes I think people born here don't appreciate what a wonderful country it is."

Growing up in a New England town meant absorbing traditional Yankee values of hard work, thrift, and propriety. But in traditional Yankeedom there is also suppression of personal emotion and a powerful streak of self-righteousness. Perhaps like a media critic.

In the Stoneham of my time a common phrase heard from many leaders in the WASP community was "the foreign element." It was not spoken kindly. They meant non-Anglo immigrants; their own newly arrived relatives from England and Scotland were instantly "Americans." Even in those years before Hitler, one was made to understand that Anglo-Saxons and other Northern Europeans were genetically superior to us "lesser breeds." The entrenched myth had a profound impact on how we young people of the "lesser breeds" tried to dress, walk, talk, arrange our faces, and hide our ethnicity in the hopeless task of trying to be mistaken for a WASP.

In most classrooms and with most playmates, I was as acceptable as any other American, but I was regularly reminded that in the larger WASP community, acceptance was short of total. One of the kindest women in my childhood, the mother of a classmate, once introduced me to a neighbor, "This is Ben Bagdikian. His family is Armenian but very cultured."

My family had its own mixed perspectives. After my mother's death, the family was bitterly divided between the original family of my four older sisters and me, and my father with his new wife and then my two half-brothers. Yet, as a young child, without any explicit word ever being spoken, I sensed a hidden special relationship between my emotionally reserved father and me. And despite unfair outbursts and periodic cruelties that left their mark, my stepmother was capable of spontaneous kindnesses toward me. My half-brothers and I had all the usual brotherly fights but we were warm brothers and as adults have been friends and mutual supporters.

My father and stepmother continued to live in old-country puritanism, intensified by my father's new vocation as a Protestant minister. But outside the home, we children exulted in American adolescent life.

As eldest son of a clergyman, I carried the loathsome burden of upholding my namesake, Ben-Hur, "the great Christian hero." Yes, my given first name was Ben-Hur. Ben-Hur, of course, was no Christian hero. He was a fictional character concocted in a simplistic novel by a general in the American Civil War who had an unfortunate compulsion to write. The book became one of the most spectacular bestsellers of all time. It was also one of the few lapses in my mother's otherwise good literary taste.

With ancient sexism, my parents assumed their first child would be a boy and would be named "Ben-Hur." But the first child was a girl, so my oldest sister was given the name of the fictional hero's sister in the novel, "Tirzah." The next three children also were girls but escaped General Wallace (Lydia was given a graceful biblical name, Cynthia the name of the nurse who attended my mother at birth, and Nora the name of the heroine in an Irish novel my mother liked at the time). When number five finally was a boy, General Wallace's invention was still waiting for me.

When the first movie of that regrettable story was made, I suffered in every schoolyard of my childhood. Horse-drawn wagons still delivered milk and ice, so I was the target of such side-splitting wisecracks as, "Hey, Ben-Hur, better clean up the pile your horse just left, hah-hah-hah." Or, "Hey, Ben-Hur, how about a ride in your chariot?" If one of my sisters was exasperated, she would send my full name echoing over the neighborhood: "Ben-Hur Haig Bagdikian, you come home this instant!"

Almost worse were elderly ladies in my father's church who periodically said things like, "You are named after a great Christian martyr and must live up to your name."

At age sixteen, when I filled out the application for my first Massachusetts driving license, I dropped—without a second thought—the "Hur" and its hated hyphen. My middle name, "Haig," is a good Armenian name with no connotation of movies, chariots, or the residue of horses.

Eventually, I was helped by having lived sixteen years with the name Ben-Hur. It made me stand out in ways I hated. It was worse that I was expected to behave like a saint. Those little childhood agonies were probably important in creating my lifetime uneasiness in the presence of praise. I love praise, of course. I luxuriate in it. But at the same time, public praise makes me nervous.

Growing up in a town of ten thousand, even in the depths of the Great Depression, was in fundamental ways the best of small-town childhoods. Friendships were uninhibited and leisurely, the environment a rich combination of orchards and close neighborly contact. Yet Boston—which back then still serenely called itself "The Athens of America"—was only a streetcar ride away.

Within the town, the family presented a double public image. Like many other American families during the Great Depression, in public we exhibited proper middle-class respectability, but within the home, the household was wrenched by humiliating economic crises. To the public eye we were like the other secure-looking families in our neighborhood, but one bitter winter when the church held back his pay my father had to chop up the grand piano to keep us all from freezing.

In childhood, I hated the divided perspectives in my family life. But now, with the luxury of looking back, I would not change them. In the end they may have sharpened my interest in journalism and goaded my social and political thinking. I think that in some vague way they moved my unthinking feet to wander into professional journalism. Despite the tensions within a split family, we all were under an imperative to be proper in public and the requirement on the family of immigrants and of a clergyman to behave like model citizens.

Those admonitions went deep. Twenty-five years later, when I was dictating a deadline story of the final Little Rock school integration from a public phone on the wall of a grocery store, two enraged segregationists ran toward me with mayhem in their eyes. One of them shouted an all-purpose epithet, "You're nothing but a nigger-loving-Jew-newspaperman-from-New-York-100-percent-for-Stalin!" I still remember with chagrin that in the moment before I ran to save my skin, this well-behaved minister's son first hung up the receiver on its wall hook as every proper telephone customer is supposed to do.

CHAPTER 5

# I Am "Dead"—Almost

It was during a celebratory dinner around the big oak table at 59 Elm Street, where most of the animated talk between my father and relatives was in Turkish, that my father interrupted briefly to lean down and whisper to me in English. Someone had just mentioned that when I was two weeks old, during the last Turkish massacres of Armenians, my father, fleeing during a storm and thinking I had frozen to death, dropped me, but when I hit the snow I cried.

Oddly, at the time his whispered story seemed unexceptional to me because family lore and the lives of other Armenians we knew were full of such incidents. Besides, my father returned at once to the lively table talk and it would be thirty years before I heard the explanation of that particular moment in the family escape.

At the dinner I was sitting beside my father, who was in his glory. I think the family dining room was his favorite part of the house. It was mine. Too many of the other rooms had associations with solitude, or tearful family scenes, or late-night whispered crises on which I eavesdropped from the bottom of the back stairs.

Somehow, evening meals were spared. There was always an opening prayer and afterward, the long Bible reading and the even longer prayer, all heads bowed. My sister Nora always peeked to catch an errant eye and made a face to force a sacrilegious giggle.

The Bible readings and prayers were often selected pointedly to indict some transgression by one of us. But after the prayer there was a regular ritual. My sisters would bait my father on biblical dogma—the immaculate conception, the miracles, Jesus' physical ascension to heaven. My father welcomed the debates with good-natured confidence. He could always outquote everyone and when needed use the terminal argument of the religious, "Some things you must take on faith."

But that night, my father's favorite cronies and eight family members were jammed around the table, the table loaded with dolmas, kooftehs, lehmajoons, moosaka, bowls of yoghurt, and great platters of almond chicken pilaf. Old Armenians are great storytellers. Like all talented raconteurs they can milk an adventure for ever-mounting climaxes until the audience has to wipe away tears of laughter. Only rarely was there a tragic story, the listeners soberly quiet, looking downward.

I would have been about eleven that night because my grandfather, one of the uproarious storytellers, was still alive. Even when I was older, I never tired of listening, even though most of their words were incomprehensible. They were in either Armenian or Turkish and I understood neither. That made me a lifetime student in the arts of the illiterate, reading hands, eyes, and mouths, watching facial expressions, interpreting emotional tones.

The full explanation for my having been dropped in the snow came shortly before my father died. During one of my visits, he gestured with his hand for me to follow him into his study where he quietly closed the door behind us. The story was told in a low voice, almost a whisper, because it involved my mother. I understood the closed door—and the long-delayed explanation. During my whole life, he had never mentioned my mother within the hearing of my stepmother.

My nonverbal interpretations of Armenian and Turkish were further honed by mandatory attendance at my father's Armenian Congregational Church. He preached usually in Turkish or Armenian, occasionally in English, and once a year in classical Armenian.

Sitting in my father's big church, on Porter Square in Cambridge, I survived the incomprehensible hours staring at the mysterious Armenian characters in gold over the altar. I tried without success to apply the decoding method of Poe's *Gold Bug*, in English the most common letter is "e," the second most common "a," etc. Or I would analyze the emotional plot line of my father's sermon, especially his false climaxes. To this day, it is hard to fool me with a speaker's treacherous, "And in conclusion. . . ." On Sundays when my father had sermonized well over the standard twenty minutes, every member of his family glared at him from the pastor's family pew. On the drive home, one of my sisters would say despairingly, "Papa, you yourself say there are no souls saved after twenty minutes." But in full cruising speed at his pulpit, my father had too much momentum. As though to reassure us as we stared from the pew, he would raise his voice and right hand in the dramatic coda of a speaker about to unleash the long-awaited conclusion. But I learned to look pityingly at my deceived sisters as Sunday after Sunday they wiggled their feet back into their shoes. I knew that my father's codas, like Beethoven's, merely inspired him to ever more resounding—and distant—finales.

Unlike the prolonged Sunday sermons, the stories that night around the dinner table on Elm Street were, with that one exception, uproariously happy.

The gaiety around the dinner table was a saving counterpoint to the horrors that most of those present had experienced. Some of them were old enough to have known the start of the Armenian genocide. It had started in the late nineteenth century, when the Ottoman Turks had sunk into decadence and corruption, losing their grip on a large empire throughout the Middle East and North Africa. Sultan Abdul Hamid, so paranoid he forbade newspapers and books ever to print the word "assassination," took out his insecurities by killing Armenian Christians in a series of massacres to "purify" Turkey. The term "ethnic cleansing" would not be created for another century but it was a process performed regularly around the world during the horrors of the twentieth century.

When the curtain of World War I fell around Turkey, its leaders began the systematic "final solution" of "The Armenian Question." In two years of mass killings and death marches they killed as many as half the three million Armenians in the Ottoman Empire. Persecution of Armenians aroused European and American Christianity with international commissions for "Near East Relief," to relieve "the starving Armenians" and start an effort that would play a crucial part in my own life.

After initial European and American outrage at the massacres, when the war was over, humanitarian concerns of the superpowers were pushed aside, as always, for profit, power, and military alliances. The United States government, to this day, will not offend its Turkish ally by officially acknowledging the genocide.

The convenient official amnesia makes understandable Hitler's reaction in August of 1939 when some of his generals asked whether Hitler's order to kill all the Jews in Poland would rouse world opposition and solidify the Nazis' enemies. Hitler rejected their worries, saying, "Who, after all, speaks today of the annihilation of the Armenians?"

Ever since the Turkish genocide against them, Armenians have suffered the open wound of murder denied.

At the time of the big dinner, there had been no time to ask my father anything more about my having been dropped for dead. Laughter returned quickly to the table. Turkish massacres and death marches are an unhealed wound among all Armenians, but traumas of the genocide never dominated our big dinners. Most of the older adults were survivors. But like soldiers who have endured the terrors of combat, they seldom made common talk of it—some sanity-keeping reserve in the psyche kept the horrors unstated, the references mostly to miraculous escapes. Direct talk of the horrors was brief, almost apologetic because so many died and they did not. It is the noncombatants who are flag-wavers. This was true for my family as well, including Lydia, who wrote a detailed private memoir but in conversation talked mostly of the good things.

It may be those family accounts, scattered in the telling throughout my childhood, recounted in Lydia's memoir, and mentioned in books, that led me to return for the first time to the city where I was born. It was sixty-six years after my father had released the bundled infant under his arm. It meant a trip into the Taurus mountains of Turkey, to the city of Marash.

Armenians from Marash are at least as proud and chauvinistic as Armenians from other provinces. And because American missionaries in the nineteenth century had established schools and colleges in Marash, there were books and references to the city written in English. My four older sisters, who were twelve, eleven, nine, and six at the time of the escape, had vivid memories that kept the exodus alive in my thinking.

The world is full of people who are drawn not only to the roots of their family, but to the house or patch of earth from their past, whether it is Alex Haley going to Africa, or Italian teenagers in Boston who day after day walked miles to stare at the redevelopment wrecking-ball rubble that used to be their old tenements. It may be heightened in our time when people in cities filled with uprooted men and women feel an urge to touch a lost vestige of a rooted past.

Something else also drew me. I have been a reporter all my adult life. Reporters learn to respond instinctively to the prime document, the crucial individual, the central scene, to be viewed with one's own reportorial eyes and ears. The old-folk stories from my childhood, the sometimes idyllic and sometimes horrifying reminiscences of two of my older sisters, and the old grainy photographs in yellowed books—all that was represented by the word, "Marash."

I had no illusion that going to Marash would be a mystical experience. Or that the trip would "solve" some deep psychological mystery. Or that I would learn anything precise. I do not speak Turkish. There are negligible numbers of Armenians remaining in Turkey and my American passport says quite noticeably that I am an Armenian born in Marash in 1920, a significant year for Turks and Marash Armenians. The passport always provokes cold stares from Turkish officials. This was not going to be an investigative trip. I had no desire to be mistaken for an aging Armenian terrorist.

Thirty years earlier I had been in Turkey as an American foreign correspondent, concentrating on officialdom in Istanbul and Ankara as I had in capitals of other Western European and Middle Eastern countries. In 1956, arrangements to visit Marash had seemed to go well, but when I checked into the new Istanbul Hilton, I found that at some point during the delivery of luggage to my hotel room from the Istanbul airport customs the manila envelope with my father's notes and a book with maps of his property in Marash had disappeared. A few days later an official said my visit to Marash was canceled.

Many years later, in 1986, my wife Marlene and I were simply tourists landing in Istanbul's Yesilkoy Airport. The contrasts of the tenth century interlocked with the twentieth were greater even than thirty years earlier. Days later we drove through the fertile valley between the coast and the mountains of Marash. The foliage and rich farmlands look remarkably like Route 99 through the central valley of California. No wonder so many early Armenian immigrants settled around Fresno.

Corkscrew roads lifted us to the high country, the loops and switchbacks crammed with double trailers and monster tourist buses. Ragged boys stood by the road selling plastic bags of cherries, cherries forbidden in nearby countries because this was the year of nuclear dust from Chernobyl.

We traced the path to Islahiye, once the terminus of Armenian death and our family's deliverance, now a sullen village with a noontime cluster of milling people, mules, and dust. We found the isolated railroad station crucial to our family history.

We drove on toward our goal until we reached a high plain where a road runs straight as an engineer's ruler toward a bull's-eye at the base of the mountains. In the distance, shimmering and faint in August heat waves, is Marash.

The parallel lines of road converge on the city. Seen from miles away, at the end of spreading farm fields of gold and shimmering in the vibrations of heated air, it is easy to imagine it in history, the ancient city of Germanica, for centuries called by Armenians, "Kermanik." Eighteen hundred feet high, set in massive mountains that reach eight thousand feet, it has been a gateway for centuries of traders, explorers, and armies, including Alexander the Great and Genghis Khan, an entry to the high mountain passes that separate Europe and Asia, which for thousands of years have brought to Marash spices, silk, gold, conquerors, banditry, and blood.

At the outskirts there is confirmation of a puzzle. In modern maps printed in Turkey, the word "Marash"—or, in the Turkish spelling, "Maras"—does not appear. What appears on the maps is repeated on the sagging enameled sign at the city line: "Kahramanmaras." "Heroic Marash"—renamed because of the "heroic" events of early 1920, events that caused the incident my father had leaned down to mention at the dinner on Elm Street, an "heroic" episode that created thousands of Armenian orphans and Armenian deaths, and made the Bagdikians American citizens.

At its entry, the city does not look ancient. A divided boulevard with flowering oleander in the median strip is lined by high-rise apartments. But the higher one drives, the older the city. Farther up is the Citadel, where the Hittite Lions of Marash once stood and where, at 1:00 P.M. on January 21, 1920, nine days before my birth, the signal of a rifle shot was the beginning of the end of the Marash Armenians.

Higher still, on the upper slopes, are the big buildings that were once the American college where my mother and father began their schooling. The large white buildings are now behind a chain-link fence and a padlocked gate.

Below, I find an area that I think may have been the location of the hospital I was born in and the site of the house the family left in the exodus. There is no certainty. It is now a spread of rubble at a street intersection away from the new city. Despite all my preparation, new buildings make it hard to triangulate with features from old photographs. I reach down for a small stone, a souvenir without rational purpose. A passing cabdriver stops, gets out and walks toward us with hostile-sounding questions. We ignore him. The stone now rests on our Berkeley mantelpiece.

When we drive upward to the highest level, the roads become dirt and the car has to push through herds of resistant goats. Trying to follow the path my family took in their escape in the death march to Islahiye, I can see where the mountain trails descend to the plain approaching the railhead, where six months after the family exodus, missionaries traced the escape paths by the skeletons.

Returning to Marash was not a transcendent experience. It is frustrating, with only a few landmarks that are unmistakably from the family's past. None of it seems to raise in me a conscious sense of racial or personal attachment to the scene. I am not aware of anger or other special emotion—a family inheritance?—until Marlene says quietly as we drive away, "I never saw that look on your face before."

Leaving Marash in our rented Fiat 131, a Turkish highway patrol stops me for speeding, takes one look at the American passport, and waves us on.

That is not the way I first left Marash.

## CHAPTER 6

# The Exodus

My sister Lydia shivered as she tramped through the snow. Somewhere a woman cried out. "The First Church is burning! The Second Church, the schoolhouse—Oh, dear God, they're all full of people!"

Lydia turned to look at the city below. A burning steeple toppled to the ground. In the freezing air, the sound of machine guns and screams carried up the mountainside.

Automatically, Lydia prayed. She turned to look for the others. Voices, disembodied in the blowing snow and darkness, called to locate family members. "Armen!" "Nishan!" "Siranoush!"

She saw my father at a wooden bridge with French soldiers, shouting for the civilians to hurry. Periodically, he argued with the soldiers to wait a little longer. He told her to keep going, that Mother and the others were just ahead.

Lydia moved awkwardly in the dark. The snow was higher than her boots. Cold penetrated her heavy clothing and against her skin she felt the cold metal of the jewelry her mother had put under their clothes in the last minutes before they ran to the mountains.

She fell. A stranger put her back on her feet. "Keep walking, little girl, keep walking."

Soon, my father caught up with her. "Will the Turks kill us?"

"The French soldiers will blow up the bridge so the Turks can't follow."

"Are there Turks in the mountains?"

"We'll be safe, as long as we stay close to the French."

They heard a horse neigh.

"That's Mozart!"

My mother was on her horse, Tirzah walking beside her.

My father told them to move ahead. He would turn back to find the others.

Once again, my father disappeared into the night, calling, "Elmas!" "Bedros!" Elmas, the strange, silent maid, was carrying the new baby. Another servant, Bedros, the strong young man, had Nora on his back. Nora was six.

What seemed like hours later, my father returned with Elmas and Bedros. Elmas had the bundled baby in her arms.

Nora jumped off Bedros' back and ran to her mother.

"He kept pinching me!"

"To keep you awake and warm, dear."

They were all there except Cynthia. Only nine years old, Cynthia was considered too young to walk a hundred miles through snow-covered mountain trails to the nearest railroad. American missionaries had taken her in a covered cart with their Armenian orphans, permitted to travel on the shorter lower road protected by the rear guard of the retreating French.

Lydia had celebrated her eleventh birthday only a month before, Tirzah was twelve, both considered old enough to try it on foot.

Lydia had a frightening thought: "Mother, is Mozart a Turk or an Armenian?"

"There are no nationalities among horses, dear."

Lydia put her head down again and walked as fast as she could. From time to time, she looked up to keep Tirzah's bright red scarf in sight among the mass of blurred grey figures struggling on the trail. Each time she caught up to her older sister, she tried not to cry.

After what seemed hours, Tirzah called: "There they are!"

They ran to a small fire where my mother and the others were melting snow.

"Where's Papa?"

Bedros said he had taken Mozart to be fed with the French Army horses. The French had said the Armenians were to stay a kilometer behind the soldiers.

The family was sharing a glass of melted snow when two French soldiers appeared carrying a man on a stretcher. The man, barely conscious, gestured for the soldiers to stop.

The man on the stretcher was my father.

The soldiers said something in French. Lydia and Tirzah started to move toward the stretcher, but my mother stopped them, whispering in Turkish, "Don't let them know it's your father."

One of the soldiers peeled back the man's outer coat to rub his arms and hands. My father was wearing the uniform of a French officer.

The soldiers withdrew into the night. At the French encampment, my father had fainted from exhaustion. But before the start of the exodus, General Querette, knowing that my father was a marked man, had lent him a French uniform.

Elmas gave up the baby so that my mother could nurse me. I had been born eleven days earlier during sniper fire in the American missionary hospital.

That morning they felt safe at last: French relief battalions with additional infantry, heavy artillery, ammunition and food had broken through the Turkish siege in the hills above the city.

The mounting terror of the previous weeks had stunned the American missionaries. Only months before, British, French, and their own government, victorious against the Turks in World War I, had signed a treaty with the defeated Turkish government. The treaty promised the end of Turks killing Armenians, and autonomy for the Armenian regions, including Marash. But there was a new Turkish Nationalist Army making an open display of postwar military strength at the city of Marash. Turks resumed murdering Armenians. Nine thousand Marash Armenians had been massacred in a matter of weeks, some with mutilations that shocked the American medical mission. The new Turkish guerrillas staggered a small French force protecting the city.

In three wild weeks of fighting, sniper and machine-gun fire penetrated homes, schools, orphanages, and the hospital. It was particularly heavy against the Armenian Protestant, Catholic, and Orthodox churches where thousands of Armenians fled for safety.

When the French reinforcements had broken through to the outskirts of Marash, the killing of Armenians had stopped and the Nationalists sent a message asking the Americans to arrange an armistice. The siege of Marash was broken. By nightfall there were quiet celebrations by the surviving Armenians, Americans, and French troops.

That night, my four sisters were saying their bedtime prayers, giving thanks for the peace, when they heard a knock on the door. A French courier said General Querette wanted to see my father. The general's personal quarters were inside the same walled compound and my father was head of the Marash committee that maintained Armenian liaison with the French. The general occasionally had taken dinner with the family.

Within minutes Lydia heard my father shouting to a gathering of men in the courtyard:

"Every priest and minister must get the news. The general has told me that he and his troops are under orders to leave the city tonight before the Turks discover the retreat. But the Turks will find out. There will be another massacre. Every Christian is in danger. Tell the Citizens Committee, the priests, the ministers that everyone who wishes to leave with the French must do so immediately. I am going to leave with my family. I've told that to the general. He promised not to stop us if we follow."

"But the Turks have surrendered."

"The French have been ordered to leave anyway."

As one man ran toward the gate, he stopped and yelled back:

"Aram Effendi, you had better go first. Your name is on top of the Turkish list."

It was the beginning of the exodus from Marash that began at 10:30 on the night of February 9, 1920, recorded in Lydia's later memoir.

The retreat order from Paris to General Querette was a reversal of deliverance and hope for the twenty-six thousand Armenians of Marash who had survived the wartime death marches and been repatriated to their home city. It began the final act of the Turkish genocide of Armenians, a coup for Mustafa Kemal's Nationalist guerrillas.

French military blunders had been notorious. But this time the secret strategy originated not from incompetent officers in the field but from the distant Premier of France, George Clemenceau in Paris. He and the British Prime Minister, Lloyd George, abandoned their promises to the Armenians in the public treaty of all the Allies, and replaced them with an earlier secret agreement between France and Britain to divide the collapsing Ottoman Empire between them and to exclude their other wartime allies, including the United States, and, of course, the Armenians—to whom they nevertheless continued to promise autonomy.

Until that night, the Bagdikian family had escaped the death marches and massacres of 1915 and 1916 in which the Turkish government killed 1,500,000 of the 3,000,000 Armenians under Ottoman rule. In those years, 60,000 Armenians from Marash alone had been killed.

During the worst of the genocide my father was a professor in St. Paul's College, an American college in Tarsus, on the seacoast one hundred fifty miles from his native Marash. Until the United States joined the war against Germany and Turkey in 1917, he and the rest of my family lived in the protection of the American college compound. But not without close encounters.

A short time later, despite the American college connection, Turkish army men seized Tirzah, Lydia, and two servants as they walked in Tarsus. They were scheduled for the euphemism called "relocation." One of the servants escaped and told my father. Luckily, my mother was teaching piano to the Turkish mayor's children and the mayor gave my father an official note. Lydia remembered the scene vividly. My father walked boldly into the Turkish Army office, angrily slapped the mayor's document onto the commandant's desk, and without waiting for the startled official to read it, stalked out with the two girls and the servant.

》

As she lay down to sleep, Lydia hoped she would wake up to find it all a nightmare, but when she woke up in the morning she was lying on the frozen ground, shivering, surrounded by snow and mountains.

Sitting up, she could see masses of people moving in a sluggish line silhouetted against the sunlit snow. My mother and father were saddling Mozart. They stuffed zwieback into the children's pockets and the family joined the long line plodding through the freezing snow.

Lydia found herself falling behind again. Each time Tirzah would come back and prod her onward. Sometimes she would pause for breath and then miss her older sister's bright scarf. Panicked, she would move faster to find it again. Once they caught up with Elmas.

"How is the baby?"

"Sleeping."

Elmas spoke in monosyllables. Years ago, she had been kidnapped after being forced to watch Turks slaughter her husband and two small children. Eventually she escaped. Silent and strange, she joined the household, devoted to my mother and the children.

"Elmas! Don't let him sleep!"

"Babies need sleep."

"He'll freeze to death! Don't let him sleep!"

Elmas jiggled the bundle and trudged on. Tirzah followed. Lydia resumed her plodding, head down, periodically looking up to keep Tirzah in sight. She tired quickly.

Lydia was cold and exhausted. She wept as she walked.

Finally, the two girls looked down at a deserted village where the mountain trail sloped down to a narrow road. Smoke still rose from blackened huts and houses. French soldiers carrying rifles patrolled the outskirts. There were red blotches in the snow.

My father had ridden back on the trail and found Elmas and Bedros and my mother, who was nursing me. They were all huddled beside the wall of a burnt-out house, the timbers still smoldering from fires after a French skirmish with Turkish guerrillas.

"Aram, I want Cynthia with us. Please try to find the missionary cart."

My father rode off again on Mozart while Bedros collected wood for a fire.

As a small fire began to spread warmth to the shivering group, they heard the icy crunch of wagon wheels in the rutted snow. My mother called, "Cynthia!" A voice under the canvas cried, "Mother!"

A precious warmth spread out from the fire. Parents and children talked with unexpected gaiety, as though they were back home in their living room. Someone had slaughtered one of the cows in the abandoned village and the family that escaped with only minutes to save their lives joked about forgetting to bring salt for the roast beef.

That night, my mother recited the Twenty-third Psalm: "Yea, though I walk through the valley of the shadow of death, I will fear no evil . . ."

My father began his usual long nightly prayer. At home, this was when Lydia usually fell asleep. This night by the warmth of the fire was not different. To her, it was like being home, warm in bed, with everyone safe. Except that now she was lying on Mozart's horse blanket and she fell asleep over frozen snow, with her blue scarf tied tightly around her head.

The scarf was a souvenir from a happy trip six months earlier to the big Syrian city of Aleppo. The war was over, and finally they could move to America. Each girl bought a favorite scarf for the trip across the Atlantic, Tirzah a red one, Lydia blue, Cynthia yellow, and Nora bright green.

They would spend the summer of 1919 in Marash, the birthplace of both my parents where my father would sell his vineyards. After years of postponement, they planned to leave for the United States in the fall.

My mother's pregnancy had been timed so that the baby would be born a native of the United States. That way, they had joked, he could become president of the United States. Once the vineyards had been sold, the gold, together with savings from his professor's comfortable salary, would pay for the family's passage and early years in the United States.

Armenians began preliminaries for the two autonomous Armenian states promised by the Allies, the major state to be in the north near Russia and a smaller one, Cilicia, including Marash, near the Mediterranean in southwest Turkey. In Marash that summer, first British and then French troops occupied the city. Turks no longer cursed Armenians with "Gavour!" the Turkish "nigger"-like oath for "infidel."

Marash leaders asked my father to organize their postwar Marash schools and named him head of an interdenominational Committee of Armenian National Union including Armenian Protestant, Armenian Roman Catholic, and Armenian Orthodox Gregorian churches. He said he would do this only for the summer, because in the fall he and his family would leave for America.

But for years Mustafa Kemal, a shrewd young officer in the Turkish Army, had quietly created a network of younger military officers and secret agents to overthrow the old, corrupt Turkish government that had lost the war. He had a strong guerrilla force, the Nationalist Army, armed by suspiciously easy raids against Allied armories.

Marash Armenians were increasingly uncertain about the weak French force protecting them; they knew too much about Kemal's agents and guerrillas, and rumors about a secret meeting between Kemal and the slippery French High Commissioner, Francois George-Picot. Later, the rumors turned out to be true. Kemal was led to understand that if he succeeded in reorganizing a new stable Turkey, France and Britain would recognize him—in return for his commitment to give them special commercial privileges.

Marash was where Kemal would first prove to the world, mainly Britain and France, that he was the Turkish leader everyone had to deal with. It would be the end for the surviving Armenians in Turkey.

It would not be new in history that powerful countries have been willing to sacrifice disposable minorities and even a small number of their own troops for national treasure and territory.

In the months of the British and French occupation, from twenty to thirty thousand heavily armed Kemalist guerrillas moved into the mountains around Marash. Soon they had seized the nearest railroad, held the good roads, and controlled the only telegraph line.

Inside the city, once more Turks yelled, "Gavour!" at Armenians. Armenian children going to the American school were attacked. The American missionaries received anonymous death threats for helping Armenian victims.

During the summer, the commander of the British occupying troops informed my father that he had received orders to vacate Marash at the end of October. French troops would replace them "a few weeks later." My father told the general that if the British left before the French troops arrived, "the French will arrive only to bury the Armenian dead."

The American mission in Marash, also endangered by the removal of Allied protection, lent a driver and their only automobile, a Reo, to my father for the dangerous trip to French headquarters. With another committee member, Mihran Damadian, they ran the gauntlet of Turkish guerrillas on the mountain road to Adana. There my father obtained a commitment from the French area commander to move up the schedule of French arrival to coincide with the British departure.

A French advance guard arrived October 29, 1919. With a small ceremony, the British left the same day. The tiny French unit consisted of 550 men, 400 from the Armenian Legion, Armenians from America and elsewhere who had fought for the French during the war, and 150 French, mostly Algerian and Senegalese cavalry with camels, all under French officers. Amazingly, the French had little food or ammunition and no radio or armored vehicles.

On January 13 of the new year, 3,000 additional French troops arrived under a new commander, this time a general. But Armenian fears were only partially relieved. The new officer in charge, General Querette, was a decent but ineffectual man, alternately impulsive and irresolute. He had spent most of World War I as a prisoner of war in Germany. His new French reinforcements were regularly ambushed with complete loss of men and supplies.

Inside Marash, Kemalist agents operated with growing boldness. As winter deepened, more Armenian villages were massacred. The French orders were to protect only French military positions, not the Armenians.

But even General Querette became angered after a Turkish ambush of more French reinforcements that had reached an outlying village. He sent 2,000 of his men, mounted on 650 camels, to punish the guerrillas. The entire French expedition was killed, wounded, or taken prisoner, its supplies and ammunition captured. A second force also was waylaid and destroyed. The general was not a quick learner.

Marash was under effective siege. It was clear that the Bagdikians could not leave for America.

One day in early January, as conditions became increasingly desperate, an Armenian boy gave a written message to my father. Lydia saw my mother turn pale. When she gathered the children in another room, there were tears in her eyes.

"Father will be away a few days. While he is away, I will be at the hospital. I will be safe there while I wait for Ben-Hur."

Hope for a boy seemed to spring eternal.

When the children asked where their father was going, she said: "The Committee needs a brave man to go on an important errand."

The whole family prayed together with my father. After a pause in the sniper fire, he took my mother across an open field to the American hospital.

When he returned, he told Elmas, "Shooting could start before I get back. Mother will be safe in the hospital. If shooting starts, take the children and everything you need downstairs and sleep in the basement rooms. The French soldiers will keep an eye on the house."

Elmas said, "The French leave?"

"They have no orders yet."

He was gone four days. On the fifth night, outside the compound gate, gunfire was heard. My father appeared, breathless and disheveled. He whispered at length in Armenian to two men who then disappeared. Later my sisters learned that Armenians, seeing clear signs of French abandonment or defeat, needed weapons to defend themselves in the coming massacre. My father, using most of his savings intended for America, made it through the mountains and purchased arms. When he reached the house, his horse, Paganini, was hit by a sniper. My father lay half under the horse as though dead. When the firing stopped, he ran inside.

The secret mission did not come too soon.

On January 21, a week after General Querette arrived, armed Turks were seen climbing the Citadel, the ancient Hittite stronghold that dominates all of Marash. At precisely one o'clock in the afternoon a rifle shot from the Citadel signalled an explosion of Turkish machine gun and cannon fire. French soldiers had been on normal patrol of streets, by agreement, accompanied by Turkish policemen. At the rifle-shot signal, all the Turkish police killed their French partners.

A few days after the start of open warfare, word came that on January 30 my mother had the child. It was, at last, a boy, "Ben-Hur." Between bursts of sniper fire, the older girls, guided by my father, ran across a field to visit my mother and the new baby. Lydia noticed bullet holes in the wall above my mother's bed. The woman in the bed next to my mother had been killed by sniper fire.

There followed quick Turkish raids to drag Armenian orphans from the American-run orphanages. Lydia became used to the dead bodies in the streets.

Events moved with dizzying confusion. Kemalist agents in Marash sent General Querette an ultimatum to surrender. Hours afterward, a strong French reinforcement succeeded in reaching the outskirts of the city and pushed the guerrillas back into the mountains. Suddenly all was reversed. Other Turks asked the American missionaries to arrange an armistice with the French. Peace was at hand.

What happened next seemed insane. From the outskirts, the new French relief force sent a courier to inform Querette that the reinforcements had decided to return and were on their way back to Syria. Querette had no radio to cancel the retreat. His standing orders were to leave Marash whenever he saw fit. With the retreat of his relief column, he, too, decided to leave. If it seemed incredible to retreat at the moment of victory, apparently it seemed reasonable to political leaders in Paris and London drawing new maps of empire and secret agreements for commercial privileges.

Inside the burning city, the Turks started to finish off the Armenians.

## »

Lydia woke up on her third morning in the mountains, once more shocked that she was not home in bed. She was cold. Cynthia was crying that she did not want to go back to the missionary cart. My mother agreed. "She can ride on the horse with me."

Into Mozart's saddle bags they repacked their diminishing food and rejoined the column of refugees. As they climbed higher, it became even colder.

More frozen bodies appeared, black Senegalese soldiers unused to below-zero weather scattered lifeless among Armenian men, women, and children.

There were so many motionless forms in the snow, she no longer stopped to stare. But as she walked head down and breathless through a sharp turn in the trail, she saw something that made her gasp. Next to the rutted path, sprawled dead on top of the snow, was a girl about her age. The girl was naked.

Lydia, took off her blue scarf and started to spread it over the body. A man called to her:

"Little girl, don't bother."

"But someone stole all her clothes."

"She's already dead. Her clothes will help someone else stay alive. Keep your clothing."

Lydia pushed back onto the trail, weeping. She saw more naked bodies. She imagined that the people she saw moving in front of her were wearing clothes from the dead. She looked desperately for Tirzah's red scarf. Twice she saw Nora's brilliant "Irish" scarf, visible as her sister rode on Bedros' back.

The sky was darkening. She felt like resting in the snow. But she heard gunfire. Turks! Lydia had thought she could not move faster, but she did. When she next looked up, she saw Mozart.

It was another burnt-out village, still smoldering. She could see French soldiers searching through the ruined village. In the midst of the scene, my mother was nursing the baby. That night they ate cold food and drank melted snow. Lydia was surprised to see her father sharing a common cup. At home he was meticulous about his exclusive glass. She fell asleep quickly.

» 

The next morning, in the winter darkness of five o'clock, there fell on them all—sleeping Armenians, American missionaries, French soldiers, and, presumably, Turkish guerrillas—yet another cruel blow, impersonal and indiscriminate. Over the already freezing masses of refugees there descended the worst blizzard in the memory of those who knew the mountains.

Lydia was awakened by howling wind and snow driven like splinters through her blue scarf. At the French Army encampment the instruments showed winds of forty and fifty miles an hour and temperatures of minus twenty Centigrade and dropping.

Everyone was up, shouting against the gale. Scarves were pulled around faces, only eyes uncovered, squinting against wind-driven snow and paralyzing cold. Around them, massive snow drifts rose as they watched.

Lydia was not reassured when her father shouted, "This will keep the Turks away."

Admonishments were called out in the darkness. Keep each other in sight. Don't stop. Don't try to rest. Keep covered.

By the time the family started again, other refugees had tramped down the accumulating snow. Quickly, the trail became a trench, sometimes higher than Lydia.

The narrow view, the swirling whiteness, and the punishing wind made it harder than ever to see ahead. Frozen bodies accumulated quickly. After a time nothing shocked Lydia. Dozens of dead camels lay frozen in grotesque forms against the snow, their supply bags still attached. Frozen Senegalese soldiers lay scattered among the stiff bodies of children and adults, some already stripped naked.

Lydia pushed against the wind, eyes desperate to keep the red scarf in view. But she could hardly breathe. She stopped, sobbing.

Tirzah came back to find her.

"If you don't walk, you'll freeze."

"Look at those people there. They're dead and they were walking."

"Lydia, stop arguing. Keep walking. Mother told us to keep walking."

The pain in her feet made Lydia cry. Sometimes the wind held her back. Other times it shifted suddenly and threatened to knock her on her face. She moved slowly. She tried counting to sixty to keep her feet moving. Finally she stood still and sat down.

Tirzah came back.

"Lydia, keep walking!"

"I have to rest."

"No! If you stop, you'll die!"

"I don't care. I'm going to sleep for awhile."

"No, Lydia! If you sleep, you'll die!"

People skirted the arguing sisters.

Tirzah gave her a push. Lydia screamed at her.

"You're a Turk! You're worse than a Turk! That's what you are. You're cruel, just like the Turks!"

Now Tirzah began to cry.

"I have to. I have to. If you stop you'll die."

"I don't care. I don't care. I have to sleep. If I die, I'll die." She glared at her sister. "But don't let them take my clothes off."

"If you die, they'll take your clothes off."

Lydia stopped crying and stared at her sister. She stomped angrily past Tirzah.

>>

Somewhere, ahead of the refugees, on a lower rutted road, the French soldiers and the American missionaries were not much better off. Even Dr. Elliott was walking, though she, like all the Americans, had been given permission to ride on wagons with the Army baggage train.

Mabel Elliott had been medical director of the hospital, and the old Marash photographs show a sturdy Boston face with steady gaze, hair pulled back in a bun, rimless glasses, firm jaw and mouth, classical WASP nose.

Most of her patients were women. In Marash, after the genocide, there were always more women than men. As a massacre came to each community, the men were marched to the outskirts of their cities and shot in masses. Soldiers returned for the women, who were marched with the children to the distant desert, most to be raped, kidnapped, or killed. In the end more children survived. Marash became "The City of Orphans."

The battle for Marash had brought out her anger. When she saw the mounting piles of butchered Armenian bodies and was told to prepare for the French retreat, she wrote in her diary:

"They had relied on us, on the great, powerful Allies. They had come back to Marash, to their wrecked homes and lived under our protection. . . ." Once more, she wrote bitterly, they faced Turkish rapes and death.

"I think that all the rest of my days I shall suddenly hear from time to time that sentence quietly said . . . 'What shall we do now, doctor?'"

Later, she found that one of her favorite patients, a young tubercular woman too weak to escape over the mountains, took off her clothes and sat by an open window, to freeze quietly to death in the night rather than wait for the Turks to enter the hospital for the sick and wounded left behind.

In the blizzard, the doctor dared not ride any longer. She walked on the trail to stay alive by moving.

"In time, I, too, was a blind machine. . . . I thought of nothing, cared for nothing, simply struggled to keep my balance. . . . The temptation of it! Just to lie down and let the snow cover us."

She saw Armenian mothers carrying small children on their backs. Typically the child's arms crossed over the mother's shoulder, the struggling mother clutching both hands of the child onto her own breast.

"I do not know how many hours we had been walking when I found the first dead child on its mother's back. I walked beside her, examining it; she trudged on, bent under the weight. . . . The child was certainly dead, and she did not know it. . . . I spoke to her, touched her, finally shook her arm violently to arouse her. When she looked up, I pointed to the child and said, 'Finished.' The mother . . . let go the child's hands. The body fell. . . . There were perhaps fifty more after that, always the same."

»

Lydia, angry at Tirzah, for the first time pushed ahead of her sister. The sudden, fierce, saving anger carried them both rapidly up the line until they saw Mozart. Lydia began to run to her mother, crying about Tirzah, but when she saw her mother, she stopped. Her mother looked sick and was swaying. Elmas, holding the baby, looked more dejected than ever.

My father rushed to my mother's side.

"Are you all right? Maybe you should ride a little."

He helped my mother into the saddle and they all moved faster to Mozart's pace.

Lydia soon fell back again. She stopped, exhausted. She looked down at the trail and cried out. Her shoes had burst. Her stiff, stockinged toes were in the snow. She stood still in the trail, staring at the open shoes and the strange bloated look of her toes.

Up ahead, the scene at the horse was even more depressed. It had stopped snowing and the wind had died down. But Elmas had been unable to get a reaction from the baby. My father, walking behind the horse, took the bundle and tried arousing the baby. Out of sight of my mother and Cynthia, my father uncovered the baby and examined it. He decided that this was not the time to tell the others that I was dead.

He put the covers back over the bundle and walked rapidly to catch up. As he approached the horse, my mother fainted and began slipping off the horse. My father dropped the bundle in the snow and grasped my mother's falling body. When the bundle hit the snow, there was an infant cry. Elmas picked up the crying bundle and kept it moving in her arms.

At the next turn of the trail they found themselves in another abandoned village. Fires had already been lit. When Lydia and Tirzah came within sight, they saw the family group around the fire. But that was the last Lydia remembered before she fainted. She did not wake up until sometime later when someone was holding her up and urging her to drink something warm.

My father said, "Don't worry. Tomorrow we will reach the railroad."

In the morning, when Lydia opened her eyes, she was dazzled. The sight was startling. Skies were clear and deep blue. The sun created a brilliant glaze over what seemed like endless stretches of new snow on the downward slope of a vast plain.

They were soon on the trail again. There were more bodies in the snow, most of them naked. Lydia looked sidelong at naked bodies of children, but only long enough to make sure the missing Nora was not among them.

In the far distance, across the blinding field of white snow, there was a black smudge. The sound of a distant locomotive whistle carried through the open fields.

Instantly, the long mass of huddled figures stopped. Something like a massive whisper rose in the air.

"Islahiye!"

The black streak was the railroad.

Hundreds of the motionless figures suddenly came to life. They began to run, stumbling through snow two feet high, seduced by an illusion of closeness, optical treachery induced by desperate yearning, by the transparent air, by the unbroken white plain made smooth by a setting sun, all of it foreshortening the unseen miles.

The next summer, after the snows had melted, missionaries located the final trail by the hundreds of skeletons of those who fell frozen and exhausted on the last fatal rush within sight of salvation.

By that next summer, missionaries already had calculated what had happened to those who had gone before: of the 3,400 Armenians who, like the Bagdikian family, left immediately behind the retreating French, 1,000 had died in the mountains. Another 2,000 left Marash two hours later, 1,800 of them killed within sight of the city in an ambush by waiting Turks; of the surviving 200 of the second wave, only 20 were known to have reached Islahiye. In their own account of the retreat, the French military records show that of the 3,000 young and healthy French troops who left Marash, 1,200 died in the mountains, 630 of them never accounted for. At least 150 of the soldiers required emergency amputations of frozen limbs.

Armenians remaining in Marash were not luckier. In the following months, missionaries counted 10,000 Armenians who died slowly of starvation, disease, or murder because the Turks permitted no one to sell or give food to an Armenian. Those who survived could thank bribes paid to Turkish officials by the American missionaries.

Lydia hurried ahead until she saw my mother, father, Cynthia, and Elmas around a fire. A neighbor from Marash stopped to ask why the family was not going on to Islahiye.

My father told him one of his daughters was missing. They would wait here. There were cows they could milk and good huts to sleep in. The family would wait for the missing ones to catch up.

That night in the mountain, Lydia was settled by my father next to the fire. He made sure everyone had milk, checked the sleeping baby, and returned to the trail to look for Bedros and Nora. The family members around the fire said their family service, praying that Nora and Bedros were safe.

When Lydia woke the next morning, Nora and Elmas and my father were not there. My mother looked sick with what looked like a bad cold. Lydia felt hot and took off her scarf. My mother said, "Don't do that, Lydia. Even if you feel hot, don't take off any clothes. You will need protection from the cold. We will soon be in Islahiye."

"Where is Papa?"

"He's looking for Nora and Bedros. They may have missed us in the night and gone on to Islahiye. We will probably see them there."

My father returned empty-handed. They started the movement downward to the railroad, plodding through the packed snow.

Suddenly, in a daze, Lydia realized they were outside a train station. A French officer approached. He had often dined with them in Marash and had always brought favors for Nora.

"This is the only train today. It will take only Army people. But my commandant said that if you will take this train, you may board with your family. You are in great danger if you wait here."

My mother said, "I cannot go without my daughter."

"Madam, you are ill. The rest of your family is exhausted and not well. There may not be another chance."

"I cannot go without Nora."

A group of women refugees had gathered around the officer and the family. One of the women cried out:

"You should be grateful! I have lost two in the mountains. You still have most of your family. I will take your place right now!"

My mother wept. She said to the woman that she was sorry for her loss, but she could not go without her daughter.

The woman was bitter.

"You had servants to help you. You have a servant now. You want everything."

My mother wept and shook her head.

"I am sorry. May God comfort you. But I cannot leave my daughter behind."

The train whistle blew.

"Madam, you must decide. I urge you to get aboard. We must leave in a few minutes."

While the officer had spoken and the crowd of women murmured, Lydia could hear her father somewhere shouting over and over, "Bedros! Nora!" Suddenly he stopped and stared toward the edge of the station.

"Bedros!"

The boy was alone.

"Where is Nora?"

"I don't know. When we started this morning she said she didn't want to be carried anymore."

My father lost his temper.

"Why didn't you hold her hand? What kind of a person are you? You gave me your word of honor! How far back did this happen?"

"I don't know. She just jumped off my back and ran."

The officer pleaded with my father.

"Sir, your wife is sick and you have your other children to think about."

My mother shook her head again.

The Armenian woman said, "Look. She still wants everything."

Another Armenian woman said, "I don't blame her. I would not leave one of mine behind, either."

Somewhere in the growing circle of people around the family, someone shouted:

"Take the train! Take the train!"

My mother, weeping, raised her head as though to answer. She stared suddenly at a woman in the crowd and gasped, "Nora's scarf!" then fainted.

My father brought her to consciousness, told Elmas and Tirzah to tend her, and ran to the woman.

"That is my daughter's scarf. Where did you get it?"

"It's mine."

By now my mother was standing again and went quietly to the woman.

"No. That is my daughter's. There is no other like it in Marash. We bought it in Aleppo. We do not care for the scarf. You may have it. But you must tell us where you found it. Was it today? How far back?"

The train whistle blew again. The officer held up his hand toward the front of the train and turned:

"Madam, we cannot wait longer."

Lydia's heart sank. My father could be seen looking wildly among the stragglers still coming to the station. Suddenly, he began to run. My mother cried out:

"Nora! Nora! Thank God! Nora!"

Nora was running toward them, crying. She was naked.

The officer said they must now get on.

My father told the officer he needed only two minutes.

"Elmas, please come with us to America."

Elmas shook her head. She had always said she would stay. She repeated it. My father reached into Mozart's saddlebag and tied a large amount of gold in a piece of cloth and gave it to her. My mother kissed Elmas. Both women were weeping.

My father gave a remaining packet of gold to Bedros.

"Bedros, you may have the horse, too. Take care of it. It is valuable."

In the confusion of the crowded railroad car, Lydia felt dizzy. It was hot and steamy. Soldiers were drinking from flasks. Somewhere one of the soldiers began singing in French. Then she lost consciousness again.

## CHAPTER 7

## My Mother

T antalizing vagueness about my mother's face and painful experiences with her photographs have sharpened my sensitivity to the power of artificial images like television's to fix permanent "memories" in our head of things we never saw.

Modern advertising surrounds us with an artificial environment that blurs the real one, and every year we all become more dependent on television, magazines, newspapers, and computers to implant someone else's images that alter our remembrance of things seen in real life. The media images can even substitute for our own sense of living and breathing reality.

The fact that I am stuck with someone else's chance image of my mother's face makes me more aware how much we are all at the mercy of the explosion of images that we confidently call "our world" but is actually a stage set created by others.

My mother died when I was three, and I began with only a meager knowledge of her because of the family division. After my father remarried, my mother was never mentioned in any family gathering. It made any photograph of her more important in my perception.

The photographs I have seen of her have considerable meaning, but they have a disturbing aftereffect. The unchanging fixed images on paper are always in danger of replacing the dreamlike memories of what little I did see of her, the way volcanic ash infiltrates the cells of live trees to turn them into everlasting stone. I have had to cope with the way a photograph can invade a void and almost convince the mind that the camera's frozen image is a living recollection.

I have seen only two photographs of my mother, one so associated with a painful incident and the other so fixed by date, that those two images, while clearly not mine but Kodak's, keep reappearing in my mind the way the eye that stares too long at a well-lighted object can close but still "see" the image after the eyes are closed.

I have real memories of being in my mother's presence but I cannot dredge up a recollection of her face. She had tuberculosis during my childhood and I know from my sisters that once she fell ill, they could kiss her only on the forehead. Perhaps when I was an infant my mother held me to one side and kept her face averted because *Mycobacterium tuberculosis* can be transmitted the same way as a cold.

My father remarried three days after the first anniversary of my mother's death, when I was four, and from that day all photographs of my mother mysteriously disappeared. My sisters periodically challenged my father about the one photo that was the sole survivor of the frantic escape from Marash and earlier had been a fixture in our new American households. My sisters would ask about the photograph even when my stepmother was present: "Papa, what happened to the wedding picture of you and Mother? It used to be right on the secretary in the living room!" My father always said he did not know. My sisters, glaring at my stepmother, clearly disbelieved him.

In my memory what remains are four real scenes involving my mother and me, but all tantalizing and vague.

One scene was in the sanitarium where my mother spent most of the time during the last three years of her life, which were the first three years of mine. It is a memory of a white bed surrounded by a group, presumably my father and four sisters visiting her on the last day of her life. Then, while the others remain in the room, I am led outside to a corridor of the sanitarium where, as I wait, some stranger hands me a penny. I can still see in my mind's eye the puzzling image of the copper head of Abraham Lincoln shining in my palm.

The other three scenes, all connected in my memory, came from five months earlier, on the day of my mother's only period in the house at 59 Elm Street. From Lydia's memoir, I know it was a month before my third birthday. I am sitting next to a woman who in memory is dressed in grey. I recall another scene the same day that follows the dinner-table scene. A frail woman in a black coat is being helped by two men down the black asphalt front walk of the house toward a black automobile parked in the street (I assume it would have been my father and Uncle Fred leading her to Uncle Fred's Model T Ford). The other scene is in our kitchen afterward where I recall my sisters weeping as they fish my mother's tubercular dinner dishes out of a pot of boiling water.

One of the two photographs of her that I have ever seen I first saw when I was about nine. Some women in my father's church were visiting our house, which meant the pastor's children were supposed to be on display and be part of the welcome. My sisters got away with serving trays of the obligatory Turkish coffee in their tiny demitasse cups and then disappearing. But I, as a useless young male, was required to sit functionless while the women sipped their coffee and gossiped.

One day, when I was unlucky enough to be at home when the parishioners visited, I sat on a chair next to a living room table that held a few books I had leafed through many times during earlier hours of visitations, and stacks of perforated paper rolls for the player piano that sat in an opposite corner of the living room. I was idly straightening out the packages of player piano rolls when I saw behind them something I had never seen before. It was a dusty album of photographs.

Anything new during these visits was a blessing. I was studying photographs I had never seen before and didn't notice that the church woman sitting next to me was looking over my shoulder. At one point she stopped me and pointed to one snapshot.

The photograph was vertical, held onto the album page with four black adhesive corners. It showed what looked to me like a very old woman in an ankle-length gray dress. She was standing on a lawn in front of large bushes. She looked sad, exhausted, and wan.

"Do you know who that is?" the church lady asked.

I shook my head.

"Yes, you do. Who is that?" she insisted.

"I don't know."

"Guess!" she demanded.

I was embarrassed. Conversation had stopped and everyone was looking at me. Given the mysterious photo I had never seen before, it was a test to which I had no honest answer. Desperate, I took a stab. I had never seen my paternal grandmother; she had been killed by the Turks in the old country before I was born.

"My grandmother?"

The woman looked at the others and announced:

"Did you hear that? He doesn't even know his own mother!"

I felt ashamed. That moment froze the album's yellowish image in my mind.

I now have unmistakable evidence, thanks largely to Lydia's memoir, that my mother was not just the pale figure in the album but a woman of vitality, spirit, and imagination. But what I cannot get out of my head is the snapshot of an ashen, clouded face of a sad, disheartened woman, a snapshot undoubtedly taken in the last weeks of her life.

I have seen one other photograph, symbolic of the beginning of her mature life, as the first one was of the end.

A few years after the living room episode, I was alone in my father's study doing the periodic penance handed down for minor transgressions. "You must stay in the sitting room for one hour and think about what you did," my father would say. It was his study but we called it the sitting room, a pleasant place connected to the living room through a double doorway in which hung a heavy curtain on brass rings.

In my father's study was a small table where he had his ancient Hammond typewriter that printed either English or Armenian letters depending on how you turned a print dial. My father used those in doing formal letters, like the ones he occasionally wrote to President Roosevelt praising or demurring from some White House action. But he wrote his sermons in longhand on sheets of white paper at four o'clock in the morning. Otherwise, the room held a grand piano, a small pump organ, a four-sided revolving bookcase, and shelf after shelf of ministerial volumes. When I had to serve time in the room, the endless rows of religious and theological books were, to me, endlessly boring.

A closet in the study was filled with still another bookcase with still more solemn volumes. Apparently overlooked by my father, at the extreme right side of one shelf of the closet, was a series of mystery novels by Mary Roberts Rinehart. Though I think I was disgustingly obedient as a child, I must have done fairly frequent sitting room time because I had read all of the Rinehart books.

This time, I was browsing the closet shelves with hopes of another nontheological find when a very large book with green binding and gold letters caught my eye, probably because of the title. It was *Heaven and Hell* by Emanuel Swedenborg. I reached for it in its far corner and when I opened it, a photograph fell out. It was my parents' wedding picture.

Even at age twenty-three, wearing a knee-length black frock coat with white tie and white gloves and sporting a grandiloquent mustachio, the man was unmistakably my father. The woman had to be my mother. It was the second of the two photographs of her I have ever seen.

My mother, like him unsmiling, has her white-gloved right hand linked through his arm at the elbow. She wears a white veil and an elaborate floor-length white gown. Her face is almost childlike in its roundness—she was nineteen when they married—but the dark eyes and firm mouth are not those of a child.

I learned later that on her wedding day my mother was in her room where her friends and older women celebrated an old tradition of singing a special song while the bride is being dressed. Her white wedding gown was hanging by a window. As the women sang, a breeze blew the dress off its hanger onto a desk where marriage documents were being prepared. Someone picked up the dress and gasped. A drop of black ink from the desk had spotted the gown.

My grandmother, still disapproving of the marriage, later told relatives the black spot was a bad omen, her marriage to Bagdikian would come to no good end. The women sewed a white patch over the spot. Naturally, when my mother died young, people remembered the black omen. After I read of the wedding incident in Lydia's notes, I studied that old photograph, but it showed only the front of the gown and that unsharply; I could not see the patch.

The print, brownish yellow in the tone of photographs taken in 1905, was cracked on one corner and along one edge, as though it had survived rough treatment. Perhaps thrown in during the last desperate Marash moments and jostled in Mozart's saddlebags during the days in the mountains? Or later, in Massachusetts, thrown away—and retrieved?

I put the photograph back into the book in what I hoped was the same general place in the center pages and carefully replaced the book as closely as I could to its original position. I mentioned my discovery to no one.

I'm not sure of all the reasons that moved me to keep my discovery a secret. Maybe it was guilt at unearthing what some adult wanted hidden. Or my dread of the periodic bitter confrontations between my sisters and my father and stepmother, with always the threat that they would break up the household. The rediscovered picture would have created one of those scenes.

The tearful, hours-long confrontations that I hated usually began with my father and stepmother downstairs at the front hall newel post and my sisters and me seated higher on the steps at the landing. They would begin at twilight when my sisters returned home from school or work and end later in darkness with only the outside streetlight on Elm Street. I was four or five and remember being very sleepy. I had no idea what the issues were except that at times my name was mentioned. One time my stepmother had a suitcase at her side.

Even in those bitter scenes, the climax came only by the power of invoking my mother's memory. It ended with a strange ritual, The Reconciliation. The two sides moved into the living room, my stepmother sat on the bench of the player piano, and my sisters lined up in front of her, having agreed to kiss her on the cheek. Nora, the youngest, was always the last holdout. She insisted it was not sincere. But one of my older sisters, I suspect as much in fatigue as in Christian love, would utter the magic words: "Nora, Mother would want it." It always worked, even though Nora preceded her kiss with the words, "But I don't mean it."

I think there was something else at work when I returned the wedding picture to my father's hiding place. Somewhere in the instinct to rebury my find was a conflict of loyalties. I was sure that my father had concealed the wedding picture and lied when asked about it by my sisters. I was loyal to my sisters, and surprised by my father's lying. But I also harbored an indefinable loyalty toward my father, and pity at his obvious dilemma trapped between two bitter and irreconcilable groups in his household.

While my father was alive, I never told him of my discovery. It became our separate secrets.

The photographs are not the only childhood knowledge I have of my mother. At the few times when my stepmother and father were not present, my sisters would recount happy old-country household episodes that reflected my mother's comforting presence or wisdom or one of her moral precepts. But I never heard any coherent recounting about her life and personality. The household habit of silence about her was too deeply ingrained.

Later, when I asked elderly relatives who might have a more objective view of my mother than her own adoring daughters, I was hampered by my inability to understand either Armenian or Turkish and I asked the wrong people. I asked former residents of Marash. Only years later, when I read Lydia's memoir, did I learn why I received only stereotyped responses, like, "She was kind to everyone," or, "She was a real lady." Apparently, the responses I evoked were not just diplomatic praise of the dead.

After her marriage, the family lived in Tarsus, one hundred fifty miles from Marash, on the sea coast, where my father was teaching in an American college. In Tarsus, they lived inside the American college compound, out of touch with the rest of the city, most of which was

Turkish, not Armenian. The family went to Marash only for the summers, to rent a cool vacation house in the mountains.

Even the Armenian adult I could talk to most freely, Uncle Fred, her younger brother, had his limitations. He was three when his sister was married, and seven years after the wedding, after his father was killed in a riding accident, he and my grandmother emigrated to the United States. He knew family stories about Daisy and Aram but knew his older sister as an adult only after she went to a sanitarium.

When she had been in the sanitarium a year, there was good news. Her doctors said she was cured and after a period of rest to regain her strength would be able to go home. Until then the family home had consisted of rented furnished houses in the Brighton section of Boston. My father looked for a permanent home and ended up in Stoneham.

But before her release there came a day when my sisters noticed a sudden change in my father. He became grim and tense. They feared the worst about their mother. At first, all he told them was not to expect her release as soon as they had thought. Unsatisfied, Tirzah and Lydia demanded an explanation. Confronted, he told them the reason.

Hospital authorities had received an order that my mother and the rest of the family were to be deported. It would mean almost certain death for her and an ominous future for everyone else in the family. A band of Armenian revolutionaries in the United States considered my father's efforts to save Marash insufficient. Apparently it was not enough that he risked his life three times in near-fatal missions and spent almost all the money he had accumulated from selling his Marash vineyards to arm the Armenians when the French became half-hearted in defending them. In Marash, representatives of the political group had asked my father to finance the weapons earlier, but my father had refused because at the time the British were committed to protecting the Armenians. It was after the British announced their withdrawal that he provided arms.

The revolutionaries were committed to vengeance on all, Turkish and Armenian, who disagreed with them. They told the American immigration authorities that my father had entered the country under false pretenses by claiming to be poor, when, they said, he was a rich man now having his wife treated at public expense in a state sanitarium. They also threatened to kill my father. The claims were found to be false and the order was rescinded. But my mother never recovered.

When next they visited the sanitarium, Tirzah and Lydia spoke bitterly to my mother about the conspirators. Lydia said she hated them. My mother told them, "You must never hate anyone, not even the Turks. Hatred cripples the hater more than the hated."

In the sanitarium, it seemed clear by late 1922 that my mother was in a losing battle. She had convinced the doctors to let her spend a short time in the family's new home on Elm Street in Stoneham. In the days before Christmas, she lay on a couch in the dining room on Elm Street to watch her daughters decorate the biggest tree my father could find that would fit under the ceiling.

The day after Christmas, a doctor examined her and said she must return at once to the Middleboro sanitarium. She left on December 27. Uncle Fred in his Model T Ford drove her and my father the fifty miles from Stoneham to the hospital. It was the day I remember being in her presence and watching her being helped down the front walk, and my sisters weeping afterward.

From her first hospitalization, my mother kept a notebook in which, over the three years, she wrote thirty-nine poems. Most are in Armenian script but in the Turkish language, an Armeno-Turkish common among Armenians who lived for centuries in areas where Armenian was forbidden as a public language. The King James Bible translated for Armenians in those regions is in that combination.

Today it is not easy to find people who can read the Armenian script, as opposed to the printed letters, and are also sufficiently fluent in Turkish to translate poetry. My mother wrote some of the sanitarium poems in English, and a few in the Armeno-Turkish side-by-side with her English translation. (She undoubtedly wrote poetry in Turkey but it did not survive the last-minute escape to the mountains.)

I first saw the notebook more than thirty years after her death. Each poem is written in a clear and precise hand, numbered and dated, sometimes with explanatory notations in English in her handwriting.

The first poem was written when she first went to Peter Bent Brigham Hospital in Boston, only weeks after arriving in America. Next to it she noted that she had sent it to Alice Stone Blackwell. I suspect that this poem was written after the discovery that she had not pneumonia but tuberculosis and it was clear she would be isolated in a sanitarium and not returning home. She has entitled the poem, "A Dispute With God."

Later that year she was moved to ultra-isolation in an outer porch for the worst cases at the sanitarium and wrote a poem in Armeno-Turkish, after which she has written in English, "Transfer from Ward F to Ward C." The poem is called, "I Do Not Want to Die."

One poem in Armenian script has her note in English, "On the 17th anniversary of our wedding, June 23rd, 1921," and presumably was given or mailed to my father. It is entitled, "No Rose Without Thorns."

On January 30, 1922, she wrote a poem with the note, "Written for my baby's second birthday." She called it, "Who Is My Mother?" in the voice of a child.

> Here I am, but who is my mother?
> Tell me about her, tell me now, dear father . . .

And then an obvious plea of her own that is spoken through the child:

> Remember, dear Jesus, I need her guiding hand,
> I am young and helpless, growing in a strange land . . .

On August 15, 1922—my father's birthday—when she must have known that she would soon have her terminal visit to the house in Stoneham, she wrote a poem called "The Homeward Turn." As she translated it, there is, in the beginning, a hopeful tone:

> Homeward I turn my longing eyes . . .
> There dwells the love that never dies,
> Home, homeward, my longing eyes.

But there are lines that become ambiguous, that could refer to a different "home" than the one in Stoneham, given her clear belief in a literal heaven where all would be reunited after earthly death. She wrote:

Homeward I turn my eager face . . .
Near seems the end of my long race . . .
The road that leads where we will meet,
Homeward, homeward, my weary feet.

The pages of her notebook are neatly numbered. Each poem and each verse is numbered sequentially. It is even divided into Part I and Part II. Part II has a facing page that reads, "Lakeville Sanitarium, Jan. 27, 1923." It was her final sanitarium after she was diagnosed as not hopeful and was forced to leave our house the day after Christmas.

If the page marked "Part II" is turned, there is page 110, Poem No. 1. It would be the first poem she wrote after her transfer to the last sanitarium. The poem is in Armenian script, but the title, like all of the others, is in English. It is entitled, "What Shall I Write?"

The facing page is No. 111, and preparation for another poem. It is headed in her writing, "No. 2." But the page is blank. So are all the remaining pages in the book.

When Mother's Day arrived in May 1923, my four sisters, following tradition at the time, wore pink carnations to church. The pink indicated a living mother. You wore a white carnation on Mother's Day only if your mother was dead. But that day my sisters confessed to each other that they did not know what color they would be wearing the next May. (As a child attending church on Mother's Days, I never wore anything but white, feeling in the quick sympathetic glances of the adults embarrassed self-consciousness and not a little self-pity.)

On the Fourth of July, 1923, my father visited my mother at the sanitarium. The next morning he telephoned home and said all the children must come at once. The girls had no money. "Go to Adzigian's store, and borrow ten dollars from Mr. Adzigian. Tell him what it is for."

Lydia ran a mile across town to the only Armenian store in Stoneham. The four of them, with me carried by one of my sisters, walked down Elm Street to the streetcar stop, paid the double ten-cent fare to Boston, changed to a subway at Sullivan Square, took the subway to South Station for the train to Middleboro and from the station took a bus to the Lakeville sanitarium.

Lydia has described the scene in my mother's room.

My mother spoke to them and my father and, of course, to what I assume was an uncomprehending me.

"Last night about eleven o'clock, I knew definitely that I was dying . . . 'I am ready,' I said, because I was tired and very sick. But I thought of you all, my dear children and husband, and I asked God to give me twenty-four more hours to live."

At that point, I was put in my mother's arms and she said to me, "God sent you to me only a few years before it was time for Him to call me. In years to come, you may not remember me, but I will try to guide you from afar."

My mother addressed my sisters and my father:

"Don't let Ben-Hur forget that his mother loved him very much."

Lydia started crying bitterly. "If you're dying now, I wish I had died in the mountains."

My mother comforted her.

"Although I do not want a tombstone—and your father knows that—there will be a spot somewhere near you which you can call 'the station' from which I left you to go home. Just a marker and a pine tree is all I want for my station. Someday, long from now, you may leave from that station where we will all be together again."

In front of my sisters, she made my father promise that no matter what the ladies in the church demanded, he would not let the girls wear black mourning clothes.

They all sang the hymn "Some Day the Silver Cord Will Break . . . My Blessed Lord will say, 'Well done!' And I shall enter into rest."

She asked that the hymn be played at her funeral, as well as another hymn with the text of Tennyson's "Crossing the Bar," and a violin rendition of the "Coming Home" theme from Dvořák's New World Symphony.

She told my sisters and my father, "We should be thankful that we are now in the New World. God sent us all safely here. And now I am going to another New World . . . I'll watch and wait for you there."

It is clear that she believed in a literal heaven where all would be rejoined. Whether she believed in a literal flaming hell, given her attitude toward forgiveness and the wages of hatred, is doubtful.

It was then, according to Lydia's description, that I was led outside. I am still chagrined that I have always remembered more sharply than any other detail of that day the penny from a stranger and the copper head of Abraham Lincoln in my palm.

The four girls, alternating in carrying the baby, took the long trip back to Stoneham. My father stayed alone at the bedside of my mother.

Late that night, just before midnight, my father called the house in Stoneham. My mother died at 11:15 P.M. on July 5, twenty-four hours and fifteen minutes after she had prayed to be given just twenty-four hours more to see her family.

When he arrived home the next morning, my father gathered the girls around him in the living room and they all wept together. It was the first time any of the girls had ever seen my father cry.

Three days after she died, my mother was buried during a steady rain at Mt. Hope Cemetery in the Mattapan section of Boston. Seventy years later, at age eighty-four, Lydia was buried at Mt. Hope Cemetery in her mother's cemetery plot, their "station."

## CHAPTER 8

# *My Father behind His Divinity Degree*

One evening while in college, I was in my bedroom studying for a physiology exam when my father walked in and quietly closed the door behind him. He asked if it were true that I was going out with a certain girl in the church. I said it was. He turned red and agitated. He looked out the window, coughed, breathed in, and said with obvious embarrassment:

"Have you . . ." his hands made vague motions, "have you kissed her?"

It was not like my father to enter into conversations about anything as directly physical as kissing.

"Yes. Of course."

The air seemed to go out of him. His face looked grim and he spoke with a hard and bitter tone I had not heard before.

"Then you must marry her."

I was stunned.

"Pa, I don't want to get married."

"You must. I cannot perform the ceremony. You will go to a justice of the peace away from the city, where you are not known, and you will marry her."

"That's impossible. You don't get married just because you kiss a girl. Boys and girls kiss all the time and don't get married."

"You will."

"I can't. I don't want to get married."

"You must."

"I'm sorry, but I can't."

I had never directly defied my father. His questions about church rumors about me had always ended with mutual relief after my explanations. But this time we looked at each other silently for a long, uncompromising moment. Without another word, he turned and walked out.

I was stunned. And angry. My first conclusion was that he didn't mean kissing at all, but sleeping together. He had never been able to speak to any of us about sex.

But it was also quite possible that he meant only kissing and whatever else the congregation gossip circuit embroidered around it. It would be consistent with the extreme puritanism he still retained from the American missionaries who educated him.

The hostile conversation shook me. I lived at home while I attended college. My father had just left the big Cambridge church to accept the pulpit of the smaller Church of the Armenian Martyrs, in Worcester, the oldest Armenian church in America. But in my four years of college, my life was centered four miles and a world away from our house, on the campus of Clark University.

I was glad to spend most of my time away from the household. My four older sisters had moved away, and for me the only remaining family gatherings were my mandatory attendance at Sunday services at my father's church, choir rehearsal at the church, and, most of the time, Sunday dinner with my father, stepmother, and two younger half-brothers, Ted and David, who already were itchy and rebellious under their parents' unrelieved rigidity. I left early each weekday morning and came back after midnight when the rest of the household was asleep.

Shortly after the troubling conversation, I made one of my periodic visits to Uncle Fred and Aunt Anna. After dinner, as usual, Uncle Fred and I settled down in their tiny living room, both of us with guitars and tumblers of Fred's favorite drink, Canadian Club whiskey and ginger ale. We were tuning our guitars when I stopped and told him the story of my father's demand that I get married because I had kissed a girl. I said he was impossibly ignorant about some real things in life.

Uncle Fred laughed and laid down his guitar.

"Let me tell you something about your dad. Grandma told me that when he was courting your mother he would come riding to our house, jump his horse over the wall into our yard, sweep up your mother and they'd ride off across the fields. Your grandmother didn't think much of that."

I was almost as stunned as I had been by my father's order to get married.

"Fred, I don't believe it."

He laughed. "That was your father," and picked up his guitar again.

I couldn't connect the grim father in my bedroom with the passionate young man riding wildly over the fields with his fiancée.

Did this impetuous graduate student kiss his girlfriend as they rode away from her home? Possibly, but maybe it was all right because they were publicly committed to marriage.

Or did they stop in some distant woods and make love? Unlikely. Both my parents took their puritanical religion too seriously.

For years it remained hard for me to merge the image of the passionate romantic with the inflexible Victorian I knew. I never saw my father or my stepmother make physical gestures of affection. They were devoted and maybe even loved each other but never in sight did they touch each other affectionately or kiss. My stepmother always addressed her husband as "Budvelli," the formal Armenian honorific for the Protestant clergy, like "Pastor." My mother, I learned later, had always called him "Aram."

My father's personal life and mine seemed forever incompatible. Despite the vague and unworded respect we had for each other, I despaired of ever really understanding him or his comprehending my personal life.

Luckily, long after the troubling bedroom confrontation, I learned more about my father. It made me realize how much I gained from the two wildly different kinds of men in my childhood. If I had not learned more about my father and not been close to Uncle Fred, my life would have been different. I'm convinced that my journalism would have been different.

From Uncle Fred, I learned that class snobbery is idiotic, and a pitifully thin world for the snob.

From my father's life, I learned that it is possible to sustain terrible loss and turbulence but retain vitality and a taste for life.

And though I learned it too late for the relationship with my father, his life taught me that men and women who present forbidding and withdrawn personalities may reveal drama and passion if only the outsider—the reporter, for example—is interested, patient, and listens with an inner ear. I lacked that patience as a child. Only later, as an adult and as a journalist, did I learn to trust that inner ear.

## »

As a young adult I wasn't perceptive about my father as a real man, but he didn't make it easy. He buried personal emotion, and he was all but silent about most things in the past, especially anything concerning my mother. I may have learned little about my father's real life because he knew remarkably little about mine.

In high school, for example, I won the state extemporaneous speaking contest and with help from Lydia and the Stoneham Rotary Club, I went on my great sixteen-year-old adventure—an unaccompanied Greyhound bus ride all the way from Stoneham, Massachusetts, to Springfield, Illinois, for the national finals. Lydia attached my money onto the lining of my suit jacket with a safety pin. I returned home flushed with victory, not in the contest which I had lost, but because I had managed successfully being totally on my own for a whole week in a strange and distant part of the country. When I rushed into my father's study to announce, "Pa, I'm back!" he looked up, surprised, and said, "Back? From where?"

There were tumults at home he seemed to miss entirely. When I was about twelve and Ted seven, we got into a rock fight that seemed our standard method of teasing each other. One of my stones grazed

Ted's forehead and drew some blood. My stepmother rushed out of the house and in a raging panic at the sight of Ted's blood broke my nose with the side of her hand.

As far as I know, my father never noticed the broken nose, or nose break number two from a junior high soccer game, or break number three from a college basketball game. (Uncle Fred once mentioned that my nose looked different from my childhood nose, and when I told him I had broken it in three places, he just laughed and said, "I guess you'd better stay out of those places.")

I was too conscious of my father's weaknesses and flaws. Though he often repeated biblical injunctions like, "Be not puffed up," he had his own vanities. It was a family joke that he kept an old heroic etching of President William McKinley that was in the house when he bought it and would periodically ask my sisters, "Don't you think I look like William McKinley?" He once said in all seriousness that if a movie were made of "The Forty Days of Musa Dagh," he would be happy to play the leading role.

He was attracted to certain kinds of showiness. He had a terrible weakness for buying big used cars that were mechanical nightmares as long as the cars had shiny paint jobs. He took for granted Uncle Fred's curative powers with automotive junk.

I saw as a weakness his endless tolerance of a few petty tyrants in the church who underpaid him and made mean trouble for him. Most of his parishioners liked and admired him, but every church everywhere has individuals who use church committees as the only arena in which they can flex personal political muscles, the churchly counterparts of academic politicians.

One experience with him shocked me. When I was sixteen a driver lost control of his car and dented our fender while I was behind the wheel, parked in front of our house. When the insurance adjuster came, my father said I should stay in bed and say I had a headache. I had not been in bed and I didn't have a headache. I refused. But I never got over his suggestion that I lie.

It seemed strangely weak of him that in the presence of my stepmother his behavior toward me was different, especially in reaction to her complaints about me.

When we were alone, if he became frustrated by my laziness or frequent neglect of errands, he would admonish me in sorrow rather than anger. He would turn in despair to his private channel to God. This pipeline seemed to be someplace over his left shoulder and he would look upward to it and say in tired supplication, "What am I going to do with this boy?"

But my father's response was different if my stepmother reported offenses to him. Though she would often show spontaneous kindness toward me, she could be arbitrary, unfair, even hysterical, and I would rebel. Once, angrily, I mocked her by calling her by her first name, Santookt, which my sisters used in addressing her but was forbidden to me because I was too young.

One of my regular minor transgressions was stealing candy and the wonderful drop cookies she made, which she usually hid. My father did not like sweets, and in our house they were always "saved for company." All during my childhood I dreamed about milk chocolate the way I later dreamed about girls.

One day I took ten cents of change on a shopping errand for my stepmother, spent it at the five-and-ten-cent store for a bagful of the fabulous chiseled milk chocolate chunks, and then claimed I had lost the dime. The lie was transparent. The bag of chocolate was in my pocket.

My stepmother was enraged. She repeated a common threat, "You are going to end in Concord! We will send you to Concord!" Around town "Concord" meant the Concord Reformatory, a juvenile prison near Boston. She called my father from his study.

I had never before seen my father so enraged. "I am going to take you outside right now! I am going to beat you. I am going to use a branch as thick as a broomstick and I am going to beat you until you think your bones will crack! I will teach you what happens when you behave this way!"

He took me by the arm, pulled me through the kitchen, slammed the door behind him, pushed me through the kitchen woodshed to the outdoors, and once outside turned me around to face him and said firmly, "You must never do that again," and walked away.

In my whole life he never laid a punishing hand on me.

On my part, I was hardly the model son. In public I followed the family command to be (almost always) the perfect citizen. But at home I was laggard and reluctant in chores. If I was told to put one cup of water next to each new tomato seedling in his garden, I saw imaginary miles of plants in the hot sun. I'd trudge lazily and reluctantly between the rows until my father would get impatient and do it all himself in minutes while he admonished, "You must learn to be more industrious."

I was more loyal to my sisters than to my stepmother, and the enigmatic positive feeling between my father and me left me with respect for him but little closeness.

The family began its division the day my father brought home my stepmother. The new couple could not have made a worse entry: on the first morning, my sister Cynthia had to serve the new bride her breakfast in bed. To the very end, neither my father nor stepmother showed any evidence of comprehending how they might have healed the split instead of widening it.

Nevertheless, now that I look back, I realize that despite that first (and last) breakfast in bed, my stepmother was not dealt an easy fate. She came new into an established household with a four-year-old boy and four growing girls still in shock over the death of their mother. Her basic model of human relations was the old Armenian tradition of unmarried daughters acting as handmaidens to the household matriarch. It was reinforced by her growing up among the rigidities of an English orphanage. She had to manage the house, do all the onerous social chores of a minister's wife, and make life as easy as possible for her husband even though his terrible management of household finances created perpetual crises.

She was understandably jealous for her own two children, Ted (Aram Theodore, Jr.), five years younger than I, and David (his mother's maiden name was Tavitian), born five years after Ted. Her partisanship never cooled the warm feelings we three boys always felt for each other.

Just as I became conscious that in his own wordless way my father clearly expected much for my future, my stepmother may have sensed it and felt that it slighted her own sons.

If I had known what I learned much later maybe I might have understood my stepmother a little better. She was six years old when Turks approached her village during a massacre. Her mother ordered her and a younger sister to hide quickly in the upper branches of a mulberry tree. From there the two girls observed the killing and butchering of their mother, father, and six brothers. After two days, missionaries found the girls still in the tree and young Santookt was brought up in an English orphanage with stern and inflexible rules. It's possible it would have made a difference if I had known this about my stepmother back then. It does now. Perhaps it explains her uncontrolled hysteria that day when she saw blood on Ted's forehead in our rock fight.

When all seven children were in the household, my sisters were important arbiters and youthful spirits for Ted, David, and me, moderating the rigidities of my father and my stepmother. When I was guilty of household misfeasances, in the absence of my father my stepmother would save her indictments for my sisters when they returned from school or work. My sisters always took pains to listen to her and if they thought I was guilty mete out punishment or admonishment. They were always fair with Ted and David. But my sisters obviously began with resentment toward their mother's replacement and never got over it.

Now that I look back, the family split made me too conscious of my father's flaws and weaknesses. As a child I missed hint after hint of a different man than the one I thought I saw.

I knew, for example, that my father was a near genius with trees and plants and periodically he would try to bring me closer to that part of his life. But if he tried to show me some of his horticultural tricks, like grafting a peach tree onto a plum, or a slice of red dahlia bulb into a blue one, I was a bored and indifferent apprentice. Maybe I was expressing what I hid from myself, a resentment of his obsessive attention to his garden compared to his distance from my life. His trying to teach me plant grafting could have become an invitation to enter other parts of his silent life.

I could see that he and my stepmother liked cooking and talking together, but I was naive about anything more in their relationship as a couple. When I was in college, my bedroom was next to theirs and one night when I was a freshman, I was astonished to hear unmistakable sounds of lovemaking. With the same reaction of self-centered youth that once led Hemingway to say that when Yale freshmen discover sex they think they invented it, I had trouble associating those sounds with the man I knew as proper, prudish, and, especially, old. Or with my stepmother whom I saw as incorrigibly sanctimonious, and old. At the time, my father was fifty-seven, my stepmother forty-seven.

I failed to catch the significance of clear evidence that my father was not all censorious puritan. He loved good food and jovial company. He delighted to play along with my sisters' joke gifts for him at Christmas and on his birthdays. He was a talented and wicked mimic. In the privacy of our dining room, he often sent us into scandalized laughter with hilarious imitations of parishioners' idiosyncrasies. My favorite was his masterful imitation of Mrs. Manzigian.

Mrs. Manzigian wore her prized ankle-length mink coat in all weather. When someone asked if she wasn't hot in August, my father did an imitation of Mrs. Manzigian's reply as she stood on the church steps in the hot sun, fluffing the fur collar as though desperate for oxygen. He was uncanny in his duplication of her whiny voice and martyred look as she whimpered, "What can you do? It's mink."

Other hints of another kind of man eluded me, like the time he picked up Uncle Fred's accordion and played jaunty tunes skillfully for a few minutes, looked embarrassed, then put it down, never to play again. When and where did my father learn to play an accordion that way?

In one of the rare times he spoke to me alone about his past, he said that when he was thirteen, during the period of the 1890s massacre of Armenians by Sultan Hamid, he was arrested for carrying a Christian Bible and was sentenced to more than a year on the Isle of Rhodes. A young boy coping as prisoner of the Turks on an island must have learned something of the unpuritanical life.

I knew the outlines of family close calls in the old country, about his accumulation of wealth after his marriage, of his heroism in the dramas of the final massacres, and that all of us owed our lives to my father's stamina, ingenuity, and courage.

But as a child these episodes seemed common among older relatives and friends who periodically recounted incidents around our dinner table. I came to think that it was unexceptional, something standard in being an Armenian of that generation. Isolated from the emotions of each individual life, the dramas became almost tribal ritual with the unworldly quality of Greek legends. Besides, it was all happily put behind us and unrelated to life as I knew it in the New England placidity of Stoneham, Massachusetts of the 1920s and 1930s.

Then, shortly after his death in 1957, Lydia sent me her two looseleaf notebooks of typed memoirs. Uncle Fred's story of the romantic young man riding wildly over the fields with his sweetheart turned out to be typical of the Aram Bagdikian I never knew.

## »

While my mother was still the teenage Daisy Uvezian living with her parents in Marash, she and Aram carried on a secret correspondence, a courtship hidden partly out of Protestant propriety but mostly for an even more formidable reason, Daisy's mother.

My grandmother was always kind with me, but she was a tall, intimidating woman who was abrasive with everyone else, except, of course, Grandpa.

Back in Marash, she did not like young Bagdikian. She said he was going to be a professor or a preacher—"Nothing but talk, talk, talk. He'll never be able to support a wife." She sneered that his parents were peasants who attended Third Church, the lowest in social status among the three Congregational churches in Marash. The Uvezians had money. The Uvezians attended First Church. (After their marriage, my mother insisted that the family attend Third Church.)

It was true. He was born not only a peasant but born into the smallest of the religious affiliations of Armenians, a Roman Catholic. The great majority of Armenians belong to the Apostolic Eastern Orthodox Church that for sixteen centuries has been the cultural glue for all Armenians scattered around the world. In the Marash region, the second largest group were Protestants, with the advantage (until World War I) of identification with the United States and Western Europe.

Because the local Catholic priest married my father's headstrong older brother to a girl against his father's wishes, my paternal grandfather forbade his entire family from ever again entering a Roman Catholic church. My father, in his turn, did not behave very differently as a parent. When I married against his wishes, he stopped speaking to me for years. Only later did he discover that he liked my wife. From far back, alas, Bagdikians have been stubborn.

The younger boys remained unschooled and unchurched until my father and his younger brother got a free education from the American Protestant schools in Marash. The two boys, including my father, inevitably became Protestants.

My father became not only a Protestant, but a member of that transcendental form of protestantism, the New England Congregationalists. From them he got his school and college education, from them his lifelong puritanical religiosity, and from them his new occupation and start in America. (It was not until 1957, the year of my father's death, that the Congregationalists combined with some Methodists and other mainline Protestants to form the United Church of Christ.)

My powerful grandmother may have disapproved, but my grandfather quietly encouraged the courtship. He like Aram's dashing energy and ambition and smiled at the way the young man came courting on his horse. The Uvezians had made their money as expert horsemen and operators of the Marash trade caravan through the mountains from Syria and the East.

When my father went to Beirut for graduate study in natural science at American University, he continued his secret love notes. They always began, "MMPD"—"My Most Precious Daisy." I had more than the usual amazement of a son that his father could have been so unabashedly passionate, a father known to me as hopelessly inexpressive about inner feeling.

My mother's replies always ended, "YMDD"—Your Most Devoted Daisy." (Her given name was "Dudeh," meaning "Armenian woman," but from some early point she was called "Daisy," thanks to the Boston missionaries who also converted my father's middle name from Toros to Theodore and dropped the "h" from the original spelling of our last name, Baghdikian.)

Affectionate letters and poems, always with the secret initials between them, did not end with their wedding. They continued throughout their marriage and to the end. They are in their letters to and from the sanitarium.

My father clearly was quick to catch the eye of the Americans. He was appointed to the faculty of St. Paul's College, the American college in Tarsus, one hundred fifty miles from Marash. He became a full-time professor, in charge of chemistry and physics. The family moved to Tarsus and lived with the Americans in their college compound.

For almost the first forty years of his life, my father seemed to rise in never-ending success, social status, wealth, and mastery despite the hostile outer society.

From the start, with the approach of their first child in 1907, my parents planned to emigrate to America, where my father, they assumed, would attend Harvard Medical School. Each time my father told the president of the college that this would be his last year, Dr. Christie gave my father a promotion and a raise and my father postponed the move.

By any Turkish and Armenian standards at the time, my father was an affluent and privileged man. He invested successfully in vineyards (perhaps it was atavistic—"Bagdikian" literally means keeper of vineyards).

Safe in the walled compound of the American college, the family escaped the genocide during World War I that killed half of all Armenians in the Ottoman Empire.

In the midst of a rigid authoritarian Turkish society that was devoted to Islam and that regularly persecuted and massacred Armenians, he was a Christian Armenian who seemed to have a special status among nearly everyone around him—Armenians, Turks, American missionaries, and regional foreign generals and diplomats. Turkish civilians addressed my father with Turkish honorifics like "Effendi," reserved for gentlemen, or the respectful "Aram Hoja," meaning schoolmaster or teacher.

As a member of an oppressed minority, he was to an extraordinary degree what he did not seem to be in the freedom of New England when I knew him—master of his own fate.

After the United States entered the war, the American college was closed but the family remained in Tarsus. They even took their summer vacations in the coolness of nearby mountains, but no longer in Marash, which the Turks emptied of Armenians during the 1915–1916 genocide.

After the Turkish defeat in World War I, the family plans for emigrating to the United States were revived. When they returned to Marash for one last summer before leaving, the returning Marash Armenians, survivors of the wartime death marches, elected my father to serve as chairman of the Armenian National Union, representing all three Armenian Christian denominations, including the majority Orthodox Church. They also asked him to organize what was expected to be the Marash regional school system after the Armenian autonomy still being promised by the Allies. Warning that he could do it only until the family's emigration in the fall, my father accepted both tasks.

But the Turkish siege of Marash in midsummer, and the sudden abandonment of Marash by the French, trapped the family. The autumn move to America was impossible.

Even when the shocking end came in midwinter, my father's daring and good luck continued.

After escaping over the mountains, the family recovered in the French-controlled port of Mersin on the Mediterranean. There Tirzah and Lydia had the top joints of frozen and gangrenous toes amputated. By then, my mother had pneumonia.

While the family recuperated in a Mersin villa owned by an Armenian doctor, my father took the long trip up the coast by ship to Constantinople. The city was still an international enclave, its Christian name not yet replaced with "Istanbul." As the interdenominational leader in the Marash region, my father had to report events still largely unknown to the outside world.

In Constantinople, my father reported first to the Armenian Orthodox Patriarch, the collection point for news about the new atrocities against Armenians throughout Turkey. My father next went to the office of the British High Commissioner, whom he knew.

The High Commissioner, in the tradition of British intelligence of the era, had the best postwar intelligence about Turkey and had always been personally appalled by what the Turks were doing to the Armenians. By 1920, the wartime American ambassador, Henry Morgenthau, who also protested personally and officially about the genocide of the Armenians, had been replaced by Admiral Mark Bristol, who was hostile to the Armenians and wooing the new Kemalist Turks to get concessions for American investors.

The Deputy British High Commissioner, Admiral Richard Webb, drew my father aside and warned him that he must not return to Mersin. My father had given a press conference accusing the French of sharing the blame for the massacre of Marash Armenians. The Paris government of Clemenceau, not yet having publicized the destruction of its own military and the Armenians in Marash and secretly planning an alliance with the Kemalists, was notoriously quick to silence press criticism. After my father's press conference, Paris sent orders for French authorities to arrest him.

The French could not seize him in the international city of Constantinople, but they could in areas still controlled by the French army, including Mersin, where the rest of my family waited for his return, innocent of the secret French orders for his arrest. It was hard to warn them because all communications systems between Constantinople and the south were controlled by either the Turks or the French.

My father met a Tarsus Turk whom he had once helped. The Turk begged my father to get him a travel permit. My father obtained a permit from the British High Commissioner and made the Turk swear before Allah he would deliver a note to my mother saying they must come at once to Constantinople.

Then my father waited. He had rented a room in an attic and each day went to the foot of Galata Bridge to meet steamers from the south, never sure that his note had been delivered.

Thirty-six years later, as an American correspondent, I visited the docks at Galata Bridge. Ferries and seagoing steamers still tied up at its pier. From the bridge's sidewalk, I handed down Turkish lire to men with charcoal braziers in low-lying skiffs selling fish sandwiches, as others before me had for decades, maybe centuries. I had no trouble imagining my father waiting each day in the same spot with no way of guessing if he would ever see his family again, waiting for boat after boat, eating a cheap daily meal from the skiffs at Galata Bridge. And I could visualize the setting when, about three weeks later, he was scanning the decks of an incoming ship and heard Nora's voice: "Papa!"

Once reunited in Constantinople, the family went through the maze of the city's Great Bazaar where my parents sold the jewels and gold buttons grabbed when escaping. The last-minute salvage brought enough money to buy steerage tickets for the trip to America and not much else.

A few weeks later, at Athens' port of Piraeus, my father presented six tickets for the trans-Atlantic passage on the U.S.S. *Susquehanna*. The purser at the foot of the gangplank counted the family and said the family needed another ticket—one for the baby. My father protested that the ship's ticket agent had said the eight-week-old infant needed no ticket. But the purser was adamant. The family had no money for another ticket. The purser told them to stand aside.

Once again, as at the train in Islahiye, the press of other refugees behind the family urged them to get out of the way. Once again my parents refused to move without the whole family. As the crowd became more restless and the purser more threatening, a man in French military uniform pushed to my father's side.

"Aram Effendi, I am an Armenian from America who came here to fight in the Armenian Legion. We came to save men like you. Take my ticket for the baby. I have money and will buy another ticket for myself."

Years later, when I was a reporter for the *Providence Journal and Evening Bulletin*, my father, as we sat at the far edge of his garden in Worcester, Massachusetts—away from my stepmother in the kitchen—told me, "It's a coincidence that you work now in Providence. The man who gave us the money for your ticket in Piraeus was an Armenian soldier from Providence."

A few weeks after my father told me the story, I was in a grocery store in the Armenian section of Providence. It was one of my periodic visits to stock up on what were plainly Armenian ingredients—pickled grape leaves, pine nuts, bulgur, long-grain rice, and a bag of lavash, the Armenian round cracker bread. Each week, the elderly Armenian storekeeper had served me with minimum words and maximum suspicion. I could tell he thought this stranger in a business suit and tie was not from the neighborhood, probably an "odar," the Armenian word for a non-Armenian, not always complimentary. After a few visits, the old man finally broke his silence.

"You live in Providence?"

"Yes."

"Where?"

"On the East Side."

The East Side was on the opposite side of the city. My answer seemed to confirm his suspicions.

"You Armenian?"

"Yes."

He looked dubious.

"What's your name?"

I pronounced it with its full Armenian sound—"Bargh-dik-yun."

The storekeeper changed instantly.

"Baghdikian! What's your father's name?"

"Aram."

I pronounced that, too, the Armenian way, "Ah-rrum."

The man's jaw dropped. He walked quickly from behind the counter all smiles and shook my hand firmly.

"I joined the Armenian Legion in World War I to save your father."

Now *I* was stunned. Surely, out of the blue, this had to be the man who had bought my ticket to the United States—an Armenian-American from Providence, Rhode Island, who had fought with the French in Turkey. It had to be the old grocer.

Alas, it was not. Astonishingly, he was a different Armenian-American from Providence, Rhode Island, who had fought with the French in Turkey.

In 1920, once on land in New York, the family's excitement returned. On board in steerage and on Ellis Island the family had lived on dried fruit and food they brought with them from Athens and Piraeus. Though they yearned for fresh fruit, food at the ship's steerage commissary was too expensive—fifteen cents for an apple.

On the sidewalk along the Hudson River piers there was bubbling wonder and euphoria. They breathed the Manhattan air and looked at the mammoth buildings.

A large sign on a small dockside restaurant read: "FRESH HOME-BAKED APPLE PIE."

My mother announced:

"Now we are in America! Our first American food will be American apple pie!"

The symbol of the apple pie must have seemed the trophy for yet another triumph in the pattern of my father's life.

In the dynamics of disaster, when you have lost what you consider "everything"—the land and culture of your lifetime, your safety, your wealth, your status, your occupation—at that point to retain simply your life and family becomes a triumph.

The final emergence from Ellis Island, as from all the obstacles for an Armenian peasant born in Turkey and from the terrors in the mountains, my father could now turn to the New World with his impressive skill, ambition, intelligence, high spirit, and endless energy. As before, he would have at his side the woman whom he still called "my most precious Daisy." She was the emotional force that made family life coherent.

Armenian Protestants in the Boston area, many of them originally from Marash, had been looking for a minister and were delighted when the American Board of Missions presented them with Professor Bagdikian, just arrived from Marash.

Even after my mother was diagnosed with tuberculosis, barely three weeks after we landed in New York, there was still hope. Doctors at the time believed tuberculoisis was best treated at higher altitudes. At the State House in Boston my father determined that the two highest towns within public transportation to his new Cambridge church were Sharon and Stoneham. He chose Stoneham, fifteen miles north of Boston. The town is one hundred sixty-one feet above sea level, a measure of the desperate hope invested in every miserly foot of altitude.

Everyone except my mother moved into the house at 59 Elm Street, almost at the top of Farm Hill. The house seemed very large, with eight rooms, and on the outside along the front and side a porch we called "the piazza." Next to it was a catalpa tree reputed to be the largest in town. Behind was a large yard perfect for children—and for my father's irrepressible green thumb that always produced large gardens and grape arbors. The family awaited the recovery and return of my mother for the start of full family life in America. She seemed slowly to improve while my father took his divinity courses and tended his new church, commuting by streetcar fifteen miles away.

When my two oldest sisters noticed my father's sudden gloom, Tirzah—now Terry—and Lydia, who had become the substitute mothers of the family, demanded to know what had happened. He told them about the deportation order.

My father, desperate to stave off the fatal order, went to the State House in Boston and walked quickly past a protesting secretary into the office of the governor.

It must have been a throwback to the Aram who saved two of his daughters by boldly stalking into the room of the Turkish commandant in Tarsus. Inside the State House, Governor Cox was sufficiently impressed with the intruder standing before him to take time to confirm that the accusation was a lie, and the deportation order was canceled.

Though the deportation order was revoked, my father was still threatened. Each Sunday my father scanned the congregation from his pulpit looking for unfamiliar faces. One night he returned to Stoneham from Boston at a late hour when someone called my father's name. When my father turned, a man came from behind a bush, pointing a pistol.

In one of the few times my father told his past history to me in private, he said he told the gunman he could shoot if he insisted, but first my father had a message for the men who had hired him. My father said he knew the names of the five perpetrators and had left their names with certain people. If anything happened to my father the

My Father behind His Divinity Degree  ❮❮ 125

group would be arrested and so would the assassin. Furthermore, the Armenian community would be ashamed to call the murderer or his children an Armenian. Apparently, my father talked long and persuasively until the man put away the gun and disappeared into the night.

When Tirzah and Lydia, after being told, begged to know the names of the five revolutionaries, my mother in her sanitarium room told them, "I hope you will never find out ... You would subconsciously hate them when you find out and you know what hatred can do. Your father and I have promised never to tell. Promise me you will never try to find out."

As far as I know, my sisters never found out, so neither have I.

My mother's death was a central blow for my father. My mother's role in his life had been inspiration and balance wheel. She gave the family an emotional life that my father, the public man, could not.

He still had his energy, resilience, and incredible optimism. But it was energy confined to an ever-smaller circle. His mastery over his fate had shriveled. The spectacular good luck of his earlier life had run out.

By the time he was forty, when most men are at the prime of their lives, my father had gone from extraordinary personal success and status to a seemingly endless succession of cruel blows that took away all his old accomplishments and now his wife.

For too long, I was aware of the way my father disappointed my expectations and too unaware of his ability to improvise ways of maintaining his spirit and keeping family life going in the face of division and loss.

Aram Toros Baghdikian was not the first peasant to reach heights against great odds, and not the first to lose it all suddenly, nor the only man who on top of so much else also lost the woman he loved. I realize now, too late, that the remote father I knew never accepted defeat. My father made mistakes. But he did not collapse or lose his taste for life or fail to hope for a good future for his children, murky as the outlines of those futures may have been to him.

Today I regret my childhood indifference toward his gentle attempts to invite me into his private pleasures, but it is comforting to me to have discovered, even late as I did, that the visceral energy and emotions of the peasant, Aram Toros Baghdikian, stayed alive in his own secret within the garden of The Reverend Aram Theodore Bag-dikian, D.D.

Mention of his first wife was never uttered in the presence of the whole family. It must have been a silence my father either accepted or enforced. But only after my father died did I learn that my mother's favorite flower was cosmos and that all she had wanted on her grave was a pine tree. And then I remembered that after my mother's death, in every house in which we ever lived, my father's gardens overflowed with cosmos and he seemed to plant pine trees compulsively all over our various front yards.

## CHAPTER 9

## *Uncle Fred*

Uncle Fred would have been puzzled if I had ever told him that he influenced my journalistic work, like the day, for example, I was listening to Francis Mahoney in an industrial suburb of Chicago.

I was sitting across the steel-topped kitchen table in Mahoney's kitchen when the muscular forty-eight-year-old machinist, a gravel-voiced decorated ex-Marine who had been talking angrily most of that grey fall afternoon, suddenly out of nowhere, began to sob. His wife, Margaret, came quickly to his side, stroked the big man gently as she repeated, "Frank, it's going to be all right. It's only a matter of time. It's going to be all right."

But it was not all right. One morning eighteen months before, Frank was at his bench in the plant when the loudspeaker announced without warning that the plant would close at the end of the week. The company was moving the factory South to a tax-free operation with low-wage, non-union labor.

Frank Mahoney is not his real name, but he and his family were real and so were about one hundred fifty other workers I talked to while preparing for a magazine article I did on what was called then "technological unemployment" or "centralizing" or "decentralizing," and later "restructuring" and "downsizing."

Aside from a few feature stories about the Frank Mahoneys, the media don't pay much attention to what happens to the Frank Mahoneys of the country who are the real ones who pay for "restructuring." Their employers increase their quarterly earnings but the employees lose theirs, some of them forever.

The news is generous with space in reporting corporate arguments for their moves, but stingy in following the human and economic disasters for those left behind.

I wonder what would happen if the economists and corporate executives—and the editors who quote them so generously—had to live the lives of the "restructured," or go through the "shock treatment" of a sudden conversion to a free market that comfortable economists glibly prescribe for other societies.

Those questions are mine, not Uncle Fred's. Fred didn't concern himself with social ideas, including mine. He had little interest in politics and distrusted all politicians. He liked the idea that I was a reporter and writer and that I covered presidents and governors and corporate chieftains and listened to ambassadors at lavishly liquored embassy receptions. But he would have been surprised if I had told him that he had a lot to do with the fact that I also spent a lot of time with the Frank Mahoneys of the world who have so little place in our news.

It was through Uncle Fred and Grandpa Kalayjian that I escaped the puritanical rigidities and proprieties of my father's household and learned the virtues, the varieties, the pleasures, and the special pains of working-class life. They have given me a lifetime impatience with the contempt of some intellectuals for "the great unwashed" who lack higher education. It was also a defense against the other side of the same coin, the romantic notion that all working people are suffused with nobility.

Like most people who find it more comfortable to work within their own miniculture, we professional journalists live and socialize among college-educated, professional people like ourselves. The resulting lopsided picture of society is made worse because modern news corporations select their news to emphasize the lives and interests of the affluent middle-class wanted by advertisers, and reward the editors and reporters who do it most effectively.

I was not that different from other journalists. But I had Uncle Fred as an important figure in my life. I respected my father and I am grateful for all that I got from him. But I loved Uncle Fred. He was an intermittent but powerful presence in my life from my infancy until he died seventy-one years later.

Uncle Fred was my mother's youngest brother and long before I have any conscious memory of him, while my mother was in the sanitarium and my father scrambling to establish a new livelihood for a large family in a new country, it was Fred who bought me my first pair of baby shoes. He had placed my foot flat on his palm, and at a shoe store in the tough part of Boston where he repaired trucks pointed to his outstretched left palm and said, "Jakey, I want a pair of shoes for my little nephew. His foot goes from here to here." It was the same hand that I held on his deathbed.

While my mother was in the sanitarium, Fred lived with us. When I was four years old and my father remarried, Fred moved out, but he still visited.

I had a number of "firsts" with Fred. I had my first taste of rough working-class life through him. He bought me my first banana split. He bought me my tricycle and later the basic makings of a bicycle. My first rudimentary car repair tools came from him, as well as a basic auto repair manual, which had detailed instructions on how to rewind a magneto—in those less lavish days, people repaired auto parts, not replaced them. I had my first drink of whiskey with him.

He even played a role in my initiation into "modern mass communications." He brought me a cat's whisker radio set, the crystalline stone with a stiff, hairline probe that you poked around until the probe found one of the few special spots that in some mysterious way brought radio waves to your earphones.

I strung the required long aerial from my bedroom window to the tall butternut tree at the far corner of our garden. Experimenting with the tiny device, I was stunned by the magical first words I ever heard on a radio. It was not a message that will ring through the ages, but it remains almost mystical to me: "This is the Shepherd Stores of Boston," and then a lady sang, "The Last Rose of Summer." In my mind's ear, I can still hear the timbre of the announcer's voice and the precise way the woman trilled her r's as she sang "Rose."

I ran outside, climbed to the top of the butternut tree, and looked south. I was sure that somehow, unknown or unnoticed by me, there must be a physical wire running the fifteen miles from my aerial to Boston. I looked in all directions. There had to be a wire. But there was none. I was astounded. As an adult I write about modern communications technology, but I am still astounded.

While our household was ruled by my father's strictures against smoking, drinking, makeup for women, and his prayerful propriety, Fred, whom I never saw drunk, used liquor, wine, and beer (never in the presence of my father) and smoked a pipe (also never in the presence of my father). Every one of his cars had the wire netting from a champagne cork screwed upside down to the dashboard to hold his pipe. When I was older, we joined each other for drinks in working-class bars, and in his home or mine for guitar playing and singing together.

Now and then when I visited him in Norwood, he took me to "his club," the Norwood Irish-American Athletic Club, the nearest friendly saloon to his house. It was a warm, beery place with faded color rotogravures of Ireland, presided over by big, taciturn Mr. Driscoll whose name the members pronounced "Thriscoll."

Most of the members looked like actors in the Abbey Players. They were middle-aged men who came directly from Ireland into the American tanneries where they did the nasty task of standing waist-deep in water working hides all day. But at night they came to "the cloob" in dark suits and ties, Chesterfield coats, and derby hats. Most of them spent the night nursing ale and playing the card game "Forty-Five."

The first time Fred took me there, he introduced me to Mr. Driscoll: "This is my nephew. He's a newspaperman." Mr. Driscoll shook my hand gravely and put two drinks in front of us. "This is on the house, gents. It's a short life."

Once, emboldened by a couple of drinks, I asked:

"Mr. Driscoll. This is the Irish-American Athletic Club. What's the athletics?"

He sighed: "Fisticoofs, my boy, fisticoofs."

The club members liked Uncle Fred. They were sure he was Irish. His appearance didn't make it impossible. What convinced them was his knowledge of Irish county jokes and songs. They were sure that "Uvezian" concealed an Irish name with an "O" in front of it.

Once an elderly club member in a derby hat came to the bar where we stood and said, "Freddie, tell the truth now, what was your real name in the old country?

Fred laughed and said, "I was born in Armenia and my name was always Uvezian."

The man patted Fred on the arm, "That's all right Freddie. You're not the first man had trouble in his youth."

I would have been about eight when he first took me to the garage in the toughest part of Charlestown where he was a mechanic repairing one of the big eighteen-wheelers for that night's run. It was a rough place, men lifting heavy crates, rolling barrels, and shouldering huge industrial reels of cable from the loading dock into truck trailers. When they backed trucks into the dirty industrial street among other roaring trucks and cursing men, now and then fights broke out.

Fred went about his business and told me, "They sound rough and some you can't trust to turn your back on, but most of them are good men." He laughed, "You know, you can make friends with almost anyone, but you may have to knock him down first."

I had been taught never to fight. It was not the "Christian" thing to do. But Fred had survived in a different world. When as a young man he came back East from my grandfather's ranch in Montana, he worked for forty-eight straight hours at brutal work few other men would do, unloading pig iron and coke from ships in Boston Harbor. He earned enough to get rid of his Western clothes for some Eastern ones, buy his first set of tools, and then pay for a Turkish bath to clean out the pig iron and coal dust. That's how he began working on the docks repairing trucks and driving them. At first he worked nights, pounding out truck brake drums on Atlantic Avenue while singing "The Anvil Chorus" from "Il Trovatore" with Italian mechanics. He remembered when the truck owners hired thugs to knock union leaders on the head with tire irons and drop them into the harbor. Truck drivers' loyalty to the Teamsters Union has a powerful historic basis.

That night when it was time for a break from the garage, Fred took me to a nearby fly-specked variety store. "Make my nephew here a nice big banana split." It was my first, and we picked our way around maneuvering trucks on the dirty street, I carefully balancing the ice-cream pyramid, to a long, dark bar that had sawdust on the floor and the shouts of boisterous talk. Fred hoisted me onto a barstool among the mechanics, truck drivers, stevedores, and guards from Charlestown Prison, ordered himself a boilermaker while he watched me work on my banana split. He laughed and said, "I wonder what the *poor* people are doing."

He always said, "I wonder what the *poor* people are doing," whenever we were enjoying simple pleasures in humble surroundings. It was a good definition of "poor": those too proper to do what we were doing.

When I was sixteen he taught me how to drive. "At every blind intersection always imagine that two fire engines, a drunk driver, and a kid chasing a ball are going to run in front of you." He taught me to shift smoothly, listening to the engine and the transmission, how to do chauffeur driving (smooth starts, smooth stops), and to drive through fast traffic in total vigilance.

Once I was with him at the Charlestown garage when he had to deliver a last-minute emergency crate in a small pickup truck. He drove with breathtaking speed through rush-hour Boston traffic. Boston drivers remind me of drivers in Rome in their talent for manic chaos, but the Romans look stately by comparison. If I had seen Fred from a sidewalk I would have thought he was a speed demon gone mad, but inside the cab it was clear he was totally synchronized with the machine, traffic, and maneuvering. (The only comparable performance I have ever seen was years later when my son, Eric, in his car racing period, dragooned me to a race in California where I saw the Australian, Bruce McLaren, in an orange CanAm, drive with the same sure precision and authority.)

Fred had lost his right eye in a teenage baseball game, but by the time his only good eye began to go blind and Massachusetts took away his driver's license, he had gone sixty-nine years as a driver of buses, trucks, and cars without an accident, moving violation, or arrest.

Fred's first real upward job was repairing the buses of the Gray Line Company. Fred quickly added driving the bus to his repair work, and then added the simultaneous job of giving the historical New England spiel formerly given by moonlighting Harvard history majors. He was serious about the history and knew a surprising amount, but he would periodically lighten the commentary. When he passed by the Gardner Museum he announced:

"The lions you see in front of Mrs. Jack Gardner's Venetian-style palace are said to be two thousand years old. Not being satisfied with their age, Mrs. Gardner is having two more made to be three thousand years old."

He had a wide spectrum of friends from the past. By the time I met him, George was Commissioner of the Middlesex District Police and ultimately a good source for me when I became a reporter. When they were young men, Fred and George sang and told funny stories at clubs, among them "Dinny Turn the Crank."

Among the bright moments at our Stoneham household was singing around the piano. When Fred visited us he and my sisters did a lot of harmonizing with sentimental songs of the times—"You Are My Sunshine," "Let Me Call You Sweetheart," "I'm Only a Bird in a Gilded Cage." They always did favorite Protestant hymns and familiar opera arias. As a child and teenager I sang along with them. Periodically my sisters would beg Fred to sing a few verses of "Dinny Turn the Crank." Fred would always laugh but never sing it in my presence. I came to realize that it must be bawdy and he thought I was too young.

By the time I was a reporter, I visited Fred one night and during our singing I said, "Fred, how about some 'Dinny Turn the Crank,'" and he obliged. It was a representation of a slide show about a zoo, with proper Latin scientific names that turned funny and usually bawdy, each verse set to a background of guitar chords and a musical refrain, "Dinny Turn the Crank," as though calling for the next slide. In their bachelor days, Fred and George had concocted one hundred verses. I never heard all hundred but I did quite a few, like:

And on your right, ladies and gentlemen [strum, strum] you will note that horse in fancy striped pajamas. It is an African mammal, *Equus burchelli*, found south of the Sahara Desert [strum, strum]. It is commonly called a zebra. The zebra's skin is so tight that when the animal blinks its eyes, it pulls back his foreskin. Unkind tourists throw sand in his eyes just to see the poor creature masturbate. Dinny turn the crank.

In a sense, my no-smoking-no-drinking father was responsible for my first drink of whiskey. I was sixteen and my father had come up with an old Pontiac—yet another mechanical wreck in a glistening shell. For a man who had taught science in college, my father was totally ignorant about what went on under the hood of an automobile and was indifferent to its care and feeding. He simply trusted Fred to fix anything.

Fred did his own mechanical work under a tree in his Dedham backyard. The Pontiac job was in the depths of winter and the ground was frozen. It had to be a complete overhaul—rings, valves, and bearings. All day Fred and I were either on our backs on the ground or standing in the wind over the bowels of the dismantled engine. We worked with freezing oily parts and tools. I did supportive minor tasks, like an intern assisting a master surgeon.

After about seven hours it was dark and we worked under a drop light. But it was finished. Now came the expectant moment. Would this collection of freezing metal become a live, throbbing organism?

Fred, showing his amazing strength, slowly turned the crank to pull the new, tight engine through a few dead revolutions, and then turned the crank faster. After about four fast twirls, the engine coughed and burst into life.

We carefully wiped and put away the tools, rubbed mechanic's soap into our hands to take off the top layers of caked grease, and with the Pontiac's engine roaring behind us, moved upstairs stiff-legged and awkward to his tiny second-floor apartment.

Fred's apartments were always overheated, but this night it made no difference. I felt a cold that makes bones seem like solid ice.

Out of a kitchen cupboard, Fred took two tiny glasses and a bottle of clear fluid. The label on the bottle read, "Old Mr. Boston." He filled each little glass and gave me one. "Drink this quickly—all the way down with one swallow."

My eyes bulged. I thought the fire in my throat would dissolve the tissues. But there followed a slow, radiating glow that spread in life-giving waves through the solid ice of my anatomy. My whole body felt a glow.

Fred watched and laughed. "Don't tell your Dad and don't make a habit of it—only when you overhaul Pontiacs in January."

When I was about thirteen, Fred, contrary to the rules of the Interstate Commerce Commission and the insurance companies, let me ride with him on his all-night truck route through southern New England in the big eighteen-wheel semi. The trailer carried barrels of fish in sea water direct from the docks in Boston, along with general cargo for stores and factories along the way.

It was a ride filled with singing and Fred's incredibly detailed commentary on local histories. There were long silences driving through a world at sleep and I fought, without total success, to keep awake every minute. The truck had eight forward gears and a second simple gearshift lever that had a low-low and a high-high to multiply the main gear ratios. As with every vehicle he drove, Fred was part of the machine and whether it was an eighteen-wheeler or one of my father's clunkers, Fred made it run smoothly as an ocean liner. When I was awake, he would say, "OK, Ben when I say so, put it into high-high. One, two, three—now," and I would push the simple lever forward and feel like Captain Nemo in the *Nautilus*.

Around East Greenwich, Rhode Island, Fred brought the truck to a stop in some woods. From the back of the cab he took a bottle of Scotch in a paper bag and buried it under some grass behind a big oak tree just off the road. It was for some friendly Rhode Island commercial fishermen. Working close to the Boston docks had unofficial benefits. When longshoremen worked the freighters, there seemed to be an extraordinary number of dockside accidents breaking open crates of liquor, imported of course, for medicinal purposes. It was during Pro-hibition, when doctors were permitted to write prescriptions for therapeutic alcoholic drinks.

At markets along the way, I marveled at how Fred could unload barrels filled with fish and sea water, heavier than two strong men could carry. Fred tipped the barrel on its edge and rolled it hand over hand to the tailgate and without any pause dropped it at just the right angle onto the street. Without losing momentum, he jumped down in time to keep it rolling on the bottom rim like a slanted hoop to the door of a darkened store.

Sometime in the predawn hours when we both got out in the cool air, we stood in the middle of the main street of a picture-postcard Connecticut village. It seemed as though we were the only inhabitants on earth, and under the town's single sputtering greenish streetlamp we happily urinated onto the colonial cobblestones.

I woke up in New London in time to watch Fred back the semi around the corners of a narrow alley. We slept a few hours in the truck and after daylight went to a diner where Fred ordered us both "the works" and bought a lemon from the cook and put it in his pocket.

When we reached East Greenwich again, he stopped in the same woods. Behind the oak tree was a half-bushel basket covered with ice. Underneath was a mass of quahaugs, the large succulent clams from Narragansett Bay.

I had never had clams before, so we sat on a fallen tree trunk while Fred took out his big jackknife and showed me how to open clams (place the knife's sharp edge into the crack and with the other hand on the dull side, squeeze it in, don't push, then cut the muscle attached to both top and bottom shells). From the lemon he had bought in New London, he squeezed a drop of juice on each clam as it sat in its open shell. "Make sure there's a small contraction of the clam when the lemon juice hits it. If it doesn't move at all, it may be dead and don't eat it." We feasted on the log under the oak tree. Fred laughed and said "I wonder what the *poor* people are doing."

It didn't occur to me until later, but my experience with Uncle Fred and Grandpa let me feel at ease in a variety of settings for which I was ill prepared by a childhood in a clergyman's household under pressure to act with stiff propriety in dealing with outsiders. As a reporter and writer who spent much of his career dealing with America's deprived, I spent a lot of time in millworkers' kitchens, dingy dives, tough bars, sweatshops, rude rural cabins, and neighborhoods where middle-class values were alien.

Uncle Fred was never without work. He had a gift for landing on his feet and being happy with what he did. All kinds of men seemed instinctively to like him, and it was clear to me that a large number of women did too.

Fred's ultimate gift to me was the joy, laughter, and excitement that both he and Grandpa carried with them through the ups and downs of their lives. That kind of fundamental exuberance was not the usual emotional weather in my childhood household. And despite easy drinking, Fred seemed to have automatic knowledge of when to stop, something I may have unconsciously absorbed.

Though he never put it in words, Fred, clearly a man of high intelligence, wit, and talent, was self-conscious about never having gone to college. Like so many workingmen I know, he never got over an illogical sense of inferiority and guilt because he lacked a degree, illogical because from the time he was ten, Fred had to work to support his mother. It angers me still when I hear intellectuals and others with degrees make sweeping disparagement of "the great unwashed" working-class men and women.

Six years before Fred died, Marlene and I visited him in Massachusetts. I had called a few days earlier and said, "Fred, we're going to take you to lunch in your favorite restaurant."

When we arrived, Fred was glowing, his round face bright-eyed and beaming, natty in a loud, bright checked sportsjacket. He loaded us into his beloved 1961 Cadillac and drove—he still had his license at age eighty-three—to the Red Barn Steak House, where over a long lunch he was lively with talk of the past.

I learned for the first time details of his coming to this country as a young boy, of growing up on the Montana ranch, of becoming a pioneer bus driver, mechanic, and some of his adventures. He was, of course, a romantic, and always looked on the bright side, and told of the rough times only if you asked.

That day I also learned some things about my grandparents for the first time.

I had met Grandpa and Grandma when I was nine. They had succeeded on the ranch and moved to Rochester, New York, where they bought two produce stores. Terry and I took the train from Boston and I filled my eyes with cinders by leaning out the window on curves to catch a glimpse of the huge coal-burning New York Central steam locomotive.

Fred's (and my mother's) father had died in a horse accident in Marash when Fred was seven, so "Grandpa" was really my stepgrandfather. Fred came to the United States with my grandmother in 1912 when he was ten. My grandmother went to work in the Charlestown chocolate factory while Fred went to school and worked nights and weekends to help keep them going.

Shortly after she arrived in Boston, my grandmother received a letter from Montana from Arthur Kalayjian. Arthur had worked for Fred's father on the caravan, and after losing his wife, had come to the United States to use his knowledge of horses by ranching near Helena. Was my grandmother, a widow, interested in visiting him with little Frederick to see if they all liked each other enough to get married?

Arthur and Margaret married and Fred spent most of his teen years on the ranch. To his dying day there were two yellowed photographs stuck in the frame of his mirror. One was an old snapshot of his Montana Shetland pony, "Princess," the other showed him standing proudly in his chauffeur's cap beside the ancient sightseeing bus that he first drove as a professional in the 1920s.

My first sight of Grandma was as Terry and I entered the store on Bartlett Street after our arrival in Rochester on the train. My grandmother stood tall, erect and imposing behind a glass bin filled with a huge pyramid of miniature ingots of Hershey's milk chocolate. She saw me staring at my chocolate obsession.

The first words I heard from my grandmother in her broken English were, "You like, my boy? Take."

My first real experience with Grandpa was also connected, in its own way, with food. We had gargantuan breakfasts in the little kitchen behind the store, and I had to decline second and third helpings with "No, thank you." Obviously, Grandpa, who had mischievous eyes, thought I was too much the prissy clergyman's son and skinny to boot.

At breakfast, he put his hand around his glass of water and with a sly smile said, "Next time comes 'No, thank you,' comes this."

I smiled and he smiled. Grandma asked if I wanted a second bowl of oatmeal and by reflex I said "No, thank you," and splash, the cold water came.

Grandma shrieked at her husband and hustled me into the back bedroom to change my clothes and reintroduced me smooth and dry to the table again, while she scolded my smiling grandfather.

Somehow it did not offend me. If it had been done coldly it would have hurt, but it all seemed different because of his mischievous eyes and smile.

That night we sat in her dining room and as I was asked if I wanted a second helping of stuffed peppers, I looked quickly at Grandpa. He was grinning and nodded below the table. Out of sight of his wife, he held a fork toward my thigh, his thumb pulled back about a quarter of an inch from the points as though the fork would go in that deep.

I loved dolma anyway and took another. He did the same fork gesture a couple of times afterward but even when I said, "No, thank you" he never used it, and it became a game. Later, after they lost their stores in the Crash of 1929 and moved to Boston, they came for one of our big dinners on Elm Street. He always sat next to me and each time a platter came around, he'd hold the fork the same way below the table and we'd both laugh.

After they lost everything and moved to the Somerville section of Boston, Grandpa, at age fifty-nine, started a new trade as shoe repairman. He opened a tiny shop in Magoon Square and every summer I spent a couple of weeks in their hot, cramped, mustard-colored tenement.

Each night, after dinner, grandpa would take out his mandolin and sing. Some songs were Armenian, but he also liked popular American songs he heard on the radio. A favorite was called, "Humm-humm-humm, Would You Like To Take a Walk?" which he played while making goo-goo eyes at his wife.

Then one day, Grandma told me, ' Tonight we make beer. You get some things from store." She handed me a list: malt, hops, sugar, yeast, and a gross of bottle caps. I stared at it dumbfounded. Prohibition was still in effect. The newspapers were full of photographs of Treasury agents with sledgehammers breaking down doors of illegal distilleries and speakeasies.

I was sure that any grocer looking at that combination of goods would phone the U.S. Marshal and a familiar horror scene played in my mind: the *Boston Traveler*, delivered every afternoon to our house in Stoneham, would be picked up by my father who would stare at the screaming headline:

CLERGYMAN'S SON ARRESTED BY U.S. MARSHAL;
ELEVEN-YEAR-OLD NABBED AS BOOTLEGGER

I decided to outfox the U.S. Marshal. I bought each ingredient in a different store. It was a very long walk during which I constantly feared the hand of the law on my shoulder. It never struck me as curious that every store seemed to have these ingredients in copious supply.

That night, after many scrubbings, the process started in the bathtub, while I waited moment by moment for the sound of sledgehammers at the apartment door. But the biggest risk was yet to come. When, as usual, I walked to Magoon Square to bring Grandpa his big, bulky Armenian lunch, this time there was a bottle of the illegal beer in it. And I had to walk right past the policeman directing traffic in the middle of the square. Already, I saw the *Traveler* headline again.

Then Grandma handed me a second, smaller bag.

"This one, give nice cop in Square."

"Grandma! Beer? To a policeman?"

She looked puzzled.

"Yes, yes. He like 'um."

Again, I saw the headlines in my head.

When I handed the paper bag to the cop, I was amazed when he looked inside and said, "Thank you, my boy. You're a good lad."

I was twelve when Grandpa died. Short of passing away peacefully in sleep, Grandpa's death was the way most people would prefer to go. His birthday was the same as George Washington's, and there was a big banquet at my father's church in Cambridge, at which Grandpa, sixty-two-years old that night, was one of the special guests of honor.

Grandpa, who had the audience roaring with his funny stories, ended his speech by saying he had lived a full and lucky life of which this event surrounded by friends was a high point, then he dropped dead where he stood.

I did not attend the banquet because I had a fever, high enough so that the next morning I did not wake up for school. When I was finally awake, my stepmother came in. She was superstitious and I think she did not want to be the bearer of bad news. "What would you say if your sisters told you that your grandfather died last night?"

I wish it had been in my power to let Uncle Fred die the same way.

The lunch Marlene and I had with Fred at the Red Barn Steak House was the last time I saw him confident, strong, and happy. From then on, he went downhill physically—hernia operations, bad arthritis, serious heart trouble, infirmity of one leg, decreasing sight in his only good eye—and lived in a room with his son and grandchildren in a neighborhood where kids stole all his tools. His letters to me could not keep out his growing despair. "My stomach looks like a roadmap." And, "I seem to be falling apart."

The next time I visited, Fred was in a nursing home. A practical nurse, Polly, was devoted to him—not unusual for most people around him, especially women of all ages—and she kept me informed about his condition.

One night in the fall of 1991, I got a call from Polly. "Ben, I think you'd better come."

Marlene and I flew from California and drove directly from Logan Airport to the nursing home. It was close to midnight. Polly told us he was in very bad shape, in horrible pain, groaning constantly and loudly and talking gibberish. She had warned me that he had started to hallucinate and often was incoherent.

Before I reached his room, I could hear his groans echoing down the corridor. He was obviously in agony. His hands waved in the air and seemed periodically to hover near his stomach. I took his hand and said Marlene and I were there, but there was no sign of recognition. His mechanic hands were still large but now the fingers were swollen.

The next morning, Fred was still groaning slightly but obviously in less pain. I held his hand most of the day. After we returned from a fast lunch, Fred seemed less desperate.

For the first time, it was clear that he recognized Marlene and me. At one point, he raised his head with difficulty and said, "Bennie, you and I . . ." and then dropped back exhausted. I leaned down to his ear and shouted.

"Yes, Fred, you and I have had a hell of a lot of good times together."

He nodded. Then in a gesture clear and unmistakable he looked straight at me, raised his left hand in the shape of a pistol, one finger at his temple while another bent back and forth as though pulling a trigger.

He stared at me beseechingly. In the wordless communication that happens when people are in a mutually intense state, the meaning was clear:

"Get a pistol and put me out of my misery."

I was overcome by the clarity and the begging. After a moment, I leaned down to his ear and yelled.

"Fred, I'm sorry. I can't. But I'm going to make sure you get medication to take away the pain."

He fell back in defeat.

Later, after Fred received a painkiller, I took his hand and yelled goodbye. Whether he heard me was impossible to tell through his groans. Marlene kissed him goodbye. I kissed him goodbye. When I got back to Berkeley I called the doctor to make sure the order for painkillers stood.

Fred died two days later. The short obituary in the *Boston Herald* was like hundreds I had written as a bored young reporter taking rudimentary notes from indifferent undertakers.

The headline read:

AT 89, FREDERICK
A. UVEZIAN SR.,
OWNED AUTO SHOP

## CHAPTER 10

# My Life as a Failure

**B**efore I was ever a reporter, I was a flop as a vacuum cleaner salesman, I flunked as a restaurant cook, I didn't have the guts to join the New Jersey mafia, and I didn't make it as a medical student. By any rational standard I would never have been hired by a newspaper in the first place except for my first employer's sole requirement that his reporters accept a life of poverty.

Certainly, my courses in college could not have been less appropriate for a life of reporting: I spent most of my academic years dissecting cats in comparative anatomy and concocting noxious fumes in organic chemistry. I was a premedical student. So in college, I took one English course and one course in European history. The rest were courses dealing mainly with numbers about objects like carbon molecules or the chromosomes of Gregor Mendel's sweet peas.

I entered Clark University as I entered the news business, in a spectacularly undeserved fluke. Being a proper eastern Massachusetts snob, in high school I had felt that the only respectable course for a middle-class male was to attend Harvard. I didn't get a scholarship to Harvard and in my senior year of high school my father moved to Worcester. I couldn't afford living away from home, so when told that Worcester was home to two Catholic colleges, an engineering school, and something called Clark

University, I looked up the address and applied to Clark. Given its distinguished scientific and scholarly history and my present gratitude to it, I blush to say that at the time I had never heard of Clark, having had no adolescent interest in any institution west of Cambridge, Massachusetts.

Given my unimpressive high school grades, today I wouldn't get into any self-respecting college, let alone Clark, but it was during the Depression and times were tough for all institutions.

I would be taught advanced physiology courses by men like Hudson Hoagland and Gregory Pincus, the geniuses who did germinal work on cancer and evolved the groundwork for the birth control pill, but the course that made the most lasting impact on my thinking about physical life was the basic freshman biology course given by David Potter, one of the faculty members without a Ph.D. He spent a lot of time on Darwin, and for someone never convinced by the six days of Genesis, the course not only explained the emergence of natural life on the planet, but helped create my view of a world so wonderfully complex, dynamic, and endlessly interrelated that to me it has all the grandeur, wonder, and tragedy of a mystical religion.

Wrestling with mating patterns of carbon molecules and the sex life of sweet peas was hardly my only concern in college. I spent too many nights putting out the college paper, performing overdue lab experiments, and not a few with dating. But there was an unending money crisis for tuition and fees.

I made some money as campus stringer for the local daily, the *Worcester Telegram and Gazette*. I was paid ten cents an inch and I stretched it by using every middle name, full departmental title, and academic distinction ever earned by visiting lecturers and anything else that would add inches of type at the end of the month. It required all the journalistic art of tacking notices on a bulletin board. I also worked on the potato counter of a local market when I wasn't padding stories for the *Telegram* and *Gazette*. That income fell short of tuition, books, and fees, but Clark was generous with an occasional scholarship and in extremis, Lydia, as usual, came to the rescue.

Summer jobs were hard to come by, so one summer I tried selling Electrolux vacuum cleaners in which the only pay was a commission of twenty dollars for every machine I sold. Each weekday morning I joined the older salesmen in a downtown office for a pep talk from Mr. Friday, the genius who ran the place. Each morning he convinced us that people of Worcester County panted behind their front doors lusting for us to ring their doorbells. I, the cool, skeptical, sophisticated college boy, actually found myself caught up in Mr. Friday's inspired locker-room performance, and joined with my fellow salesmen, mostly middle-aged and portly, singing our greedy hearts out on selections from the Electrolux Song Book. My favorite was to the tune of "On Wisconsin" in which we belted out in full throat, "On Electrolux, On Electrolux, Onward to the sale . . ."

I didn't have a car, so I had to take trolleys to my assigned neighborhood, carry one box with my demonstrator machine and another with the brand new one to be left behind in the happy event of a sale. It was the first time I ever had the beginnings of the shoulders of a halfback.

In some ways, I was a smashing success. I could get into Worcester County houses no other salesman had ever cracked before. Until I arrived, that was considered tantamount to making a sale a day, but despite my record of successful entrances I always made saleless exits.

In the long run, my experience as an Electrolux salesman made an unanticipated deep impression. I spent the summer in the world of housewives, most of them in working-class homes with little money and endless drabness and loneliness. Our technique for getting into the house was to say we weren't selling anything but wanted to demonstrate a new rug shampoo by making like new any carpet without charge in some of the city's "better" homes. After we were admitted, we explained that the shampoo showed better results if the rug were first vacuumed thoroughly. After a few passes with the housewife's older machine, looking at the pile closely with signs of growing frustration, we asked, apologetically, if she minded our using the machine we had left on the doorstep. As planned in the Electrolux strategy, when we pulled the machine out of its big carrying case it looked magnificent—a beautiful blue body with streamlined chrome trim, low and sleek as a crouched leopard, and as it worked it spread a hygienic-smelling "clean" odor. We were supposed to wait until the housewife volunteered a question about the machine and casually answer that it was called the Electrolux and could also clean drapes, reach unseen dust over door lintels, and by reversing the hose and attaching a bottle full of moth crystals, "demotherize" a closet.

Twice I got a signed contract, but each time, come nightfall, there was a phone call from an angry husband just home from the factory, "You get here right away and pick up your goddam machine," and when I arrived the carton would be on the front steps with a contract torn into small pieces.

I worked all summer, never sold a machine and, of course, made no money. But I left Worcester County cleaner than I found it.

Only later did it dawn on me why I was so successful in getting into homes. In those days, house-to-house salesmen were common, but experienced housewives took one look at me and knew instinctively that I was never going to sell anything to anyone.

The Electrolux summer sent me into tenements, middle-class apartments, and a few cottages to discover what later reporting also told me, that on the whole people wanted to be kind, wanted something better in their lives, and worked hard at it. Underneath self-protection, most are not cynical. They are terribly vulnerable to the promise of something better in life.

The life concerns of the people who lived in the hundreds of houses in the neighborhoods where I failed to sell a machine simply did not exist in the news back then and neither do their counterparts today. The realities of their daily lives and environment is seldom "the American household" that you see in the newspapers and magazines. Fifty years after my Electrolux summer, as I watched a televised news conference on the Federal Reserve's increase of interest rates, all the reporters asked what it would do to the stock market and bank rates, which is fair enough, but no one asked the similarly relevant question of whether it would not raise the price of necessities for the ordinary households like the ones I cleaned in Worcester County.

The next summer I actually made some money. Someone who had been there told me there were summer jobs in Asbury Park, New Jersey, a bus ticket away. Its boardwalk was a smaller version of Atlantic City, filled with tourist restaurants, shops, and hotels. I arrived with very little cash and used almost all of it to pay two weeks' rent on a furnished room in advance. But in my eagerness, I was too early. The tourist season had not begun, and I ran out of money.

For the first time in my life, I was hungry and had no money for food. I stretched things out as long as I could, buying a bakery's nickel "stale bag" of leftovers, which could contain anything from old doughnuts to stale bread. I discovered the demoralization and self-contempt of being truly hungry but having no food in sight.

But desperation is the mother of lies, and at a hash-house I saw a sign: "Wanted, second cook." I had no idea what a second cook was, but I walked in and announced to "Charlie," the owner, that I was a second cook.

Charlie, who happened to be an Armenian, asked where I had worked as a second cook and I rattled off every hotel I could think of: the Bancroft Hotel in Worcester, Copley Plaza in Boston . . . He said, "Grab an apron from the cook and get going for the night crowd."

It was not a big place, a long counter with stools and a few small tables at one end, two short-order countermen in front, and a cavern-ous kitchen in back. In the kitchen, the sole cook pointed his big knife at the aprons and said, "Make a Waldorf salad."

I didn't know what a Waldorf salad was. In the strategy of all fakers of experience, I asked, "How do *you* like them made?" He looked an-noyed, "A Waldorf, a Waldorf, lettuce, apples, walnuts—a Waldorf!"

I knew what lettuce, apples, and walnuts looked like and I began chopping some lettuce with a big triangular knife in slow, careful strokes. The cook was busy chopping onions in lightning-like move-ments and he glanced over when he heard the slow crunch of my cuts. "Come on, come on! The crowd starts any minute." I tried the lightning-like strokes. I cut my knuckle. There was much blood.

The cook stopped what he was doing. "Kid, you never did this be-fore, did you?"

I admitted the truth. The cook threw down his knife and yelled, "Charlie!"

Charlie used some highly original language and finally yelled, "Goddammit, lucky for you I need a dishwasher. Get going."

I began working on the tub of greasy pans in greasy water. And then Charlie added, "The only reason I'm doing you a favor is you're an

Armenian." I got twelve dollars a week for washing dishes and mopping floors from 8:00 P.M. to 8:00 A.M. seven days a week. I was delighted.

It was while on this job that something helped steer me away from my original ambition. I passed up a chance to finance my becoming a doctor.

The twelve-hour shift meant that in daylight I got to know the boardwalk and some of the local haunts, one of which was an illegal dice game in an anonymous-looking place near Charlie's hash-house. Almost every afternoon, I dropped in, fascinated by watching dice players who live high-tension psychodramas as they play, associating their fate in life with every roll of the dice. I still enjoy reading faces of people gambling.

I never played but got to know the staff. The young croupier was stuck on himself, had curly hair and looked like Allan Jones, the tenor who sang in the slushy romantic scenes in the Marx Brothers' "A Night at the Opera." Another fixture was Louie, an elderly man who sat quietly in a chair in the back and, like me, never gambled.

Every morning at 3:00 A.M., when Charlie's was almost empty, I mopped the floor. And every night, shortly after 3:00 A.M., the staff from the dice table came in for lunch (all night-shift workers, including newspaper people, call the dinner break "lunch" even when it's at 3:00 A.M.). And every night without fail, Allan Jones opened the door of the hash-house as I mopped the floor and asked loudly, "Hey, kid, whattya hear from the mop?" and laughed hysterically at his never-changing exercise in original wit.

One night as Allan Jones was returning to his labors he said quietly, "Louie wants to talk to you. Come see him tomorrow."

It turned out that fatherly-looking Louie controlled all the illegal gambling and slot machines in Asbury Park. He had noticed that I never gambled. He asked where I lived. I told him I was going to college in Massachusetts and was in Asbury Park for the summer. He asked what I planned to do after college and I told him I planned to go to medical school. He called me to a small bare desk he had in the back and said he needed an honest young man to make regular collections from slot machines around the city.

"A good boy like you, don't gamble, good worker, smart, going to be a doctor, you shouldn't be washing dishes. I need someone like you, works hard, don't steal. I like that. I need someone to collect from my machines every day. Forget the job at Charlie's. You be straight with me, you don't steal from the machines, I pay you well. And I pay your college and I pay your medical school. What do you say?"

I was flabbergasted.

I was heading toward my last year in college. The hope of medical school had begun to fade. All medical schools, especially Harvard, were extremely expensive and we were told there was no financial help in the first year. That alone made it dubious that I could get in, even into "one of the other" medical schools. Competition was fierce and my grades were not that competitive.

I liked Louie. He seemed worldly-wise but kind, even gentle. I was, of course, inclined to think well of a man who said he thought well of me. Back then, I wasn't knowledgeable about what men had to do to become big bosses in the rackets, and the Louie I saw had an appealing personality. I had spent a lot of time in the past two years agonizing over how I could possibly afford medical school tuition and now suddenly the problem seemed to be solved.

Nevertheless, I knew that I wouldn't accept Louie's offer. Maybe it was the desire to obey a lifetime's preachments against breaking the law and Calvinistic strictures in favor of hard work and rejecting "the easy way out." It was also timidity. Among other things, I mentally saw the feared headline in the *Boston Traveler* my father read every day:

CLERGYMAN'S SON NABBED
AS BAG MAN FOR CRIME RING

I was embarrassed to turn down Louie, but the next day I told him I was sorry, but I had decided to stick with my job at Charlie's. He shrugged and said, "You change your mind, you come see me."

I didn't change my mind and I kept going to watch the gamblers, exchanging nods with Louie when he was in his chair. But shortly afterward, I found the dice room locked. The word around town was that Louie had been raided by the state cops because, according to the crowd at Charlie's, some politicians in Trenton got a better payoff from a different mobster. Sure enough, two weeks later, the dice table opened with a different crew. But by that time I had graduated from Charlie's and made a less shadowy set of friends.

One day, strolling the boardwalk before 8:00 P.M., I had seen a sign at a big lunch and soda counter, "Need soda jerk." I had never been a soda jerker. At Charlie's I had learned how to fill in at the counter during rush hour, fry eggs, broil hamburgers, fill a mug of coffee at the urn, and then swing it quickly in a smooth arc to the customer at the counter without losing a drop. Three things enraged coffee drinkers at Charlie's—if their coffee was slow, if it was cold, and if the mugs were less than full.

The proprietor of the soda place was Mr. Andropolis, and when he found out I was a college boy and had already worked the counter at Charlie's he took me on. It was wonderful. I had daytime work in the fresh air. The place had doors that folded back each day to open onto the boardwalk. And I got fifteen dollars for six days plus tips.

In back of the shop, on a small stoop overlooking the ocean where no one could see me, I learned, after a few splashings, how to pour a milk shake in a dramatic rising spiral from the big whipping can into the customer's glass.

Mr. Andropolis was pleased and soon asked me to write out each week's menu. Spelling was not his strong point. His old menu listed a salad with "redish and lettish."

In addition to simple sandwiches and ice cream in all its permutations, he had a locally popular orange drink. He showed me the secret formula so I could make it every day. But first he swore me to secrecy and warned me against answering any questions from strangers. I thought he was being paranoid, but sure enough, one day two unpleasant-looking men in dark suits uncharacteristic for boardwalk strollers ordered their orange drinks, lingered over them at the counter, and engaged me in what they obviously regarded as shrewdly casual conversation about how the stuff was put together. I wondered if they represented Louie's replacement and told myself that Louie would never put the move on a nice man like Mr. Andropolis. I shrugged off the question as though it were too complicated for little me. (The secret ingredient was exactly the right amount of ground orange rind but otherwise my lips are sealed.)

I made a number of friends on the boardwalk, the best ones Manny and Dr. Beetjuice. Manny was a weasel-faced little guy with a Brooklyn accent and fascinating stories about Jewish life in Flatbush. Dr. Beetjuice was a big, florid, blond man from Toledo, Ohio who knew things from Shakespeare and whose professional life required a terrible phony German accent. Evenings over beer and pizza at a local indoor bocce court, we had long talks on life, literature, and how their two families back home were struggling with the Depression.

Manny and Dr. Beetjuice had a collapsible stand barely large enough for two men, a small shelf for demonstrations, and at their feet a bag full of plastic devices. Every day they set up the stand in front of Mr. Andropolis's store.

Manny was "the factory representative" who explained that his firm did not believe in "wasting money on advertising" but instead wanted only to demonstrate its products "to people of a better class who came to this upper-class resort." The products were not for sale, but the company hoped the finer housewives vacationing here would remember these health-giving appliances when they appeared later at the best stores in major cities.

Manny then introduced Dr. Beetjuice, the company's "research scientist." The good doctor wore a white coat.

The chief audiences for this pitch were the ladies from the town of Ocean Grove at the southern end of the boardwalk. Ocean Grove is home to a Methodist camp meeting where the streets literally were chained against automobiles on Sundays and no smoking was allowed at any time. Its visitors, most of whom seemed to be middle-aged women, were highly interested in clean living and good health. Most of them wore sensible shoes and white dresses and were drawn irresistibly to the science lectures by Dr. Beetjuice and by the health-giving devices he demonstrated.

"Ladeez," he would warn ominously, "iff it iz mit night vision you haff problems—DO NOT DRINK BEETJUICE!" The ladies looked alarmed. "Drink garrot juice!" The ladies nodded in relief.

With that Dr. Beetjuice drew into view a vegetable press into which he put sliced carrots and squeezed an orange stream into a paper cup. He went on to lecture on the way aging could be stopped and "ze vidalidy reztored" by drinking raw vegetable juices, eating raw vegetables, and letting nature's own uncooked vitamins prevent disease and early death. It so happened that this life force was extracted from vegetables by the amazing devices that kept appearing on the little shelf. The gadgets in Dr. Beetjuice's hands did marvelous things, like make radishes look like roses and cucumbers look like straw hats.

Sooner or later, some lady would ask how much these devices cost and Dr. Beetjuice would look offended. "Ladeez, I am zorry. I am a ziendist, not a zalesman." At this point, if Mr. Andropolis was not around, I would take off my apron, walk to the stand and ask for the most recently demonstrated gadget and slip fifty cents on the shelf.

Dr. Beetjuice would bristle, "Young man, vee are not zalesmen. Zis inztrument iz not for zale."

I would persist and Dr. Beetjuice in exasperation would turn to Manny.

"Mizter Vilson, pleez take care of zis young man."

Manny would shrug in irritation (glares at me from the ladies), snatch my fifty cents, hand me the gadget, and point for me to please leave. Then Dr. Beetjuice, in a gesture of helpless beneficence, would say,

"Ladeez, zis iz embarrazzing. Vee are not zupposed to zell zese, but Mr. Vilson zold vun to zat young man and not to you who haf been zee vunderful audience." He would look beseechingly at Manny. Manny would shrug in resignation, say "It's against the rules, but . . ." and the ladies quickly emptied their pocketbooks and walked off with bags full of junk and I got my fifty cents back.

I didn't feel so bad being their shill. Raw vegetables really are good for you. At least I hadn't joined the mafia.

More important, between Manny and Beetjuice and a couple of other pitches I watched regularly, I became a lifelong connoisseur of pitchmen and skilled countermen. I learned the pitchman's secret —keep talking, keep the eyes and ears busy, and give the viewer's brain no time to reflect on what has just been said. It is precisely the same technique of commercial television, where endless quick talk and scene changes are a threat to each generation's capacity for quiet reflection.

I have to confess that as a reporter I have not been above using a form of the technique when dealing with people who are experienced in dealing with reporters and sophisticated in the arts of public persuasion. Once I asked an Oklahoma senator who had sponsored legislation to increase the profits of oil and gas companies if it was not a conflict of interest since his family firm would be a major beneficiary. He exploded with indignation. He yelled at me that oil and gas was his state's biggest industry and it was his duty as a senator to defend and promote it. He carried on at great, guilty length, so when he paused for breath, I tried to mollify him by agreeing that he did have that natural senatorial duty, then shifted the context to the inevitable difficulties all members of Congress have who have been successful on their own in business and also represent a state's business as part of their public function. I asked how he dealt with that when confronted by such a question from the public. He gave me an unexplosive answer. I reported both his explosive and unexplosive response and added the context of the conflict-of-interest laws.

I treat differently men and women who do not share the senator's sophistication and who understand that responses to a reporter's questions, no matter how calmly or even sympathetically asked, probably will appear in print. Gaylord Nelson, when governor of Wisconsin, used to tell his staff always to assume that anything, anything at all, said to a reporter will appear on Page One the next day.

Less sophisticated men and women dealing with a reporter for the first time are very different. They probably see as a kind of visiting neighbor this friendly, warm man or woman speaking sympathetically, always nodding as though personally agreeing.

Once, for example, I asked a welfare mother on the West Side of Chicago if she tells the social agency that she earns extra money housecleaning weekends to make ends meet. She said of course she did not report it all, telling me all her budget figures, including housecleaning earnings. I reminded her that I was a writer for a magazine and if I used this with her name, her social worker probably would see it and the woman could get in trouble. This surprised her, and I ended up not using her name or any identifying circumstances. I used the useful and fruitful reporting device of interviewing many similar people, making it easy to give a representative picture without identifying any one source.

I felt no obligation to treat the senator from Oklahoma the same way, and I didn't mind using the pitchman's technique with a sophisticated and powerful politician.

In Asbury Park I moved to a busboy's job at a fancy soda and lunch restaurant where I could also fill in at the counter during slack midafternoon hours. Customers don't tip busboys, so Maizie, a hard-boiled experienced waitress, took pity on me. She was part of the Miami Beach-Asbury Park movement of professional restaurant workers who each year migrated en masse like geese, north in the summer and south in the winter. Like Mrs. Manzigian in my father's church, Maizie ostentatiously wore a fur coat every day in every weather and always hung it up in the waitresses' closet so that the "Lord & Taylor" label showed. She made it clear to everyone that the coat was the gift from a very rich gentleman in Miami.

After a week, Maizie asked me, "Kid, are the girls leaving you some money at the end of the week?"

When I said they weren't, she asked if I was stealing their tips and taking my time clearing their tables. When I said I wasn't, she was disgusted.

"For God's sake, what do they teach you in college, anyway?"

I'm not sure what Maizie did, but pretty soon on payday the waitresses started giving me a dollar.

I made enough that summer so that between Lydia, the potato counter, and padded stories in the *Telegram and Gazette*, I came through with most of the second-semester tuition, but not enough to go to medical school.

The next winter during a heavy storm I took a trolley home from the campus. I had to transfer in downtown Worcester for the Newton Square line and during the wait took refuge from the driving rain by strolling through the Woolworth five-and-ten. Inside, working at the end of a counter, were Manny and Dr. Beetjuice. Manny again was "the factory representative" and Dr. Beetjuice, in his white coat, this time giving a scientific seminar on the metallurgy of a new, exclusive replacement for fountain pen points made of "zee zegret medal, zindomium."

I sauntered to the edge of the gathering and Dr. Beetjuice spotted me. Without missing a beat, he said,

"Ladeez und chentelmen, dis iss amazing. In zee audience is my brilliant young azziztant from zee University of Heidelberg. Vondervul to zee you, my boy."

He shook my hand and I got out of there quickly. I didn't have fifty cents for another sentimental shill for my old friends and I couldn't risk being seen by a classmate at Clark who would know that Dr. Beetjuice's brilliant young assistant from the University of Heidelberg was struggling with German I in Professor Bosshard's class.

For a boy growing up in a proper household of a clergyman, my summer work, like my times with Uncle Fred and Grandpa, gave me an immediate sense of the life and personalities in working-class and lower middle-class blue collar life. But it was hardly the case that I started my local reporting as an act of high social responsibility, or that I performed it with brilliant insight.

Once out of college and into the newsroom of the Springfield, Massachusetts *Morning Union*, even on a paper with less than towering standards, I was forgiven more often than I deserved.

Paul Craig, the editor who hired me, was a kindly man who told me not to tell anyone that I was going to get eighteen dollars a week because others might be jealous.

My City Editor, Mr. Hatch, a manic personality perfect for a B movie about newspapers, had a bristling grey mustache and constantly wore a green eyeshade, possibly even to bed. Waiting for us when we came to work at 3:00 P.M. was Mr. Hatch's sloppily typed reaction to our labors of the night before. His reviews usually began, "And you call yourself a reporter!"

Luckily, standards on the *Morning Union* were sufficiently eccentric to let a stumbling novice sneak by. The paper crowded as many short items it could onto Page One, which looked like a badly arranged scrapbook. I had the federal and hotel beat, which normally meant ten or twenty short stories each night on anything from the date chosen for the next meeting of the Western Massachusetts Chapter of the Tall Cedars of Lebanon to the vote for increased dues for the Dump Truck Operators Association of Hampden County.

On dates for the next meeting, I was superb. On big stories, I was a disaster. In 1941, there were four dailies in Springfield (population: 100,000), two morning papers and two evening ones. I had competition from the best of the four, the morning *Republican* and its experienced reporter, Henry Berliner. I learned a lot from getting beaten by Henry.

When Henry and I covered the regional meeting of the American Society of Mechanical Engineers, we began by eating the society's free dinner (short of stealing the poor box from a cathedral, there were no ethical niceties for reporters). The president announced the date for the next meeting, after which he said that the meeting was now closed due to military secrecy and the "gentlemen of the press" should please leave. I was nothing if not a perfect gentleman and I left.

At the end of my beat, I wrote a brief story whose central message was that the engineer's annual picnic would be held at the Quabbin Reservoir. The next day Henry Berliner had a bylined story above the fold in the *Republican* about the engineers' meeting. The guest speaker had been John Garrand from the nearby Springfield Armory. Mr. Garrand had invented the Garrand rifle, which became the standard weapon of the U.S. Army in World War II. After I left, he had told new stories of the rifle's creation and ended by disassembling and reassembling the mechanism in less than a minute while blindfolded.

My story prompted Mr. Hatch to stray from his standard opening in my daily note. "When I assign a story to a reporter for the *Springfield Morning Union* I do not want to read it in the *Springfield Republican*."

At the meeting, Henry had stood up as I had, but he lagged slightly behind me and unobtrusively sidled into a chair at a different table. That was when I learned the reporter's knack of looking like wallpaper.

My next big story was a textbook case of how not to succeed.

In the eerie complacency of America on the verge of World War II, the big issue in Springfield was whether old Memorial Church would be torn down to make room for a new Coca-Cola bottling plant. Thus, there came to town the famous James Aloysius Farley, architect of Franklin Roosevelt's first presidential campaign, former postmaster general of the United States, and now a high-ranking official of Coca-Cola. His appearance was treated like a state visit. Mr. Hatch told me to hustle over to the Highland Hotel dining room and get a definite answer from Mr. Farley, yes or no.

Mr. Farley was dining alone, except for a large lobster that he was quietly demolishing. Presenting an outward demeanor of a cool big-time journalist, I apologized for disturbing his lunch and said I needed just a minute of his time to ask about Memorial Church.

Farley was the most famous man I had interviewed for the Springfield paper, and I was relieved that the big man had an honest, open, shining face with a beaming smile and was delighted to be interviewed.

"Why, certainly my boy, certainly. Here, let's get you a lobster and we can talk while we eat."

I quickly begged off on the lobster. On an issue as grave as Memorial Church versus a new Coca-Cola bottling plant, I doubted my ability to wrestle a lobster and Mr. Farley at the same time.

"Sit down, son, sit down. What would you like to know?"

I already felt the excitement of a reporter moving in for the kill. I took out my notebook and questioned him shrewdly for a half hour. After I was satisfied, I put away my notebook and thanked him profusely, knowing I had a terrific story.

I entered the newsroom flushed with victory. I sat down at my typewriter and went over my notes. I went over my notes three times. I couldn't believe it. I had nothing.

Farley had given me carefully enunciated emphatic sentences, but no sentence ended the way it began. It was a collection of dazzling U-turns. Coca-Cola had always respected an historic city like Springfield, especially its places of worship, just as it was concerned with a city's economic well-being. . . . Everything added up to zero. One of the century's greatest political artists had left me and his lobster in the same condition.

I had other similar triumphs. My first feature story was about anti-aircraft spotlights the Army was displaying at the big Eastern States Fair. The lights are now used to advertise discount carpet sales, but back then they were considered infallible protection from air strikes. The high point in my story was colorful language about the small demonstration plane trying to escape the crisscrossed spotlights, which I wrote twisted and turned "like an animal in travail."

The next day, I modestly entered the newsroom waiting for that highest of accolades, an old-timer wandering by my desk with a quiet, "Nice story, kid." Instead, when I took my seat, I heard a strange chant. It was my older deskmate, Elliot Stocker, repeating over and over as though in a requiem mass, shaking his head in melancholy disbelief, "Animal in travail, animal in travail, animal in travail . . ."

Maybe the only reason I didn't get fired in Springfield was that Mr. Hatch had no anger left after venting his spleen in his devastating notes. Another was the big boss's indifference to the newsroom. The owner, Sherman Bowles, regularly strode long-legged through the newsroom on the way to the composing room, but he looked uninterested in the news. He seemed mostly interested in the back room, where he could see, and for all I know, count, the metal slugs of type produced by the linotype machines for the measly money he paid his workers. The workers in the composing room were deaf men who communicated by sign language, hired after Bowles had broken the regular composing room union.

The town was full of Bowles stories, some whispered in fear, because Bowles owned all four dailies. People said he loved breaking unions and had even tried to run down a picket line of striking workers with his pickup truck.

The big conglomerates who now own most newspapers, including the surviving one in Springfield, usually do what Sherman Bowles did but are more couth. Now they accomplish the same thing with high-priced law firms and union-busting specialists dressed in custom-made suits who arrive in limousines at legislators' offices bearing loopholes and permissive amendments in federal regulations. At least Bowles took pleasure in doing his dirty work personally.

When the country declared war after Pearl Harbor, I decided I would be a flier and tried to join a Navy program for flying officers.

The recruiting officer turned me down because at that early date they were accepting applications only from native-born Americans. So I enlisted in the precursor to the Air Force, the Army Air Corps, which didn't mind that I didn't arrive in the country until I was four months old.

I didn't realize it then, but World War II would so alter my thinking—and the nature of American newspapers—that at war's end I knew I would never again work for a publisher like Sherman Bowles.

After the war I worked for the Providence papers, very different from working for Mr. Bowles. But my own sins, not Bowles's, followed me. The first time I entered the Providence newsroom, there was my old Springfield deskmate, Elliot Stocker, who was now Assistant City Editor of the *Evening Bulletin*. Stocker took one look and said, "Why, here comes animal in travail."

## CHAPTER 11

# "Your Kind," "Their Kind," and World War II

I t was not a happy trip. It was the summer of 1945 and I was
on the way back to Biloxi, Mississippi where I would train
in one of the more eccentric air operations of World War
II. I was glad Betty was with me; on some pre-overseas assignments, wives had not been permitted. We tried now
and then to talk about something relaxing or funny.

We laughed a little about my role in the crew of an ancient amphibious PBY plane, part of an air-sea rescue
squadron; in addition to navigating, my job was to jump
into the water and rescue crew members from B-29s
that fell into the sea after being shot up in bomb runs
over Japan. I was the only member of our crew who
couldn't swim, and we expressed the traditional wonder
at how the military assigns tasks. I was deeply devoted
to my Mae West inflatable life vest. That was worth a
small smile.

But no matter what we tried, the sadness intruded. For
the first time since 1944 when Chris was born, he was not
with us. Up to then, the three of us had been vagabonds as
I was transferred from air base to air base, each time turning the 1939 green Mercury convertible into a traveling
nursery. But now, for the first time, we had left the baby
with Betty's family in Worcester until we could find housing in Biloxi. After the special training in Biloxi, I would

leave for overseas and Betty and the baby would live in New England. Being without Chris for the first time was very hard.

Riding with us in the car was another heaviness. As we drove south, the news came that Franklin Roosevelt had died in Hot Springs, Georgia. We passed railroad tracks where silent lines of men and women waited patiently, sometimes at night and sometimes in the rain, to view the train carrying the dead president back to Washington.

Franklin Roosevelt had been President of the United States since I was twelve years old, and the politics of social justice had been the only politics of my first years of political awareness. It was hard to believe the sudden disappearance of the man who had been the center of national life for thirteen years and leader of the war effort.

It had been a long, tiring drive and at nightfall I called ahead to a hotel along the Gulf coast. I explained that I was a flying officer in between bases and that my wife and I needed a room. The "flying officer" touch was always a plus in getting difficult accommodations, especially in the South, which regarded military people in wartime with even higher esteem than the rest of the country. The clerk reassured me that a fine room would be waiting for us.

The clerk was smiling as we came through the doors but when I reached the desk, his face changed.

"Oh. We don't take your kind."

"You told me on the phone, we had a reservation."

"Yes, but I didn't know."

I understood, of course, what he hadn't "known." He hadn't known that when he saw me he would think I was a Jew. I was not about to tell him otherwise. But I insisted on making him explain.

"What do you mean, 'my kind'?"

Most anti-Semites who consider themselves genteel have a curious reluctance to use the word "Jew." Apparently, to them its consonantal single syllable sounds too harsh, like an epithet, and since they do in fact think of it as an epithet, in polite company they try to avoid it by using the word "Jewish" instead.

Today it is easy to forget that through World War II, anti-Semitism and the idea of racial purity and superiority were common and casually expressed throughout white Gentile society. "Your kind" was simply the sugarcoated expression of a widespread certainty that all human beings were divided into two camps forever apart by nature, the superior races—Anglo-Saxons with roots in Great Britain and northern Europe—and the inferior races—those who originated everyplace else in the world.

It was not just a Southern problem. Ten weeks after we were turned away from the Mississippi hotel I was on a quick trip back to New England to locate an apartment in Providence for Betty and the baby. It would be close to Carl and Edith in Providence, two of my best friends from college days, and at the same time close enough, but not too close, to both our families in Worcester "in case something happened."

We answered an ad for an apartment on Angell Street, a pleasant neighborhood next to the Brown University campus. Yes, the lady said on the phone, the place was still available and, no, she had no problem with a mother and eighteen-month-old child, especially the family of an officer going overseas.

A white-haired woman smiled at us through the curtain of the small window in her door but when she opened the door and saw my face unfiltered by lace, she said:

"Oh, I'm terribly sorry, but I don't rent to your kind."

She seemed genuinely sorry, as though there had been an unfortunate natural phenomenon whose inevitability we both accepted.

It revived many memories from childhood. In grocery stores and other public places where adults assumed that children do not hear anything, I heard remarks about "your kind" and "the foreign element." "Our kind" often grew up trying desperately to look like "their kind."

As a child, I tried to emulate the preferred "American" images I saw all around me. The most desirable men pictured in *National Geographic*, *Saturday Evening Post*, and in the movies, were handsome WASPs with evenly shaped features, usually blond and blue-eyed, depicted in their supposed habitats, like exclusive clubs, or escorting beautiful blond WASP girls to the tennis courts.

In the privacy of the locked bathroom, I would try to comb my hair like Clark Gable or Cary Grant and to assume the cool and confident expressions of my media models of male desirability. I wished my name were "Bill Summers" and that I wore white, striped tennis sweaters and could eye with irresistible charm the eager, lustful blondes from the movies and ads.

But, alas, much as I stared at the mirror head-on with my gablesque leer, when I caught sight of my profile, it all collapsed. My hair was too messy, my eyes unblue, my nose, even before its collection of breaks, too un-WASP. Without the fantasized imposition of Clark Gable's face onto mine, I was inescapably myself, not just in looks but in my inner conviction that I was undebonair, unconfident, unattractive and unacceptable inside the charmed circle of "real Americans" that I imagined.

The feeling was not diminished by a great deal of straight-faced assertions in serious literature. As a child I had read magazines sent free to the homes of clergymen in which periodic articles warned against the contamination of America by "the polyglot races." Sober-sounding college anthropology texts still classified each race as having absolute qualities of mind and personality.

In college, our class of premedical students was taken to interview an assistant dean of Harvard Medical School who explained the criteria for selecting students. In addition to looking for high general marks in chemistry, biology, German, and, preferably, Greek and Latin, the dean added, "Sons of doctors are given preference and, of course, we have a very small Jewish quota. Also, we tend not to take children with Southern Italian parentage because so many people of that extraction perform illegal operations." African-Americans, of course, were not even considered by the dean or most of the rest of white America.

When it was clear to President Roosevelt that sooner or later we had to enter World War II, the chief reason he gave was not to stop Hitler's persecution of Jews and other "inferiors" (after all, he did sign the order sending loyal West Coast Japanese-American citizens to inland camps) but because Hitler was an aggressor and we should come to the aid of "our British cousins." It was a safer way to mobilize general support.

In the Army we regularly saw one of the series of military films on "Why We Fight." We fought not because Hitler was carrying out a massive subjugation of the "inferior races" of the continent, but because Hitler broke treaties and dive-bombed civilians in cities. When the films showed Nazis trashing Jewish neighborhoods, you had to look fast and know German or Yiddish to notice the painted sign "Jude" and the Star of David scrawled on the broken storefronts.

Nazidom's anti-Semitism and its endemic undercurrent in my own country played a role in my quick enlistment when the country went to war. I volunteered after Pearl Harbor for a number of reasons, but one of them was a sense that the mentality of condemning "your kind" had become a world threat. It was the aggressive doctrine of a military power, led by Hitler, promising a thousand years of barbarity. I felt that sooner or later those "thousand years" would be a threat not just to civilization, but to me, my family, and my closest friends.

The country's prewar failure to make fighting anti-Semitism and racism a national cause had a high cost. The failure extended to our news. It was not surprising to me one day several years ago, sitting comfortably on the deck of our Berkeley house in a privileged neighborhood, no longer excluded as "your kind," to hear the historian Deborah Lipstadt describe what she had found in a study of four hundred American daily papers of the 1930s. She had looked to see what our prewar news carried about the Nazis' persecution of Jews and other minorities, looking for evidence that would have better prepared the country and the world to face the threat of Hitlerism earlier rather than later—and to make less violent our own internal struggle against racism.

As she detailed later in her book, *Beyond Belief*, Lipstadt discovered that if you read closely enough and knew more from other sources, you could have learned years earlier the magnitude of the horrors developing in Germany and Eastern Europe, but the news was reported in small, obscure stories that usually emphasized the official German denials. There was little evidence that American journalism regarded the early Hitlerian racism as having prime importance, or took steps to pursue the reports or to look at the total picture that was scattered in bits and pieces buried in back pages.

When I look back, my failed impersonations of WASPs inside the locked bathroom of my childhood had a purpose. They were reminders, much later, that there is no sense in trying to run away from your ineradicable self and inheritance.

But it also reminds me how powerful our mass media images and figures are as models of what is acceptable, desirable, and successful. They influence the self-identification, confidence, and aspirations of whole generations. That realization and my own experience of being discriminated against as "your kind" would make a difference in what I did thereafter as a journalist.

Those experiences had been simmering for a long time before I moved to enlist after Pearl Harbor. The war was both personal and national, though I chose the Air Corps for a less convincing reason. I had been a pacifist and I doubted that I could kill another human being whom I could see as a real person. It was hardly honorable: the victims of aerial bombs are just as dead as soldiers shot face-to-face and, worse, more likely to be civilians as well.

It was not even valid escapism. I had not yet come to understand that in kill-or-be-killed confrontations, the psyches of most people quickly resolve that delicate dilemma.

My hope in 1941 that flying would release me from the intimacy of killing came to mind years later when the country went through a kind of blood-lust in expanding the death penalty in criminal cases. What would happen, I wondered, if those politicians were required personally to administer the electricity or poison to every condemned criminal and watch the results to the end. Some politicians I've met would relish it, but most, I think, would be less glib about voting to impose the penalty on other human beings if, in addition to voting in the comfort of their legislative chambers they were required to take part in the death chambers.

My decision to pick the Air Corps was influenced by my fantasy about flying. I had never been in an airplane before and assumed that it was a serene experience of gliding noiselessly among brilliantly blue skies and soft white clouds. On my first flight, from our training base in Monroe, Louisiana, I was shocked that the plane smelled of gasoline, grease, and vomit, the engines coughed, snorted, and rattled, and the plane bounced and jiggled like a wounded bird—or an "animal in travail." There was no gliding smoothly in extreme weather or serenity in flying with oxygen masks in unheated planes at temperatures of ten below zero.

There was, nevertheless, a different kind of poetry. In daylight the incredible variety of shapes, colors, and textures of the American landscape spread out from horizon to horizon. When they were not the thunderheads I came to hate, the small cumulus clouds were dynamic white sculptures against a brilliant blue. At night from high altitudes the skies were an astonishing display of massed stars never seen from the ground. They put earthly ego in perspective.

I had qualified to take my pick of being a pilot, navigator, or bombardier. I didn't want to be a bombardier—still the obtuse ethicist who wanted someone else to release the deadly stuff. And I thought aerial navigation might be more intellectually interesting than driving a machine.

I came to regret that decision. The more I flew, the more I wished I had chosen to be a pilot. I would have had more control over my fate instead of the luck of the daily draw in which I sometimes got a competent, mature pilot, and, as the war used up crews, some who were immature and careless.

I entered flight training with the same illusions as my fellow air cadets. Before Pearl Harbor, we had seen the movies and *Life* magazine photographs of glamorous air cadets in full dress uniform, eating meals on white tablecloths and standing white-silk-scarved beside aircraft in "The West Point of the Air." We all had the same surprise. We were the first trainees on a base still half airfield and half sorghum field. We studied, marched, did calisthenics, took exams, and tried to breathe in the constant cloud of dust kicked up by the roaring bulldozers all around us. For weeks, we lived in tarpaper-covered barracks without electric lights and our choice of fluid intake was either Coca-Cola or treated water, dispensed from suspended canvas sacs, that tasted like discarded chemicals. Coca-Cola became the fluid of choice.

The ads said we were an elite, and in some ways perhaps we were in the simplistic way our national educational techniques define the elite: we had passed long mental, physical, and psychological exams.

But when we first gathered dirty, disheveled, and unshaven after three days and nights in an ancient passenger car on a low-priority train, we gathered in ragged formation in Montgomery, Alabama to be told by a pained drill sergeant, "You are the sorriest looking specimens of humanity I have ever seen in this man's army." It turned out he greeted all newcomers that way, but it helped dilute any sense of elitist superiority.

In those first few months after America entered the war, the new Army Air Corps was extremely fussy. It did not want to waste expensive training, costly airplanes, the lives of crew members, or the success of missions on what it considered flawed specimens.

The most rigorous physical exam occurred after months of basic training and studying theory. Now we started flight training, the most expensive kind, and the Air Corps didn't want to waste it on men with hidden weaknesses. A young doctor in the orthopedic section of our naked assembly line sent me into a panic when he announced loudly, "Hold it, Mister. Turn to face the wall. I thought so: 'perfect pronation.'"

The doctor was so delighted with his discovery that he kept trumpeting, "a textbook case, a textbook case." I stood facing the wall and over my shoulder asked what was pronation. "Outward-turning ankles, Mister. Textbook case. Sorry," and he stamped my papers a big, red "Disqualified." The doctor was so proud that he called the head flight surgeon to observe his perfect textbook case. I argued with the flight surgeon that I had run cross-country in school and never had any foot trouble. The flight surgeon, an older colonel, took a quick look, scratched out the "Disqualified," and told the small audience of doctors, "The German Air Force won't mind if he has a little pronation."

Nine months later, when we graduated with wings and commissions as flying second lieutenants, our names included the ones the country accepts when wars must be won regardless of race, creed, or national origin: Atkinson, Bagdikian, Baumgartner, Bonano, Brick, Cahoon, Carmody, Cohen, Cooper III, Dabrowski, Facteau, Fasanelli, Frankel, Graczyk, Grandpre, Guinsberg, Zucherman. . . . We were the sons of subway track walkers in Brooklyn, clergymen in Massachusetts, oil roustabouts in Texas, coal miners in Pennsylvania, hillbillies from Appalachia, and Ivy League graduates from New Haven.

If we were some kind of elite, standing there in the base theater pinning on each other's wings and bars, we were "superior" only in our performance on conventional tests of usefulness in a technical operation of war. In the qualities that might prevent wars in the first place, we were not necessarily any better than people picked at random.

But it was hardly an unfettered exercise in full democracy. Neither in the base theater that day nor later in our crews was there a single African-American. The national exorcism of white racism had not yet begun. Women were in segregated noncombat units.

The only black soldiers on our base worked in either the mess hall or labor battalions. Late one night, when I had the once-a-month duty of being in charge of base security, there was an emergency call of "bad fight with weapons in the colored barracks." A master sergeant military policeman advised us flying people about everything we did during our security duty, and that night he drove me to the barracks where we could hear angry shouting and cursing inside.

The sergeant said, "Sir, take out your .45, and if they don't obey your order to come to, send a round through the roof, then shoot a couple of them in the foot right away." I made the sergeant feel better by just unbuttoning my holster, but I waited for the sergeant to enter the barracks and yell, "Ten hut!" and then depended on walking rapidly toward the center of the fight and in the momentary surprise saying as calmly as I could, "Drop your weapons." Luckily, there was a clatter of dropped weapons on the floor just as a large backup of MPs rushed in. But I wondered if it had been an all-white unit if the sergeant would have advised me to shoot them in the feet.

We were ruled by flying officers in classrooms and in the air, but everywhere else we were governed by Army ground people, most of whom had contempt for the strange air people who acted as though they were still civilians. As a result, every day during my training we had close-order marching drill, but in three-and-a-half years of flying no one ever showed us how to use a parachute.

We wore a parachute every time we flew, and a couple of times I thought mine would be put to use, but all I ever heard was the civilian lore that you jump, count to ten, and pull the ripcord, until an older pilot told me, "Tighten your leg straps if you don't want to be a boy soprano."

When it was clear that I was going to get my wings and a commission (and a fifty percent bonus for hazardous duty), Betty planned to come down so we could be married. When I was in college she had been in the choir of my father's church and we had started to date. Some evenings I studied at the Ogasapians' where her white-haired, blue-eyed mother had the same reaction my grandfather had years earlier, sending me back to campus late labs with a twenty-pound bag of Armenian food for what she regarded as her daughter's emaciated boyfriend. I even relaxed from time to time to join her crowd in an Armenian card game called "Euchly," where I discovered that my future mother-in-law, this warm, white-haired blue-eyed gentle woman, was the most skilled card shark I have ever met. Mrs. Ogasapian always won legally but when she became bored doing it honestly, she also added the skills of an outrageous cheat, making me win against my own best efforts.

Betty and I had planned to get married in Louisiana after I received my commission but for a moment Louisiana mud interfered.

In the early weeks of overcooked goo in our Selman Field mess hall there appeared one day a wonderful novelty—a crate of fresh oranges. A stern officer in charge of the treasure announced as we filed out, "Each cadet will take one, and only one, orange as he leaves the mess hall." My friend, Elmer, marching beside me, had concealed from the Air Corps that oranges make him throw up. As we left the mess hall, Elmer desperately thrust his orange into my hand as though it were a live grenade.

As we formed outside the mess hall, the officer yelled at me in a rage.

"Mister, you heard my orders! One orange to a man. What are you doing with two oranges?"

As prenatal officers and gentlemen we had been instructed that when accused of an infraction we had only three permissible answers, "Yes, Sir," "No, Sir," and "No excuse, Sir." I said "No excuse, Sir."

The officer demanded that the man who handed me the orange step forward. Elmer also said "No excuse, Sir."

That Saturday while our classmates were in town eating civilian food, going to dances, drinking, dating girls, and otherwise engaging in the varied joys of weekend civilian life, Elmer and I were assigned to spend the weekend digging post holes in a swamp at the far edge of the runways. In the hot Louisiana summer sun it was not long before we were mud-caked automatons.

We were rhythmically grunting and cursing, when we became conscious of a tiny figure far out on the field running toward us. We ignored him. We were not in the mood to interact with the rest of the human race. But the figure reached hearing distance:

"Bagdikian, long-distance call in the day room."

Long-distance emergency calls during the war usually meant a death in the family or an impending one. I threw down the post-hole digger and walked in the sun toward the distant day room. It could be my father or Betty's father. My father often had medical emergencies but always walked away from them. Her father was old, ailing, and almost blind. When it was clear that my dating his daughter was getting serious, the only questions he had asked me were how was I doing in my studies and had I read Victor Hugo.

In the day room the receiver was hanging on its long wire from the wall phone. I left a trail of mud on the floor and when I grabbed the receiver, caked mud from my hand fell to the floor. The sergeant at his desk was apoplectic. "Stop messing up my bad word day room with your bad word mud!" I ignored him and spoke into the phone.

It was Betty. She was on the verge of tears.

"What's wrong?"

"My sister thinks we should have a white wedding."

It was as though I had received an unintelligible alien signal from another planet. More mud fell from my clothes and arms. The sergeant was yelling obscenities in the background. For a few seconds, my brain could not process what my ears were hearing.

"What did you say?"

She repeated it, closer to tears than before.

The alien message gradually took shape in my head. Her sister thought we should have a white wedding.

"A white wedding? A white wedding? Do you know what it's like down here? I'm covered from head to foot in mud and just walked a half mile to answer an emergency call. I thought this was an emergency. I thought your father had died. Tell your sister she's crazy."

And I hung up.

So we had a white wedding. Betty's gown was long, white, and satin. She also thought it would be nice to have a military wedding, which meant we would leave the church under crossed ceremonial sabers held by my squadron friends.

We had an ecumenical ceremony, two Armenian Congregationalists being married in a Presbyterian church by the Methodist base chaplain, with my best man a Jew, Betty's maid of honor the Irish Catholic wife of a friend in the squadron, and Betty "given away" by our squadron commanding officer, a pleasant ground officer from a high Episcopal WASP family in Chicago.

Elmer and his wife, Esther, and Betty and I shared half a tiny cottage on Lee Avenue a mile or so from downtown. We had long arguments with our neighbors about the treatment of blacks. On Emancipation Day both neighbors stayed up all night with shotguns at a second-story window overlooking a distant black cafe, convinced the blacks would get drunk and run amok among "our women." Both white neighbors had done their gun watch every Emancipation Day for years and so had their parents. The black community did celebrate Emancipation Day in their segregated neighborhood, but there had never been any attempt to approach whites and neither neighbor knew of any of the past. But they stood watch every year, convinced that it could happen anytime.

I was especially friendly with Joe Monte next door. We went fishing together and his kids called me, in all seriousness, "Mr. Aviator." We had to agree to disagree about race. Joe insisted that all blacks were radically inferior children whom he felt should be treated with Christian kindness as long as they stayed in their place.

Fifteen years later the Supreme Court spoke and the Archbishop of Louisiana invited all races to his cathedral and preached what at the time was a courageous sermon declaring racial prejudice immoral. In 1957, while covering the school desegregation struggles in the South, I revisited my old wartime Monroe neighbor, Joe, for the first time. It was a warm reunion with a lavish dinner in his home. But first he insisted on showing me the sparkling new neighborhood of black workers and artisans, and boasted that the crew chief in his contracting business was a black man supervising his white crews.

I said, "Joe, what happened to all the low brain development and childlike natures you used to say they had when we argued during the war?"

Joe, a Roman Catholic, looked hurt. "Why, I never said a thing like that."

Arguers against change like to say, "You can't legislate morals," but it is hard to convince me that authority figures can't evoke more humane attitudes, just as they obviously do the opposite.

I had received my wings and commission in February of 1943, still early in the war, and I was ordered by my instructor to train the incoming flood of new air crews.

While air combat losses over Europe were fearsome, those from training were not insignificant. Betty told me what it was like at the housing project for military families when one of our planes would crash. A wife would see an olive-drab Army sedan moving very slowly down the unpaved streets of the project, uniformed men inside the car looking out windows on both sides. And every wife in the neighborhood was soon peering through the curtains. "Don't stop here, please God, don't stop here." Inside the car, the base chaplain was looking for a particular street with a particular number so he could ring the doorbell and tell someone that her husband had just been killed in a training crash.

One evening when I returned from a long flight, the operations officer stopped me as I left to check out and go home.

"Hey, Bag, we need a volunteer navigator to take a C-60 for one of our crews stranded in Evansville."

A plane from our squadron on a training mission had crashed at Evansville, Indiana, but somehow the crew of eight got away unharmed. I said I'd do it and left to call Betty to tell her that I wouldn't be home until the next day. As I was collecting maps and getting briefed on weather to the north, the operations officer came back.

"Forget it. Another navigator needs his four hours flight time. Do you mind?" I didn't mind. I had just finished an eight-hour flight and now felt that I wasn't letting down the stranded men whom I knew.

The next day we learned that our rescue plane had successfully picked up the stranded crew and then crashed on takeoff and exploded, killing everyone in both crews. I felt the usual succession of emotions: relief, guilt, grief, then resignation—you do the best you can, but there is good luck and there is bad luck that does not discriminate between the good and the bad, or the "superior" and the "inferior."

In early August 1945, I completed air-sea rescue exercises at Biloxi and my newly formed crew was ordered to Mather Field, California, no families permitted. The night before we headed over the Pacific, we were briefed for a dawn takeoff to Honolulu and from there Okinawa. But the next morning we were told that the flight had been postponed. Then we got the news. A new "device" had been dropped over a Japanese city called Hiroshima. Three days later another more powerful "device"—a new kind of bomb, called an atom bomb—was dropped over the city of Nagasaki. With the two cities wiped out, the Japanese were suing for peace. We waited weeks for the armed services to sort out what it would do with its sudden excess of people.

During the first weeks of peace in those strangely suspended California days, it was possible both to look backward and to think about the future. In the wartime military you think in terms of hours, days, and weeks—the distant future is too uncertain. Planning your life too far ahead is tempting fate. During the fighting, I had heard month after month about lost former companions and friends, of fellow navigators and students I had come to know personally, routinely killed in combat or in training for combat. The casualties among the ground forces were even worse. Their wives and families had seen the olive drab sedan stop at their front door or a Western Union delivery man on a bicycle delivering the dreaded yellow telegrams.

During the fighting ground troop casualties everywhere were in numbers hard to grasp, but while the battles were occurring I had drawn all the grim satisfaction of a former pacifist at reports of high numbers of enemy dead. With added self-interest, after each air raid I read the papers to find out whether they had lost more planes than we did.

But during those first peacetime weeks of enforced idleness what had been only a philosophic background thought now became overwhelming. As the urgency of winning receded, the enormity of the cost all over the world became more stark than ever. In the weeks of brilliant California autumn, waiting for my number to come up for discharge, I was struck with the sickening cost of racial and group hatreds. Millions of the world's young men were dead, other millions of civilians killed in their homes and concentration camps, great cities around the globe devastated—the habitats mostly of widows, orphans, and old men or ones crippled in the war. Once the us-versus-them struggle was over, it was easier to think of the recurring cost of centuries of great powers' arrogance, greed, and hatreds.

Something else looked irrational. My whole adolescence had been spent in the Great Depression, when every attempt to get society to pay to put people back to work and place food on family tables was politically resisted. Every dollar for purely constructive purposes was squeezed out grudgingly: the country couldn't afford it and it would mean raising taxes. Yet when war came, every year we found ten times the dollars to create weapons and train men to kill and destroy. There had been little choice once Hitler and Japan attacked us, but was the creation of widows and orphans our only generous priority?

These were hardly original thoughts, and I was far from being the only person thinking them. World War II ushered in among other things a change of popular values and attitudes in the United States. With war's end and confirmation of the Holocaust, all leaders in the United States for the first time inveighed publicly and repeatedly against the poison of racism and social prejudice. That was new; before that racial and gender sneers were a part of unthinking conversation and common public speechifying. Respectable, god-fearing people did not bargain, they "jewed down" the price. They talked casually about niggers, wops, kikes, frogs, and polloks. Unlike the Republicans after World War I, the best known Republicans at war's end urged Americans to join in international efforts to prevent wars and promote global justice.

American children born in wartime and in the decade that followed did not grow up as their parents had, in a society of casual racism and antisemitism. Hitler made public antisemitism and racial insults less fashionable.

To the postwar young, the atom bomb was not what it was to me in the first hour of that first day in California when I heard of the new "device." During years of wartime, I cheered every time we developed a blockbuster bomb bigger than the enemy's. The atomic bomb, at first, seemed only another bigger bomb for our side. But the postwar reaction among young people who had not experienced the survival emotions of soldiers was closer to the truth: it was an intolerable weapon that changed everything.

Baking idly in the California sun and able to think without reservations about the future, I knew in a vague way that my view of my future life work had changed. It was not so much an explicit decision as the slow emergence of an assumption. Before, any newspaper job seemed wonderful. But now the kind of paper made a difference. When I received a letter from my old paper in Springfield asking if I would return, I wrote back a firm no.

Whatever the nature of that misty assumption that the world had to change, the war created another internal change. A generation of black servicemen drafted into the armed services to defend democracy had to deal with the stark contrast between what they were asked to fight for abroad and what white America denied them at home. They were segregated in civilian life, they were segregated in the armed forces, and now millions went home to civilian life and found they were still segregated there. That, too, would change and with it much of my future reporting.

In 1962, I spent an afternoon talking to Medgar Evers, the civil rights leader in Mississippi. I asked him why he was spending his life fighting for black rights in Mississippi.

"I'll tell you exactly why," he told me. "I'm thirty-six years old, but the scars started piling up a long time ago. I was born in Decatur here in Mississippi, and when we were walking to school in the first grade, white kids in their school busses would throw things at us and yell filthy things. This was a mild start. If you're a kid in Mississippi, this is the elementary course. . . .

"I went into the Army in 1943 with the Red Ball Express in France and Germany. I got back in 1946 and so did my brother, Charlie. He'd been in the southwest Pacific. It was his idea that he and I and four other Negroes who'd been in the Army ought to vote in the next election. . . . We went down and registered with no trouble at all."

Friends visited the Evers house that night to warn that white men had spread the word that he and the others had better not vote. The warning was not subtle, and the threat came from, among others, a United States Senator from Mississippi, who had, of course, taken office with an oath to support the Constitution.

"Just before the election—this would be in 1946—Senator Bilbo came to town," Evers told me. "Word went out that no Negroes were to come to town that night. But my Daddy, another man, and I went anyway and we were standing across the street from the rally and we heard Bilbo tell them, 'The best way to keep the nigger from the polls is to visit him the night before the election.' I remember looking into his mouth while he said those words."

When Evers, his brother, and four others went to vote, they were directed to the county clerk's office where fifteen or twenty white men with knives and guns informed Evers and his friends that they did not want them to vote. Outside the office, a mob of two hundred white men had gathered, blocking the door to the polling booth. Evers heard one man say, "You shove him and I'll hit him."

We knew we were in trouble and might end up dead. We had all seen a lot of dead people in the war. I had been on Omaha Beach. All we wanted to be was ordinary citizens. We fought during the war for America, and Mississippi was included. Now after the Germans and Japanese hadn't killed us, it looked as though white Mississippians would.

That was too much, and he and his brother, unable to vote, began organizing the first Mississippi chapter of the National Association of the Advancement of Colored People. One year later, Evers was dead from a white segregationist's bullet, shot on his front lawn as he returned from a church rally for black voting rights.

Within a year of my returning to civilian life and to journalism, a far milder experience than Medgar Evers' helped clarify my sense of what was important in the rest of my own career.

A few months after shedding my uniform, I took a job as editor of a new air travel magazine in New York. I alternated weekends commuting back to the family in Providence and house hunting in New York. I was part of the inevitable postwar surge of young writers, journalists, and artists, including my old bohemian crowd from Providence, flocking to New York to make it in the national center of cultural life.

Finally, I found the ideal house for the family, a pleasant duplex in Jackson Heights. It cost $9,750, and rent from the other half of the house plus my salary would more than take care of the monthly payments. Under the G.I. Bill, all I needed was a $250 down payment.

The final closing had the formality of a small version of signing the Versailles Treaty. The principals gathered around a polished conference table in the paneled office of the real estate firm. We were all in our best business clothes, smiling official smiles and waiting for the man from the bank. When the banker arrived he had unexpected news.

"Mr. Bagdikian, I'm sorry that the bank can't give you the mortgage we thought we could. You'll need a larger down payment."

I protested that we had a deal that had been carefully worked out and confirmed in every detail. Besides, I couldn't afford a larger down payment.

"Why this last-minute change?"

"I'm sorry, but there has been an invasion."

"Invasion? What do you mean, 'invasion'?"

We had won the war. There could be no more invasion.

"A colored family has moved into a house only two blocks away and your duplex is no longer worth what it was before."

There was no arguing with the banker, who, like the sweet old lady on Angell Street, acted as though this were a regrettable natural disaster beyond anyone's control.

It was no longer "your kind" about me. It was now "their kind."

"Their kind" probably was a veteran, like me, a man with a family, and, like me, an American. But blacks, Hispanics, and newer foreigners had replaced me as one of "your kind."

Shortly after the scene in the real estate office I had my fill of working for the repulsive owner of the new magazine and returned to being a newspaper reporter. The "invasion" of a black family into their own country was a reminder that postwar America had a lot of unfinished business in a different kind of battle. Our journalism also had its own struggles ahead. I never consciously planned it that way, but for most of the next fifty years, I found myself, like many others, reporting and writing on what I saw as the unfinished business in our society and in my own profession.

## CHAPTER 12

## *The News as Seen from Wall Street*

Until I was a young adult, I believed in one of the powerful American myths—if left to themselves, social and economic problems in the United States would take care of themselves. Some self-righting business mechanism would see to it that the poor would become unpoor and everyone would be better off. I supposed that business people were too smart to let their customers run out of money, but if they did, the newspapers would point it out and it would all come out just fine.

The only things about the economy and business I remember seeing in my father's *Boston Traveler* during the Depression were articles saying things were getting better all by themselves—except, of course, when government interfered. The free magazines my father received as a minister were all full of praise for the automatic efficiency and wisdom of the business world. But they all had ferocious warnings against government "meddling." Radio preachers sermonized that it was unchristian to waste taxpayers' money to pay "idlers" to rake leaves when "the bureaucrats in Washington" should be doing more to "help private business" and encouraging "idlers" to show more "gumption."

It seems that government was the problem. Anyone who had enough "gumption" could get rich in America as long as they weren't always wiped out by taxes. Taxes were usually mentioned in phrases like "ruinous taxes." The worst horror was something called "socialism," a disease of President Roosevelt's New Deal which they denounced because it rewarded "idlers" and punished hard-working Americans who had "gumption."

For some reason, liberal magazines didn't send free copies to clergymen, even though I knew my father admired Franklin Roosevelt, and the rare political ideas I remember him mentioning did not sound like the stuff that came to the house.

Advertisements did their part to form my boyhood impressions of the outside world. Someone must have given us a subscription to the *National Geographic*. Photographs and articles described half-naked African tribes, but closer to home the ads I remember showed handsome WASP Americans in tuxedos playing billiards in paneled rooms decorated with pictures of red-coated aristocrats riding to hounds. The men playing billiards gave me the feeling that this is what one was supposed to be in America, including us, since we were all doing our best to be super-Americans.

The *Boston Traveler* and the men preaching on the radio kept saying that American free enterprise was threatened by the government "dole"—a word that puzzled me except that it seemed to be a bad thing, like "welfare," that government gave to lazy men. "Dole," it seemed, was the enemy of "gumption."

All those words and cartoons had a strange effect. They formed my picture of the real world beyond Stoneham though they didn't describe the world I knew, yet I held the two conflicting images in my head at the same time.

If being a real American meant getting rich from working hard, all the people I knew best worked hard, but becoming comfortable financially did not seem to be the result.

I never knew any man who was less of an "idler" than my father. From four in the morning when he wrote his sermons, articles, and letters until late at night, he had endless "gumption." He worked in his garden to raise our own vegetables and fruit and raised chickens for our own eggs and meat. His Armenian parishioners were scattered all over Boston and its suburbs, and in the years before the Board of Missions lent my father money to buy a secondhand car to reach them, my father did his rounds by trolley and bus and on foot. He saved money by doing almost all of the shopping to feed a family of nine for a week by going to the wholesale markets around Fanueil Hall in Boston. That meant taking two trolleys and a subway, combing the endless, noisy carts and meat wholesalers, haggling over prices and accumulating bargains. On the return he was heavily laden and at the end of the Stoneham trolley line had to walk up Elm Street hill half a mile. My father carried the loops of three packed shopping bags in each powerful hand while I, even as a teenager, had to struggle to carry only one. He helped my stepmother cook, tended his big garden, and did all the repairs and maintenance around the house. My father never threw away a bent nail, but straightened it with a hammer.

Part of the charm of our third-floor attic, a favorite place of mine, was its rich odors in winter, thanks to my father's money-saving: he grew his own spices and in the fall spread them to dry on newspapers in the attic. We also stored the large crop from our two apple trees in the attic after the first frost (needed to give Baldwin apples their best taste). My father and stepmother, a couple of my sisters, and I tore newspapers into squares to wrap each apple and filled the two barrels that supplied us until January. My father never was "on the dole."

My grandparents worked just as hard. When my oldest sister, Tirzah, and I spent the summer of 1929 with them in Rochester, New York, the two of them, without help, were running two grocery stores. We lived in the tiny apartment behind the store my grandmother ran, and Grandpa Kalayjian did all the wholesale shopping and running of the other store. They, too, worked from dawn to nightfall. They weren't "on the dole."

Uncle Fred was always repairing cars and trucks, or driving the big eighteen-wheeler longer hours than ICC rules permitted. When I was eight, a drunk driver ran into Uncle Fred's car and after the accident Aunt Anna needed serious plastic surgery on her face. The other man's insurance was going to pay the big hospital bills, but in 1929 the man's insurance company went bankrupt and Fred and Anna, stuck with the medical bills, lost their small cottage and forever afterward lived in tiny second-floor apartments.

They all seemed to have this thing, "gumption," and they were never on the "dole." But my father was forever in danger of our house being foreclosed, the Depression wiped out my grandparents, and Uncle Fred stayed ahead of the bill collectors after losing his house by taking on nighttime repair jobs. They never came remotely close to the world of the men playing billiards in the *National Geographic* ads.

A lot of people other than our family also seemed excluded from the visions of "real Americans" in the ads. In Boston the elevated train ran past Charlestown tenements where bedclothes were aired over windowsills and their owners leaned outward to escape the heat of the dark space inside.

»

In all my years in the Deep South, it was clear that if there was a self-righting mechanism in the business economy, it had missed African-Americans, who seemed only a half-step beyond slavery. Even most of the whites in the Deep South were poor by New England standards; they lived in shabby small cottages, satisfied to feel racially superior to the black people who came to cook, wash, and tend their children from before breakfast to after supper. Ironically, the notion of white superiority diverted the attention of the majority of Southern whites from their own poverty. After I began covering the civil rights movement in the South as a reporter, I realized that it did more to liberate poor whites more than it did poor blacks.

Maybe my paradoxical optimism was enforced because for most of my growing years Franklin Roosevelt was president, and he looked and sounded like the "real Americans" in the *Geographic* ads yet was confidently taking charge to make things better for the people who weren't in the ads. We listened to him on the radio and, while politics still struck no conscious chord in me, the president's personality did. The music I heard on the Atwater Kent radio when my father listened to the Democratic National Convention was the theme song, "Happy Days Are Here Again." When my father listened to the Republican

convention, the message was that happy days would come for everyone—including us—only if the government let business alone, ended
"ruinous taxes," and stopped "the dole."

》

I was never much interested in abstractions about politics and even
now am easily bored by them. But during the war I had periods in
which I did what a lot of people in the services did—read everything
in sight. Military life is full of the G.I.'s universal complaint: "Hurry
up and wait." Intense scheduled activity is interposed with long periods of idleness, and a hunger for new ideas was not easily satisfied.

One man in my navigating training squadron was a Marxist and another a philosophic anarchist. They were both friends and I constituted an audience of one for their running debate on how to achieve
the ideal society. The Marxist argued for a change controlled in some
vague way by the working class. The anarchist wanted some of us to
sign up for his postwar plan for a "new society" in the British Columbia woods, away from the devil he saw, the impure influences of modern cities. I found the two of them interesting but too theoretical for
me, some of the debate carried on in terms I didn't really understand.

After I began to get officer's pay plus fifty percent for hazardous
duty, one of my first splurges was to order a set of the *Encyclopedia
Britannica*. Any arrival of a package of books still fills me with antici-
pation, like mental CARE packages. But none have I greeted with
such delight as the two heavy boxes of twenty-four volumes from Chicago delivered to the tiny cottage on Lee Avenue in Monroe.

In the long flyless days of winter's low clouds and storms in Louisiana, I read my *Britannica* articles from aeroplanes to X-rays. It was like
being hungry in a fabulous cafeteria. I found myself stopping to read
whatever was on the pages in front of me.

Listening to my utopian political friends I heard terms and ideas I
didn't understand, so Marx was among the subjects I looked up.
"Marx" led me to "Economics," but that was as dense to me as Marx.
Much later I read books by other people, like John Kenneth Galbraith
and others I now recognize as middle-of-the-road or liberal econo-

mists who write in my brand of English. And the more I read, the more difficult it was for me to hold the opinions from my father's free magazines in equal regard or to reconcile them with what I saw and experienced on my own. After a time I learned, to my intense surprise, that the Depression in which I grew up was nothing new in history. Before there was ever an income tax or government "meddling" in business or the "dole," the country had suffered regular recessions and terrible depressions about every four years. People died of hunger and disease; many had rebelled, including factory and mine workers who had gone on strike and been shot down by the owners' private police or tax-paid state militia.

How could it be that American families starved and went homeless when business ran the economy and government wasn't "meddling"? Why did all this happen long before there was an income or other "ruinous" tax, or a government "dole"?

A large part of the answer is the failure of the news to tell us.

After the war, it took a few years for me to appreciate fully the power of the mass media to create a world that I—and the audience —could not see on our own. What we experienced in our own lives and saw with our own eyes, and even some of what we thought in our own heads, could be made to seem meaningless or dumb or even un-American by the news and advertisements.

Much too slowly, what I saw and read as a reporter told me that the self-righting mechanism I had once believed in was too simple-minded. If it worked at all, it took too long for too many people. Our modern ghettos are only one demonstration of what appears to be too true: when it comes to the welfare of the country and their own long-term interests, the business community is full of slow learners.

Reginald, a neighbor in Providence, added to my doubt about the ability of businesspeople to handle things "without government meddling." Reginald had been a department store executive for one of the largest retail outlets in New York. He and I spent time needling each other by trading sins of journalists and businessmen. I thought he was too harsh on reporters, but he was brutal on his own former colleagues in business. He had taken early retirement in disgust.

"You guys gripe about big business, but what a lot of you journalists don't understand is that most of those big shots are the dumbest bastards imaginable when it comes to the big picture."

He kept blaming me and all journalists: "You guys never ask the business executives the right questions. If you did, you'd find that most of them can't look beyond their own noses."

In the 1980s, thirty years later, I remembered Reggie's accusation that journalists don't ask the right questions when, like millions of other Americans, I began walking daily through painful gauntlets of homeless men, women, and children holding out paper cups, begging for money.

Newspapers and television had lots of stories about the homeless. Most of the news was sympathetic about some heart-rending case. But I kept waiting year after year for our best newspaper or broadcast journalists to ask Reggie's right question and highlight the answers: "Why, in the midst of this wonderful prosperity of the 1980s do we have for the first time since the Great Depression, growing numbers of men, women, and children living in the streets?"

There were plausible, factual answers but they remained unasked, or at least hidden, in the news, like the 1980s reduction in annual subsidized housing from two hundred thousand units a year to seventeen thousand. Or that by 1987 the richest one percent of families had increased their income by seventy-four percent, while the income of the poorest one percent had dropped by eleven percent.

The regular news also seems to shun models of problem-solving that might cast doubt on the conventional wisdom of not meddling with private enterprise.

The news every day tries to explain variations in the stock market and lets economists, brokers, and assorted gurus, and even journalists, speculate on their probable causes and cures. Whole sections of newspapers and entire broadcast programs are devoted to possibilities for a quick killing or a safe bet on Wall Street. That is, in our definition, good, respectable, professional news. But there is no speculation or broad spectrum of opinion offered about the causes and cures of unemployment, homelessness, and the continued long-term poverty of millions of Americans who are filled with "gumption" and are neither "idlers" nor dependent on the "dole." These are spasmodic, presented only on dramatic occasions.

In 1989, 327 economists issued a public statement, and Nobel Laureate economist James Tobin testified publicly in Congress, that the country urgently needed to spend money on the public infrastructure—repairing schools, roads, bridges—and to allocate more money for children's education and health. The repairs were necessary but they would also provide needed jobs and housing, which would be the only permanent way to increase the tax base. When I searched the standard news data banks, I found only brief and indirect references to Tobin's testimony in the back pages of two newspapers.

If those answers had been given half the airtime and front-page headlines the ups and downs of the Dow Jones Industrial Average receive, they might have cast doubt on the standard dogmas that favor corporate life.

Instead of asking "why the homeless now and not before?" our main news in the 1980s was full of speeches and headlines about politicians and economists singing the familiar hymns: "get government off the back of business" and "taxes will hurt business and cost jobs," as though both were immutable natural laws that only fools would question.

There is another mantra in the news that leaves the country stumbling blindly into failures in public policy: private enterprise is inherently more efficient and effective at all tasks in society and tax-supported public services are inherently inefficient and unintelligent.

Like most other reporters, I have spent hours reporting on the sins and omissions of municipal state, and federal agencies. Like others, I have been praised by editors for scoring little victories like finding the public works commissioner's nephew on a summer paving project. Most newsstaffs spend a lot of time on that kind of fearless investigation. But reporters are not often assigned to be as diligent and persistent in looking for examples of wasteful, dumb, and dangerous greed in private industry. Those stories get into the news only when there is a criminal indictment or a multimillion dollar lawsuit.

Most daily news about business reports successes in corporate ventures, raising to high public visibility those said to be responsible. There is no daily section in the newspaper or program on television on how every day there are clever and effective school projects and public agencies that daily solve interesting and important public problems.

The interest of the news in public agencies mainly is in what is wrong, which is necessary, but the imbalance has made it difficult to get public support for public services that private enterprise cannot or will not provide on terms that society needs.

Or if there is a flaw in a policy favoring business, an editor's standard excuse for not running a story is "Too complicated. No one's interested." A memo suggesting such a story may go back to the reporter with the editor's shorthand: "MEGO" for "My Eyes Glaze Over." Megos tend to go on stories with lots of numbers—except for stories concerned with the health of the stock market and business life in general.

But in the mid-1980s, two reporters for the *Philadelphia Inquirer* proved that if the facts and figures go to the heart of what people struggle with daily, and if they explain what has been worrisome but mysterious, the audience will demand more. Donald Barlett and James Steele actually read the 1986 "tax reform" bill, fine print and all, that was passed with the announcement that it would tax the rich more and relieve the burden on the working class and the working poor. The *Inquirer* ran the Barlett and Steele series for days, seventy-five thousand words in a series full of statistics and graphs. It showed that the tax bill did the opposite of what it claimed. It gave the richest million families a tax cut of $84 billion and created a deficit of $160 billion.

The paper received four hundred thousand requests for copies and had to call the police to keep order in the lobby among people trying to buy copies of the articles. The reporters wrote a book, *America: What Went Wrong*, that became a best-seller.

Even the *Washington Post*, more willing than most to run a story that might irritate business, reflects the assumption that business leaders are more legitimate sources than their critics. Once at the afternoon conference when editors propose stories for Page One play, I offered a Ralph Nader study that exposed embarrassing actions by industry, and Executive Editor Ben Bradlee sighed, "Jesus, Nader again?" Neither there nor in the many news conferences I have attended as a guest have I ever heard an editor say something like, "Ford Motor Company again?"

There is no conspiracy among the men and women who govern the news business to protect private enterprise at the expense of public agencies, but there is something harder to combat—shared values. Stories of individual corporations in trouble do appear among the waves of positive corporate news. Bradlee did run the Nader study on Page One. But the imbalance day after day and decade after decade leaves the public's picture badly distorted.

>>

I wish I could say that mean, old Sherman Bowles was an exception in his one-sided treatment of taxes in the news, but year after year on better papers with more sophisticated owners, when it comes to the subject of taxes, the usual news practices seem to be suspended. Taxes that unfairly burden middle-class and poor families for the benefit of corporations and the wealthy, provoke little comment or emphasis in the news.

I wish I could say that when the Night City Editor tore up any of my stories that might put Bowles's properties in a poor light that I quit in moral outrage. I was too excited doing the stories that were acceptable. I just assumed that the torn-up and unassigned stories were part of "journalism" and I accepted it the way most journalists today tend to accept whatever happens to be the news policy in their newspapers and broadcast stations. More important, the public tends to accept what standard journalism deems important or unimportant.

I no longer see the media's treatment of taxes as either quirky or inevitable. It is a reportorial sin of our standard newspaper and television news. When there is a popular "tax revolt" it comes most often from the bottom up, from angry individuals, not exposés in the news.

The way Congress and White Houses have pushed taxes downward is like Uncle Fred's story of the Cambridge cop who found a dead horse on Massachusetts Avenue but dragged it to Main Street because the cop couldn't spell "Massachusetts." Politicians drag and push taxes to someone else's street. Whenever possible, federal taxes are pushed onto the states, and the states push them down to counties and cities. There, stuck with only limited tax possibilities, the end of the line becomes sales taxes, which are grossly unfair to working people, and property taxes, which, like sales taxes, usually get so onerous that property owners use their superior political cohesion to rebel.

That game is seldom made clear in the news, as I rediscovered when I became a California resident. The hottest political and media phenomenon that year was Proposition 13 because California, with all its tradition for innovation and progressive politics, was not immune from the national tax game. Maximum avoidance of the income tax had cascaded the burden downward to sales taxes and property taxes. People who spend the greatest part of their disposable income on sales taxes are the poor, the working poor and the nonaffluent who have the least political power over legislation. But property owners of both residential and commercial buildings do have the sophistication and power to protect themselves, and in California, property owners rebelled.

"Prop 13" would drastically cut back property taxes. The crucial question was, if it passed, how would cities and the state pay for the education and other services taxpayers wanted. The pro–Prop 13 forces said it would not hurt services because it would only "cut the fat." Opponents said there was not that much "fat" and basic services would suffer.

Almost as a conditioned reflex, the news media of the state favored the arguments of the forces that would protect corporations and let everyone else take the consequences.

Recently, with the help of researchers Peter Leonard and Michael Levy, I looked at news treatment of Proposition 13 when it was on the ballot in 1978: The front pages of the ten largest papers in the state—a third of all state circulation and the basis for most television newscasts—did not produce an honest or balanced picture for the voters.

We found that in the two weeks before the vote, front pages and headlines were dominated by the backers of Proposition 13 and their assertion that the tax cut would simply "cut the fat" in government without cutting services. Opponents who argued that Proposition 13 was so radical, and the demand for public services so pressing, that there was no way to avoid crippling public services like schools and police and fire protection were mentioned only in the back pages.

The *Los Angeles Times*, for example, the largest paper in the state, had Page One headlines and stories on the issue for a number of days in the two weeks before the vote, all on news and speeches by those who favored "Prop 13." No front page story headlined opponents' arguments or speeches.

But two weeks after the proposition passed by a large margin, the same front pages reported—based on the same information that was available before the election—that Proposition 13 would require drastic cuts in schools, police and fire protection, and other services because agency heads said their new budgets simply would not support continuation of the same level of activity.

One post-election front page headline in the *Times* was curious. It was on a story of the drastic cuts coming in public services: "Voters Didn't Believe Warnings." The paper's readers might have asked, "What warnings?"

Other leading papers either did not bother with front page reporting on the coming vote or they used one or two stories that highlighted arguments by backers of the proposition.

The effect on California was not so different from the impact on the whole country of a larger imbalance of the tax system. After Proposition 13, California schools, which had been among the best in the country, quickly plunged to among the worst. The state and cities lost $200 billion in revenues, and since then many cities and school systems have lived on the brink of bankruptcy. Neighborhoods, schools, and housing for lower income families went into a rapidly accelerating downward spiral.

Sixteen years later, a Page One headline of the *San Francisco Chronicle* quoted Wall Street:

CREDIT RATERS SAY PROP 13
AT ROOT OF STATE'S WOES

And the year California's famous higher education system had its first large budget cut despite a growing population, the proposed state budget increased prison budgets by 9.8 percent.

I was no longer working for the daily news, but it had not been the finest hour in the profession I had just left. But neither was the tilt to favor business very different from the unbalanced journalism I found as a cub reporter.

## CHAPTER 13

## I Discover I Have a Union Problem

I t took a week before the thought dawned on me that the City Editor wasn't absent-minded. I was being punished.

Every morning I had told the City Editor I needed a story to do, but he hadn't assigned me anything. The *Providence Journal-Bulletin* newsroom was constantly busy and the City Editor could always use an unassigned reporter. My idleness had lasted too long to be an oversight. I was in the official deep freeze.

My punishment in 1954 was for an offense close to unforgivable on any daily paper then and to this day. I had joined with other reporters in trying to bring the reporters' union into the newsroom. I knew that all newspapers abhor unions but I didn't think *my* paper would go this far.

In Providence, as I sat idle for weeks, it became clear that the management hoped I would quit. If I did that, my leaving would circumvent federal laws that make it illegal for a company to fire an employee whose only offense is trying to organize a union.

I was about to learn the peculiar pain that comes to a reporter suddenly frozen out of newsroom activity. In the special culture of a news staff, every individual task is part of a choreography as synchronized as clockwork; but, unlike clockwork, each man and woman does something individualistic, usually complicated and sometimes creative, and each task is different from what was done the day before. Yet, with all this unpredictability and variation, it all must come together at a precise moment, what newspeople ironically call "the daily miracle," when all the individual contributions come together at the split second the newscast goes on the air or the presses start to feed the fleet of trucks waiting at the press room platform.

The daily miracle requires a traditional decorum in the newsroom. It is what produces much of journalism's occupational humor and the surface of mutual respect between superiors and subordinates. Though pressure and inner tensions are constant, whatever disagreements and explosions occur along the way, the same deadlines must be met again among the same people, edition after edition, day after day. The quiet, lubricated synchronization of diverse tasks by diverse personalities can be repeated without fail only if arguments appear to be forgotten after each deadline. For that to happen, congenial relationships must be restored daily between editors and reporters.

But suddenly, I was frozen out of the newsroom decorum and clockwork. As a union-minded reporter, I was being treated by my editors with unchanging coldness. It was shocking. Life at "work" became painful. It was worse than being called in and told, "You're fired." I suppose the paper's law firm had warned them not to fire me but to make life for me so miserable that I would quit voluntarily and be a warning to other reporters harboring thoughts of joining the union.

The sudden change could not have been more dramatic. Up to then, I had been favored in ways most journalists envy. I had wonderful assignments. More often than other reporters I had periodic freedom to research and write national stories in depth and detail. I was encouraged to do long series, like a study of the wreckage Senator Joseph McCarthy was leaving in his wake, or a series on the shoddy journalism of some of the country's leading commentators. After I won a national prize, the paper took out a full page ad in the trade magazine *Editor & Publisher*, with my photograph and the headline, "We're Proud of Ben Bagdikian, but Not Surprised." A fellow reporter had said to me, "I could get all those prizes if I had your assignments. You're the fair-haired boy around here."

Not long before, I had been taken for a literal "walk in the woods" at the summer place of one of the owners, who told me that if I would start up the ladder on the editing side that I could go "to the top." I was flattered and thanked him, but said I enjoyed reporting too much to leave it for editing.

Reporters taken out of the daily routine to do special series do not always warm the hearts of city editors who resent superiors "stealing" one of their reporters. But I stayed in the City Editor's good graces because between the special series I liked the relief of daily stories—with their hourly unpredictability and gratifyingly quick appearance in the paper.

I also liked doing what made most other reporters groan, like being the "gate" man, the reporter who talks to the extraordinary variety of people who come to a newsroom with "an important story." Few have important stories and some are delusional, like the man who came in one day to reveal a conspiracy against him by the United States Patent Office, which would not issue a patent on the man's "revolutionary invention," an ungainly set of wheels, gears, and weights that he said was the world's first perpetual motion machine but which, unfortunately, had to be plugged into an electrical outlet.

Another daily assignment I never tired of that others regarded as suitable only for a cub reporter was covering Sixth District Court, the lowest-level police court where the city's unlucky, unhinged, and unwanted appeared. It was a daily parade most citizens never see. With few exceptions, defendants were represented by the city's laziest lawyers, like one incompetent attorney who pleaded his man innocent of homicide but kept referring to "my client, the murderer." Arrested prostitutes were routinely represented by a prominent state politician who, before approaching the bench, passed in front of the women lined up at the back of the court, and murmured, "Now girls, that will be twenty-five dollars each." The women would dutifully hand over their meticulously prepared packet of twenty-five dollars and were then lectured by the judge to go home and help their mothers.

But whether doing special or routine daily assignments, I had the same problem that all the other reporters had, low pay and negligible benefits. The *Journal* and *Bulletin*, for the times, had high news standards (except for its sacred cows, like Brown University, Republicans, and the management side of all labor disputes). But their depressed pay and lack of benefits for reporters forced me to augment my salary with outside free-lance work for national magazines, including assignments in southern New England for *Time* and *Life*. Nevertheless, the paper's work was so interesting that when, after a year, *Time* offered me an editing job in New York at almost three times my Providence salary, I turned it down. I didn't like *Time*'s national politics, and I didn't want to leave reporting for an inside job editing. But I turned down the offer with guilt about my family's finances.

The low salaries for reporters contrasted with the higher pay and better health, pension, and vacation benefits for production workers at the *Journal* and *Bulletin*. They had a union and we did not. The message could not have been more clear.

The management fought relentlessly to keep out the reporters' union, The Newspaper Guild. Every reporter was told the standard management horror stories—the union would end quality reporting because the union favored "hacks," there would be red tape and corrupt bureaucracy, it would end pay rewards for "the best reporters" because everyone would be stuck with the same pay as the "drones and deadwood." Victory by the union would mean layoffs, and when layoffs came, the management would remember who had been a "reliable" worker.

The management was shrewd in playing on what it knew about each of us. For some people in the newsroom, the idea of joining a union was associated with the factory work of their fathers, whose social status the sons were trying to escape. Those reporters were asked if they wanted to be "like the CIO strikers at the textile mills?" The Newspaper Guild is an affiliate of the AFL-CIO. One editor told a colleague, "You don't want to be like those slobs in the back room," the "back room" referring to the composing room full of skilled linotype operators.

I met socially with the top editors from time to time and they, too, hinted that if the union won, their jobs might be jeopardized because a successful union drive would be cited as evidence that the editors lacked "staff loyalty." They were telling me I would be disloyal to them.

At the time, I hated going idle for weeks. I would have preferred the more common form of punishment in which the editor suddenly assigns the offending reporter to a beat like night police. On night police, the reporter sits alone at a desk all night and into the early morning hours calling every law enforcement agency in the region for any news of crimes or arrests. At least it's an activity.

Reporters undergoing The Treatment usually hang on for the same reasons I did back in the 1950s. Their families can't afford to go without a period of pay. Or they fear that if they quit and apply for another newspaper job, they will be followed by the label "union agitator," and most newspapers do not knowingly hire such reporters. Today, some big chains even give prospective reporters hours-long personality tests to see, among other things, if the would-be reporter is a "team player" who will accept corporate rules and resist unions. Some even ask applying reporters outright what they think about unions.

But I also hung on because I was angry. I resented approval being turned off like an electric switch. I knew that my editorial superiors were under pressure to follow the company's anti-union techniques, but they had their decision to make and I had mine.

In Providence, the union lost that first election badly, 89 to 127. But most of the bad things management had said the union would do—like inflate the bureaucracy and promote obedient hacks—the triumphant company did on its own by way of showing who was boss, and five years later the union won easily.

And like so many other unearned breaks in my life, my punishment resulted in one of the best turns in my career. In my enforced idleness, I had time to read all the out-of-town papers from cover to cover, including the still lively *New York Herald-Tribune*. One day, on the bottom of an inside page, a three-paragraph story in the *Trib* announced that applications were being accepted for Ogden Reid Fellowships designed to let a mid-career journalist spend a year abroad.

I applied for the fellowship and received it. In March of 1956, while I was still in the newsroom deep freeze, there came in the mail a check for $5,000 made out to me. I had never seen a check with that many zeros next to my name. Betty and I looked at it as though it were an artifact from outer space. We lost little time in driving along with

Chris, then eleven, and Eric, four, to the Boston offices of the French Line, where we booked passage on the Ile de France, cabin class, with an open return.

When I told the paper that I was going to Europe for a year, the attitude of management changed. I was suddenly being spoken to. Why didn't I become their (low cost) foreign correspondent: they would pay me $15 for every story that they printed. (No expenses. After all, I had a fellowship.) During the year in Western Europe and the Middle East I wrote a lot of serious pieces, family adventure stories, and articles for magazines to stretch out the $5,000.

I never saw the results of what I mailed or cabled to the paper and had no direct knowledge how many $15 fees had been deposited in my bank account. So periodically I wrote to Bill Morrison, an Irish import who was vice president of the Rhode Island Hospital Trust Company Bank, a novelty in a hierarchy usually cluttered with relatives of the bank owners. Bill and I had struck up a friendship exchanging anthropological notes on heirs of old Yankee families and the banks they ran. During my European stay I would drop Bill a postcard from, say, Athens, asking "How much longer do I have?" and he'd write to my scheduled mail drop in, perhaps, Cairo, with messages like, "Don't worry." But after fourteen months, his message was in a cable: "Time to come home." The $15 deposits were running out.

I came back a year later not only rehabilitated in the eyes of the *Providence Journal*, but, to my puzzlement, with job offers from four other papers waiting for me at American Express in Paris. Years later, I discovered that I had been one of four finalists for the Pulitzer Prize in foreign reporting, and the offers came from editors who had sat on the Pulitzer juries and read my stories. In Providence I had great assignments again.

I was lucky that my union episode had a happy ending.

Today there is finally something like proper professional pay for reporters on papers in the largest cities or where they have newsroom unions. But for the ninety percent of papers outside the major cities and those without a newsroom union, reporters' pay is still appallingly low, and hostility to unions still appallingly high.

The low salary of contemporary reporters has a special irony. In

Providence, as in other newspaper cities, our strongest potential allies had been the powerful union of linotype workers. Papers needed the men with specialized skills to operate the masses of great, ungainly, clanking contraptions full of wheels, chains, pulleys, moving arms, and the heated hellpots that squirted the hot metal that turned reporters' typed words on paper into raised letters in metal. Often, a linotype operator would catch a grammatical or historical error missed by editors. Under duress, a struck paper could replace reporters with supervisors cutting and pasting together wire service stories that came from afar on teletype machines. The resulting papers would be thin on local news, but they could maintain their publishing schedule if reporters went on strike. But if the big linotype machines fell silent, the paper had to shut down.

By the 1960s, smaller papers with their limited press runs and small number of pages were able to use new printing processes and computers. It was harder to convert the largest papers. Even in the 1970s, when I was at the *Washington Post*, we, like other large dailies, still used typewriters and had masses of the complicated linotype machines in the factory part of the plant. But several years later, even the largest papers, including the *Post*, had converted to computers, and there began to appear in the lobbies of some newspaper buildings a cleaned-up, polished linotype machine as an exhibit of "the romantic past," for which newspaper lore has an irresistible impulse.

But there has been nothing romantic in the irony for all the reporters I know in the nonunion and smaller newspapers. Now that they all use computers, their keystrokes are also setting type, and the old arrays of linotype machines and their unionized operators have been replaced by men and women pasting reporters' laser-printed stories in column form into full pages easily made into printing plates. Gone is the strongest single ally of reporters fighting for better pay and benefits. The irony is deepened because the conversion of reporters' keystrokes gave the newspaper industry an unprecedented increase in profits and simultaneously made it easier for companies to break unions by refusing to renew contracts or to prevent their election in the first place. Now that the business is dominated by big chains of papers, one company's strike-bound paper can be temporarily staffed by workers (and profits) from a different nonunion paper owned by the same corporation.

Most news reporters in the country have suffered the consequences. When I left news work to teach journalism at the University of California at Berkeley, I found myself sending trained journalism graduates into underpaid and insecure jobs at a time when even small papers were making higher-than-ever profits. A 1990 Michigan State University survey found the starting pay for journalism graduates second from the bottom of twenty-eight categories of jobs for university graduates.

Where reporters' unions already existed, the management techniques turned brutal. In 1984, old friends at the *Washington Post* sent me a memorandum from the paper's executive in charge of labor relations. The memo, intended for supervisors and editors, was a guide for punishing union-minded reporters and employees taking union leadership. It read, in part: "The only discipline which will ever work . . . that . . . leads to self-discipline . . . is to demean the employee, in his eyes, in the eyes of his family, and the eyes of his fellow employees— make the demeaning stick with him, by putting the reprimand in writing and mailing it to his home with copies to the union and to the chapel chairman."

(Newspaper production workers in the nineteenth century, before protective labor laws, avoided retaliation by using prayer meetings as a cover for discussing unionism; their local union units are still called "chapels.")

When a delegation of reporters protested, the company refused to repudiate the memo. In the early 1970s I would have considered the existence of the 1984 *Post* memorandum as unthinkable. But by 1984 it had become thinkable.

The unchanging depression of reporters' pay made me break a rule I had stuck to for most of my career—to steer clear of accepting government and other kinds of commitments that would put me on both sides of the reporting transaction.

A newspaper publisher in New Hampshire, with the sympathy of publishers nationally, was trying to exempt reporters from the Wages and Hours Law that provides minimal standard work rules, including compensation or compensatory time off for overtime work. The news-paper claimed that since modern reporters called themselves "profes-sionals" they should be exempted from the Wages and Hours Law and should instead be treated like tenured professors and independent art-ists. The Department of Labor asked me to testify in favor of keeping reporters covered by the law. I was no longer a reporter for newspa-pers and I agreed.

Modern reporters do, of course, call themselves professionals but they do not have tenure; promotion, demotion, and assignments are governed by management, unlike independent artists' work. It was hard for me to believe the publisher's arguments, given papers' high profits and professional reporters' scandalously low pay outside the big cities at a time when managements demand that even starting re-porters have not only college degrees but also prior news internships and published stories to prove their competence and talent. Further-more, reporters' devotion to their stories, to meeting deadlines, and to handling news emergencies for their papers is traditional and close to universal. If their paper needs them, reporters don't quit at the end of a day when their story is still unfolding. Most consider it a professional obligation to drop vacations or family dinners if the paper calls to say they are needed in an emergency.

Furthermore, the Department of Labor had always been lax with newspapers, leaving overtime or compensatory time off up to the most informal verbal discretion of the management. "Dave," I would say at the *Post* to a reporter who worked three hours after usual quitting time, missing his family dinner or seeing his children into bed, "Why don't you come in late on Saturday?" And if Dave said he'd rather take off half a day on Friday, if his presence on Friday was not crucial, I'd agree. It was nothing unusual. It happens that way on most papers with most editors. If anything, editors have a way of forgetting report-ers' extra hours. Now in the Department of Labor case, management wanted legal freedom to deny reporters any overtime compensation or compensatory time off. This was too much and I agreed to testify, but I refused to accept any compensation.

The case was tried in New Hampshire. I am happy that in 1990, ap-pellate courts upheld the victory for the Department of Labor in pro-

viding at least minimal protection for tens of thousands of news reporters in places without other defenses against cavalier treatment by
employers.

>>

There is an unhappy connection between news companies' hostility
to unions and the way they treat unions and ordinary nonunion wage
workers in the country. It remains one of the unadmirable characteristics in our standard news.

Unbalanced treatment of work life in the news is not a recent development; it is now simply more sophisticated or, like the 1984 *Post*
memo, more arrogant.

In my father's daily papers in the 1930s, the management was always the hero and the workers or their unions the villains and the slobs
in worker-management conflicts. When Walter Reuther was organizing the CIO in the auto plants, General Motors argued that it was
ridiculous to ask for higher pay for assembly line work that had become a series of simple, boring tasks. I remember Reuther being
quoted, "Then you shall pay them for their boredom." My father's
*Boston Traveler* ran an editorial cartoon showing an auto worker with
money overflowing his pockets, pushing a simple handle up and down
as he read a newspaper. But by then, my own assembly line experience
had left me entirely sympathetic to the factory worker.

One high school vacation I had a job in a tiny back alley shop near
the Stoneham Fire Department. For hours at a time, I sat at a simple
machine putting five lurid-colored celluloid plastic "petals" on a
grommet, then pushing down on a foot pedal to rivet the petals in
place. I was paid by the hundred. To make any money, I had to make
at least a dozen a minute without interruption. One day going home
from work, a girl in my high school class waved from across the street
and called, "Hi, Ben." I had a secret passion for her and ordinarily
would have been overjoyed to cross the street to talk. But I could only
stop and stare. No words came to my mouth. All my reflexes were still
frozen in the hundreds of mechanical motions of grommet-on-spindle-
petals-on-grommet-push-down-on-pedal I had been doing for hours.

Later I saw Charlie Chaplin behaving the same way in *Modern*

*Times*, repeating his assembly line motions in public. And later still I could understand the incident with Marshall Jones.

Marshall was a popular pilot in our air-sea rescue squadron who got tired of sitting idly every day at Mather Field in Sacramento. It was near war's end, and day after day we'd report to the flight line for yet another dawn briefing on our trans-Pacific flight, always postponed until the next morning. We didn't know that in Washington they were getting ready to use a new "device" over Hiroshima.

Marshall Jones tired of the idleness and got a daytime job at a food canning plant in nearby Sacramento. He would come back after his day at the plant, wearing his combat ribbons from the Italian air campaign plus a newer badge: "Essential Civilian Worker." One night, when Cal, our pilot, asked, "What did you do for your country today, Marshall?" Marshall was unusually somber.

> Something funny happened on the line this afternoon. I'm the last inspector of the whole peaches before they go into the big cans of syrup. Just standing there staring at all those whole peaches coming down the assembly line for hours does funny things to you, and right before quitting time today I did something that just came out of nowhere. I grabbed a peach off the line, took a bite and put it back on the line, and before I could stop it, the peach with my teeth marks on it went into the can and the cover was stamped on and wrapped with the label. I should've told someone, but I didn't.

We all laughed but I thought I understood Marshall's impulse.

By this time I knew that assembly line workers were not like the one in the *Traveler* cartoon, but I also knew that most of the news seemed to regard them and most other wage workers with either disdain or indifference. By the 1980s, that same attitude was apparent when a new affliction struck, among others, workers in the news industry itself.

When electric typewriters and then computers made their way onto business desks, including those of reporters and editors, certain kinds of workers began to have tingling and then paralysis in their hands. Some had to stop working. Computers' easy keyboards permitted long continuous hours of typing while hardly moving one's arms or changing the position of one's wrists and hands. That creates unrelieved stress on the tendons and nerves involved in making the same unvarying movements for hours, day after day. It became a standard medical diagnosis, Carpal Tunnel Syndrome or Repetitive Stress Injury; the overused tendons pass through a restricted "tunnel" in the wrist and become damaged as they swell against it. Carpal Tunnel Syndrome is now a common occupational hazard for supermarket cashiers, chicken pluckers, assembly line workers, data processors, and some kinds of surgeons, as well as many journalists.

The long history of the news industry's indifference to reporting general workplace dangers for workers made it easier to ignore the new worker safety problem in its own industry.

The problem grew in newsrooms all over the country, and some individual papers, like the *Los Angeles Times*, were quick to take the new epidemic seriously. But though the National Academy of Sciences had confirmed the growing incidences as early as 1983, the trade magazine of daily newspaper publishing quoted an industry leader as late as 1987, saying officially, "We know of no major problem in the newspaper industry."

I have Carpal Tunnel Syndrome creeping into my hands. In the 1970s and increasingly in the 1980s, I found myself being awakened at night by an irritating tingling in my arms and hands that would not go away. It became progressively worse until, in the mid-1980s, I went to a specialist who diagnosed it in two or three minutes and prescribed special exercises and night-time braces to slow down the evil.

My problem would undoubtedly have developed sooner if not for an object of religious devotion among newsroom nostalgists, the old reliable cast-iron workhorse Royal. Those typewriters relieved the tendons in the typing fingers because you had to interrupt typing to reach up and push the carriage return bar at the end of each line, then pull out the sheet of paper and stick in a new one as you completed each page: very old-fashioned and very therapeutic.

My earliest workhorse had been my father's ancient bilingual Hammond typewriter, averting any possibility of my developing early Carpal Tunnel Syndrome or, for that matter, becoming a true touch typist. The Hammond had a circular band of type on a wheel, each semicircle adjustable, one side English, the other side Armenian. When you pushed a letter key, it turned the dial to the proper letter, after which a tiny hammer in the back struck the intervening paper and ribbon against the letter. The machine, old and sticky, required a spearlike attack on each key, and after each keystroke, you waited for the print wheel to take its own sweet time to get back to neutral. I blamed the ancient Hammond for giving me a technique common to a lot of reporters, a ferocious combination of hunt-and-peck and touch typing that looks to outsiders like a manic organist out of control.

The sticky Hammond and the old typewriters were an unrecognized blessing. Once, when asked to do so, I calculated that so far in my life I had composed on typewriter and computer keyboards over fifteen million words, an appalling number. Perhaps Carpal Tunnel Syndrome is proper punishment. But the poor chicken pluckers are blameless innocents.

>>

Carpal Tunnel Syndrome quickly put white-collar professionals in the same distress as a lot of blue-collar workers. But the news seldom stresses worker issues, compared to daily concerns with issues affecting corporations, banks, and professional life.

A study of the three networks showed that in 1989, of 22,000 minutes of network news and public affairs programming, two percent was devoted to workers' issues and problems, like childcare, workplace safety and health, and the inadequacy of the minimum wage to keep full-time workers out of poverty. In the same period, the three networks spent more than twice as much time on the problems facing business.

Many corporations and their executives are found in violation of the law, but—except for "glamor" figures in business such as Donald Trump and Leona Helmsley—once the cases are reported the embarrassment is not repeated each time some unrelated development places them in the news. Few convictions of a corrupt union leader, however, seem ever to be forgotten by the news. In the years from 1950 to 1970, twenty-five percent of all network news and documentaries about unions was about corruption in one union, the Teamsters.

Strikes continue to be the main news about workers even though work stoppages that last more than one day have been dropping drastically in the last generation. There was an average of 340 strikes a year between 1965 to 1974, 172 a year from 1975 to 1984, and 46 a year from 1985 to 1992. But during all that time, in the news, strikes were the subject of fifty percent or more of all news of any kind about unions.

In 1984 there were only 62 work stoppages in the country, and as usual the vast majority of union contracts were renewed peacefully. But on CBS that year, there were 184 stories on strikes and 40 stories on peaceful contract negotiations without a work stoppage.

Even the language of labor-management news stories creates associations of aggression by unions and generosity by management. In news of contract negotiations, unions "demand" but companies "offer."

It is not surprising that one researcher at the University of Southern Illinois found that the pattern of news leads the public to associate phrases like "violent, socially unresponsive, elitist, undemocratic, and ridden with crime" with the word "union."

Unionists have reason to be bitter about the contrast between the sparse and largely negative news about American workers and generous positive treatment of American employers. The imbalance changes—if the workers and employers are far away. In 1989, for example, 1,700 members of the United Mine Workers in the United States went on strike for nine months over the withdrawal of benefits in mines in Pittston, Virginia. Over that period of time, the three major networks gave the event a total of twenty-three minutes of news coverage. At about the same time, miners in the Siberian coal mines also went on strike and the three networks devoted thirty-seven minutes to the Siberian strike. Both CBS and ABC dramatically depicted the bitterly degrading living and working conditions of the Siberian miners in contrast to the lavish comforts of their bosses. No union official could remember any American network ever reporting on American workers on strike for better working conditions, and simultaneously comparing their personal lives with those of their employers.

A century ago, the country had large papers that highlighted the problems of ordinary working people. Two of the late nineteenth century's most powerful chains, those of E. W. Scripps and the early

Hearst, fought in their news and editorials for the rights of working people and against their unfair treatment by big corporations and sweatshops.

More than a hundred years ago, a Scripps memo to his editors around the country reminded them: "I have only one principle and that is . . . to make it harder for the rich to grow richer and easier for the poor to keep from growing poorer." One of his editorials recommended, "Tax luxuries, inheritances, monopolies . . . the privileged corporations." Hearst in his early years campaigned regularly in his papers for the rights of unions.

But for the last seventy years there has been no such editorial or news selection policy on any standard daily news outlet, printed or broadcast. In one-newspaper cities one does not expect advocacy all over the front pages. But neither should there be hostility or indifference toward an important segment of the community.

≫

I was punished in the 1950s for joining a newsroom union; forty years later, the attitude of publishers had not changed. Neither had underpayment of reporters.

For about sixteen years I was part of the faculty at the Graduate School of Journalism in Berkeley, where we taught some of the brightest college graduates in the country in two graduate years of training in print and broadcast journalism. Meredith was one of the best students—talented, intellectually sharp, and a good reporter. In my ethics seminar I mostly used real cases of ethical dilemmas in the news, and each student independently had to come to a yes-or-no decision: when deadlines arrive in the news, there are no maybes. Meredith was notable for her ability to present a sharp set of lawyerly rationales on each side of an ethical news dilemma but still come to a reasonable decision.

In her reporting classes she had a talent for quickly identifying the significant news in a complex scene, for rapid fact gathering, and for good writing. When she received her Master's degree in journalism, she already had behind her four years of highest grades from one of the country's most demanding undergraduate colleges and two summers as an intern reporter on a California daily paper. She landed a job on a midwestern daily with a salary of $16,000. The salary aside, she loved her job.

Meredith telephoned from time to time to describe the great beat she had and the way her editor kept giving her terrific stories, but she found it hard to make ends meet on her salary. Then she discovered that some of the paper's pay and benefits were not in compliance with the state law. After failing to get a change, she and a number of other reporters had started to petition for a union contract. I had never told her or other students about my own experience joining the union. But now I warned her that her paper's management would not be happy. I wished her well.

Not long afterward, Meredith called from the Midwest to say that the NLRB was going to hold a union election at the paper, "But guess what? I've been put on night police."

## CHAPTER 14

# Wars and Society—Bottom Up or Top Down?

I had landed during an air raid blackout and was moving in total darkness up a narrow spiral staircase to the Ministry of Defense press office for my credentials. My right hand followed the iron rail upward while my left hand, groping for possible obstruction, came against the unmistakable form of a woman.

"I beg your pardon," I said.

"Perfectly all right, old chap," a cheery British accent said, "You're a Yank from the States. What paper?"

"The *Providence Journal* from Rhode Island."

"How quaint," said the lady descending the staircase as she and I passed chastely in the dark.

We were in Israel where I had just landed at the start of the 1956 Israeli-Egyptian War. I had been based in Rome during that year and was confronted with two big stories that broke at the same time, the Middle East War and the anti-Communist rebellion in Budapest.

From Rome I told editors in Providence that I wanted to go to Israel because I had been there a few months earlier and knew the territory and some of the people. I chose Israel instead of Egypt because in a war it's best to cover the winning side; winners have fewer reasons to lie and their communications to the outside remain more intact —and I was sure Israel would win. Israel had the best army in the Middle East and they had the backing of the West, including the British who had once controlled the region.

Immediately after my phone call with Providence, I received a call from our Rome embassy. It was the Deputy Chief of Mission, who said I should bring my passport down to be stamped not valid for travel to Israel. Our government was limiting all travel of Americans to the war zone.

"Even for correspondents?" I asked in disbelief.

"Sorry, old boy, even for correspondents."

I said, "Thanks for the call," and started packing. Before rushing to the airport, I had to face the fact that I didn't have enough U.S. dollars in hand to finance what a correspondent might need in the unpredictable circumstances of a war zone, where cold American cash could be important. I had told Providence that they would have to pay my expenses on this story and take out a special life-insurance policy on me. But I had to leave long before any money wire from Providence could arrive.

At a parents' meeting of the International School of Rome where both Chris and Eric were enrolled, I had met a young Italian couple who ran a small bank. I made a quick call.

"Elaine, I have an assignment and I need a thousand dollars right away."

"Of course," she said. "Come on down."

"I can give you a check but there isn't enough money in my account in the States to cover the check right away."

"Stop worrying," Elaine said cheerily. "Come down and get your money."

On the way to the airport, with Betty and the kids crammed into the cab, I stopped to give Elaine my worthless check, picked up the money, and headed for the plane. At the gate, Betty disappeared momentarily and came back with something in a paper bag. It was a bottle of Scotch—it's not easy to get my favorite Kentucky bourbon in Italy. The Scotch would end up being a godsend out in the Sinai Desert.

During the Israeli-Egyptian war, I learned all over again what I had learned in the United States and in most of my reporting life: there are real advantages to looking at the world from the bottom up, compared with looking at it solely as a country's leaders see it, from the top.

Most of the best-known correspondents from major news organizations are hard-working and skilled, but almost by the nature of their work, they need to report the overall scene and their quickest source is top political and military leaders. Too often it stops there. Each hour or day there has to be a new dispatch or update, which means correspondents spend their time at the door of leaders whose view of reality is secondhand and one-dimensional. Since many reporters and their editors measure their own status by the status of the people they cover, most journalists aspire to cover presidents, prime ministers, and kings. It then becomes easy to assume that the job of reporting is complete once the view from the top is recorded, but top leaders often do not know the whole truth, or if they do, seldom disclose all of it.

"The view from the bottom" has its own pitfalls. It requires extensive reporting and homework as well as meetings with leaders. Journalism has an ignoble tradition of phony views from the bottom, as in the caricature of the foreign correspondent new to a country who talks only to his cab driver from the airport and immediately files a story, "The people of Transylvania are restless tonight. . . ."

Covering the war also confirmed that sometimes news celebrities have journalistic feet of clay. In Tel Aviv, as elsewhere, many celebrity journalists spent most of their time at the best bar of the best hotel, feeding off the crumbs of other reporters after the daily official briefing. For some, their first move on arrival was to visit the best tailor in town to be custom-fitted for a natty, military-looking khaki costume. They then pursued an unvarying triangular daily circuit: the official briefing, a visit to their typewriters (for a novelistic first-person account based solely on the briefing), and the bar of the Hotel Dan.

And not all the correspondents had their minds focused on the war.

One man from the London bureau of a major wire service was an amiable fellow who made most of his money writing popular songs and lyrics. Once as we were walking away from a military briefing on the outskirts of the desert, I saw a fighter plane with smoke pouring out of one of the engines. I poked him.

"Bob, look! I think there's a plane going down."

But the man was distracted, staring into the middle distance, and he held up his hand to hold me at bay. He was not to be disturbed from his work by a mere fighter plane in trouble.

"Hold it, I think I've got it."

He nodded his head and jounced his body rhythmically:

"A smile is just a frown—doo-dah-de-dah-turned upside down! —dah-dah-de-day."

Later in the press room, another man soon to be famous for historic novels complained about his "stupid" bosses in New York. He had been sent to cover the war for an American syndicate. At the moment, he was a "color man" for his syndicate, which meant he was supposed to produce vivid background pieces and human interest stories as a backdrop to the main events, even after the fighting was over. I was in the press room one day as he typed his second cable to New York. It began:

"The Bedouin in their black tents continue to wander through the deserts ignoring war and turmoil of the great nations . . ."

His phone rang, he listened and said, "Ok, ok."

He turned to me, "The idiots in New York want more color." And he turned to the sheet in his typewriter and in pencil inserted a few words so that the story now began:

"The *colorful* Bedouin in their *fabulous* black tents. . . ."

Such men had their reportorial satisfactions, but us small-fry corre-spondents had our own satisfactions and excitement usually denied the men from the majors.

At the first military briefing in Tel Aviv the Army spokesman was giving the official account for the day with simplistic flip charts and I'm afraid my face showed impatience. Sitting across from me, also bored, was a tall, thin, Israeli photographer who caught my expression and smiled. That's how I met Beno Rothenberg.

We agreed to work together. Beno had a jeep, an Uzi submachine gun, a .45 revolver, and an oversupply of chutzpah and ironic humor. Beno wanted me to carry his .45, but as a correspondent I didn't want to be armed, so he laid the weapon beside me and said, "If we get ambushed on the road at night, we both start shooting and yelling—we have to sound like a regiment to scare them off."

He also knew Israel better than most Israelis because he had been the official photographer for some important archeological digs. Without him I would have had more trouble getting to significant places far from Tel Aviv, and I would never have been able to accompany tank crews a few miles from the Suez Canal while the British and French bombed Egyptian targets on the other side of the canal.

The first night we camped six miles from the Suez canal, near an Israeli tank outfit. The British and French had secretly planned the war with the Israelis and we could see them bombing Egypt along the canal. But I heard small arms fire somewhere on our side of the canal. I asked the young tank commander where it came from. He said, calmly, "Egyptians."

"Is there a battle near here?"

"Oh, no. They're out there by the hundreds, waiting to surrender."

"Why don't you take them prisoners?"

"We have just enough water for ourselves. There's not enough water for them, so we let them stay out there. We don't want them."

All through the desert I had seen bodies of dead Egyptian soldiers. That's when I felt I had to inspect them closely to see if they had died from wounds or from thirst. Most had bad wounds but some seemed simply to have dropped dead. None of the dead men were officers.

Later I interviewed an American lieutenant with the United Nations contingent who told me with visible contempt that at the first sign of hostilities, dozens of Egyptian officers had abandoned their men and had run to the U.N. compound where they removed their military uniforms and asked for protection.

Out in the desert, I was grateful for the large supply of oranges Beno brought to stave off thirst. And he became grateful for the bottle of Scotch in my small bag. When we had to sleep in the sand near the Canal, I was introduced to the shocking cold of the desert at night. Wrapped in a blanket abandoned by a fleeing Egyptian, I worried only briefly about military histories I had read in which retreating armies had deliberately left behind typhus-infected blankets.

In the night, we shivered so much we couldn't sleep, so out of my bag I took Betty's bottle of Scotch and, like a couple of winos, we put the bottle between us and took turns taking swigs and sleeping until the warmth wore off and the shivering woke us up again. The newly awakened man would reach over, take another swallow, and dig the bottle back into the sand upright for the other man when his alcohol wore off and he woke up shivering.

It was Beno who helped translate when I covered my only totally censored story. We ran across an Israeli Army encampment in the desert that looked in uncharacteristic disarray. Beno talked in Hebrew to a couple of soldiers. Still in shock, they wept as they described how they had just been strafed by their own planes and some of their men were killed or dying. As part of the three-country plan for the war, the French had sneaked in some pilots to fly unmarked French Mystère fighters, and the soldiers assumed it was "a Frenchie" who didn't recognize their markings on the ground. The story remained so well buried that it was missed by a well-known American military writer in a detailed history of the war.

The censor of the Ministry of Defense held back my story, but thereafter I was treated with elaborate consideration, confirming the old journalistic rule that the more you know the more you'll be told.

When I returned to the hotel from the desert, I was unshaven, dirty, greasy from looking into disabled tanks, and disheveled from having slept in my clothes. I was a surreal passenger in the elevator to my room in a luxury hotel, my only companion in the elevator an elderly American woman tourist who at first shrank from me. When I apologized in American English (not the British English heard in most of Israel), she realized I must be an American correspondent and asked me what was happening in the desert. I noticed that she was carrying a copy of the *Jerusalem Post* and remembered for the first time that while I had been out in the desert there had been a presidential election at home.

"I'll tell you," I told her, "if you'll tell me who is now the president of the United States."

She told me that Eisenhower had won the election but she left quickly without asking about the desert. She probably doubted the value of a correspondent who didn't know the name of his own president.

Journalistic little fish competing with the whales are not beyond guile. An old friend, Dick Dudman, from the *St. Louis Post-Dispatch*, also was covering the war and one night he motioned me to a corner of the hotel lobby for a conspiratorial conversation. The active fighting was all over, but now the news focused on what would happen between the Israelis and the thousands of Israeli-hating Palestinians in the captured refugee camps in the Sinai. There were rumors of a riot or rebellion in one of the distant camps. If true, did it mean that perhaps the Sinai violence was not yet over?

Dick told me he had overheard two correspondents, one from the *London Times* and the other from the *New York Herald-Tribune*, boasting to each other at the bar that they had made a deal with the Israeli Army to allow only one car to reach the troubled camp. The Army man had said they should be at the Defense motor pool for their exclusive car and driver at 6:00 A.M. the next morning.

Dick and I looked at each other happily and at 5:30 the next morning we presented ourselves to the officer at the motor pool gate, saying, "We're here for the car and driver."

There had been a serious disturbance at the camp. It had been controlled by the time we arrived, but we were able to get important interviews with Palestinians in the camp that illuminated both the refugee problems of the future and the illusions that years of isolation had permitted the camp Palestinians to harbor about Israel and the rest of the world. It was the only real story from the war zone that day.

A few days later I suffered one of the hazards every correspondent risks, but particularly one from a smaller paper. The United States had forced the British, French, and Israelis to stop their invasion. The United Nations would send forces to divide fighting troops in a war. Dick or I, I've forgotten which, had picked up quiet word that the Canadian general in charge of the new U.N. mission would be in Jerusalem that night at the American diplomatic mission building.

What was the U.N.'s plan? Would its troops go in armed? Had the general assurances from fighting units on both sides? How many and what nationality of troops would separate the forces at what location in the now-disputed territory? They were questions still unanswered in world news.

Dick and I hired a cab for a wild ride up to Jerusalem, where we entered the American mission and spotted the Canadian general at a bar across a large room from us. We started to walk across the floor but were held back as a blare of trumpets introduced a ceremony for the annual celebration of the founding of the U.S. Marine Corps. Marching between us and the general was a slow honor guard of Marines in full parade dress, followed by an embarrassed Marine holding a massive birthday cake covered with lit candles, the poor man moving with as much military dignity as he could manage while trying to march in step and simultaneously keep the candles from blowing out. The formation seemed endless, at least to us, each of us, I am sure, imagining our Sunday paper deadlines in the United States falling one by one with each verse of "From the halls of Montezuma to the shores of Tripoli . . ."

Dick and I could see that the Canadian, not terribly interested, killed the time with a few drinks. By the time we finally crossed over, we had a quite talkative general who gave us the plan for the U.N. intervention. Both Dick and I rushed to cable our stories, but Providence handled it in a way that periodically gives correspondents apoplexy.

That Saturday a subeditor on duty at the *Journal* was one of those editors who believe that serious news, including any story with a foreign dateline, is unimportant and the only real news items people are interested in are the latest sex episode in the life of a celebrity or a zany accident in Twin Falls, Idaho. My story was on a deep inside page of the Sunday *Providence Journal* and the rest of the country's front pages had stories that began with phrases like, "The *St. Louis Post-Dispatch* said in a dispatch from Jerusalem yesterday that the United Nations will . . ."

»

My preference to view events from the bottom did not come from superior wisdom. My love for Uncle Fred and Grandpa Kalayjian may have sensitized me to how remote most of our news is from the lives of ordinary people and I had the disguised blessing of spending years on a serious medium-sized set of papers in a small state before I went to national publications. Still, I was as eager as most new reporters to have the easy access to famous newsmakers who are most readily accessible to big-time reporters.

The Providence papers had close to a monopoly in Rhode Island. I probably learned the dynamics of politics and politicians more quickly than if I had started as a cub reporter on a national paper reporting only on narrow slivers of other reporters' big stories. Once you have covered a lot of mayors of towns and small cities and the governor of a small state, and absorbed ordinary citizens' reactions to them, you are less dazzled by famous national and international holders of power who, as James Reston once wrote, draw on their trousers every morning one leg at a time like lesser mortals. You discover that the more powerful hierarchs too often differ mainly in having a different brand of rhetoric, more secretaries, more skilled media handlers—and greater personal remoteness from the realities of ordinary life.

By the time of the Little Rock school crisis in 1957 I was only momentarily envious as I watched Dr. Benjamin Fine, the solemn education editor from the *New York Times*, descend the stairs of his airliner from New York, leather briefcase firmly in hand, and be ushered into a waiting municipal car to be driven immediately to City Hall for a briefing and exclusive interview with a waiting group that included the mayor, the chief of police, and the superintendent of schools. Later, he and the *Times* did, of course, report some of the popular reactions in Little Rock, but the initial view was heavily weighted as seen from those on top.

Having no choice, like most of my peers gathered in Little Rock during that unfolding crisis, I landed in anonymity and took a cab to the second best hotel where a group of older men in wide green suspenders sitting in the lobby rocking chairs suddenly stopped their conversation and eyed me coldly as I approached the desk clerk. I immediately visited the offices of the top officials in the city and the State Capitol, where I was handed a day-old press release and told I could join group briefings the next day.

But by then I had learned the advantage of getting a feel for what was going on away from the executive offices. I spent time talking to lesser officials who knew as much or more than their bosses and talked more frankly. I talked to people in the working-class homes in neighborhoods around the school and discovered that they were not all the people in the news photographs, screaming hysterically at black children. They weren't happy with integration but some were resigned to it, and a few even found reasons to accept it.

(My ego was massaged by later seeing a footnote in a sociologist's book about the Little Rock crisis that said I was the only correspondent in the news he examined who discovered that one source of the public anger was that top city officials had transferred their own children from Central High before ordering the school to enroll black students. That came from talking to ordinary people in the small cottages around the school. It let me ask leaders questions about a matter they would never have volunteered.)

Not being a famous reporter from a famous news organization has its technical problems. At Little Rock, when the final day came for the black students to enter the school escorted by the United States Army, something like two hundred reporters and foreign correspondents gathered to watch. The telephone company had put in a few temporary phone booths on a nearby corner but they were all for the wire services and biggest papers. When Central High opened and the black children did or did not enter successfully, it would be deadline time for a lot of Eastern afternoon papers, including my own, and for all radio and TV stations.

I went to Park Avenue in front of the school at 6:00 A.M. and already the residents were on their porches and front lawns, watching the solid line of Army soldiers standing stiffly a few feet apart around the school property. The soldiers looked formidable. I struck up a conversation with a kindly-looking, elderly Ms. Flowers who lived in a tiny cottage directly across the street from the front steps of the high school, a perfect vantage point. We discussed what it must be like to wake up with soldiers on your street and what she thought this all meant for the future. It was an amiable chat and in due course I told her that at about nine o'clock it would be very important for me to have a phone to call my paper and I would be happy to pay her to use her phone for a collect call. She seemed quite agreeable and was delighted to take my five dollars.

At nine o'clock, as the students successfully entered the school, I ran to Ms. Flowers' front door and there I bumped into Stan Opotowski of the *New York Post*, also reaching for the front door to Ms. Flowers' house, but I interposed.

"Sorry, Stan, but I've reserved this phone with the lady who lives here."

"What are you talking about!" Stan demanded. "I've got it reserved. I paid her to reserve it for me."

At that point, a third man, from NBC Radio, ran up. We both told him we had the phone reserved. He was indignant because he, too, had paid the gentle lady (both of them had paid a lot more than I had). In the argument, I rushed in to the phone only to find it was a party line in the neighborhood, busy with some other correspondent who made it clear that I should get off the line. Nice Ms. Flowers had oversold her phone three times and all three scheming reporters got their comeuppance.

That's when I ran to the nearest public phone blocks away and had my dictation interrupted by two angry segregationists, whom I beat in a highly competitive road race until I reached the perimeter of soldiers. There I immediately assumed a more dignified pace as I passed a fine young American private first class.

»

It is inevitable in coverage of large public issues that the words from the top will dominate the news. But it doesn't follow that these words are the whole story or even the true story. Leaders know only what their underlying chain of communications filters upward, and even when they know most of the story, they seldom tell it all. Periodically, they feel it necessary to lie "for the public good," and when they do they sometimes come to believe their lies.

Furthermore, top executives are more likely to be wedded to policies or ideologies that influence their interpretation of whatever information they get. Leaders of democracies have some restraints to prevent them from suppressing bothersome information, but they are no less vulnerable to theories they believe in. Herbert Hoover was demonstrably a man of intelligence but he sincerely believed in policies that drove the country deeper into the Great Depression.

Lyndon Johnson and Richard Nixon were men of considerable intelligence and knowledge, but these two relentless politicians found themselves the victims not only of their own lies but of their own self-delusion. Those lies and delusions cost more than a million lives in Vietnam and threatened to shred the American social fabric.

The journalist's antidote to the fallibility of leaders is to look as honestly and diligently as possible at the world over which the leaders have power. That is not always easy. The view from the top often is also the view of the news entrepreneur, who tends to share the values of others who administer pyramids of power. The results in the news can be dismal. In economic affairs, the greedy strategies of junk bonds and takeovers based on crushing debt in the 1980s were reported in terms of the glamour kings of Wall Street, largely as "miracles," "imaginative financing," and "discipline in the economy." It was a flawed view that nevertheless appealed to powerful leaders in the news media who were loath to take persistent pains to examine the evidence of the flaws in those official versions of the real world.

Those shared values among the country's leaders prevailed so persistently in the 1980s that by the time reality crashed in, the country was broke, deeply in debt, and in a stubborn recession. Yet, it was a debacle most news treated as though it had come unbidden from heaven.

It is no accident that smaller magazines and isolated stories in large ones often discover flaws in the top-down view of the world that dominates standard news. An annual exercise called Project Censored (of which I have been one of the several judges during many of its years) lists the ten most important stories that the judges feel the mainstream news failed to report or treated with casual neglect. Year after year, most of the stories became public only through small publications and reports. If those stories finally received proper attention from the major media it was too late to help the public, or the stories never did appear prominently.

In 1993, for example, the unreported or underreported stories in the mainstream news included important public information that as a result of deductions the largest recipients of government tax benefits are major American corporations, and that for years the CIA had been working cooperatively with drug-dealing high Haitian military dictators.

Most of these stories appeared in small magazines, a few in large newspapers, but all quickly disappeared in the standard news in favor of more glamorous ones or news more congenial to high public and private holders of power. The truth does not reside exclusively in the offices of the high and mighty around which most journalism is clustered.

»

Like so much else good and bad in the news, television has magni fied everything. The medium, nationally and locally, in conventional broadcasting and in cable, competes for something "new" and "dramatic" every moment in order to freeze the hand tempted to change channels. The winners of that competition are quickly rewarded with higher revenues from commercials. That obsession makes it easier than ever for sophisticated newsmakers to fashion the timing and wording of their announcements and photo opportunities, knowing that in the race to be first, the staged event is reported, often on cam era, without taking time to put it into a larger context and without examining realities outside the newsmaker's office.

That first perception of a news event, whether in the mind of a reporter or of the public, tends to be the frame in which everyone fits everything that follows, like the human eye that stares too long at a brightly lighted image and continues to "see" its afterimage.

The rush to be first with news from the top did not originate with television. Papers have always done the same thing with a vengeance. But television with its near-universal audience and its ability to implant vivid images in the mind is more long lasting.

I saw the way television would change the role of American news in my first year as a Washington correspondent. I covered the last press conference of President Eisenhower in January 1961. As I look back, even its location was symbolic of a dying era. The conference was held in the Indian Treaty Room, a small chamber full of sixteenth-century-style baroque decoration, inside the Executive Office Building, that great Victorian pile next to the White House to which the president could stroll for his periodic press conferences.

Inside the Indian Treaty Room, the leading print correspondents were in the front row of seats, only a few feet from the president, with receding rows of reporters arrayed according to the size and power of each correspondent's newspaper. Jammed into the last rows were the television cameras, great bulky machines on tripods, their film not releasable for television news until edited by the White House.

The conference ended, as usual, when after roughly a half hour, the senior wire service correspondent, Merriman Smith of United Press, said, "Thank you, Mr. President." In that instant, the doorkeeper opened the doors and there began the bizarre event that ended every presidential press conference.

The wire services used to boast that they had "a deadline every minute" because they provided the news to thousands of newspapers and broadcast stations in every time zone of the world. They competed by seconds and minutes. As their correspondents burst out of the Indian Treaty Room, they ran pell-mell at an unseemly speed, many of the men middle-aged, stout, and red-faced, all rushing to a nearby phone where someone held the line open for their man. Muffled fast talk could be heard as the correspondents rapidly dictated the leads and first several paragraphs of what they had mentally composed as they made notes on the president's unfolding questions and answers.

Those of us who did not have such urgent deadlines at the moment could employ the more dignified long-strided half-walk-half-run that reporters use when leaving a news scene to get to their offices as rapidly as possible without looking like bank robbers fleeing the police.

One week later, I covered the first press conference of the strikingly photogenic new president, John F. Kennedy. It was televised live from the cool State Department auditorium, half a mile from the White House. The presidential microphone was up on the stage, and the correspondents at a distance below in the auditorium's blue-cushioned seats. After thirty-six minutes, Merriman Smith called out his "Thank you, Mr. President," the doors opened, and Smith, his main competitor, Marvin Arrowsmith, of the Associated Press, and a few other correspondents started their all-out run toward telephones across the lobby.

But as I watched the habitual foot race, halfway down the lobby the running figures suddenly froze. It looked like a science-fiction movie in which a mysterious ray instantly stops people in their tracks, except that the frozen figures slowly developed embarrassed grins. It had just dawned on them that no rush was needed. Their shouted words into the nearest phone would be superfluous. So was their primacy in the role of giving the country the first word on a major news event. The whole press conference had already been seen as it unfolded in the living rooms and business offices all over the world.

In the correspondents' home offices—including mine—freshly purchased office TV sets had been rolled up to editors' desks, and reporters were knocking out stories as the questions and answers were shown on the screen, while editors constantly substituted new leads as they perceived that some new presidential response had greater significance—all while we correspondents were still seated in the auditorium.

National news would never again be the same.

Newspapers can no longer ignore what television news has shown about the world. By the early 1970s I was the first editor in charge of national news at the *Washington Post* who had to watch the three network evening newscasts in order to see what the public would have already heard the night before our paper came out. The idea was not to duplicate the news or discover something we had missed (that was rare), but to see what would be on people's minds before they ever saw our paper in the morning.

## »

I wish every executive producer of network news and editor of a major paper took a sabbatical in places like the hometown of a friend of mine, Dave Mitchell.

Dave owns and edits the *Point Reyes Light* in California, which won a Pulitzer Prize for pursuing a troublesome story about a drug treatment program in the region that had become corrupt and violent. The national networks and big metropolitan papers had dropped the story because they feared libel suits or simply lost interest.

Smalltown papers can be a delight to read because they so often get across the flavor of a real human community Once in the old Point Reyes Station Cafe, whose patrons sometimes arrive riding in a pickup truck or on a horse, I asked Dave how he stayed in touch so closely with the spread-out, semirural end of his county. He laughed.

"Right now, we're sitting at Table Six. Every morning, all the people who think they run things around here have coffee together at Table Six and either we sit with them or, like everybody else, we just drink our coffee, listen in, and talk back. It's hard to keep a secret in a town like this."

After Dave's paper won the Pulitzer, he was hired by the *San Francisco Examiner* as an investigative reporter, but after a while he quit and went back to the small *Point Reyes Light*. He missed Table Six and his constant immersion in community reality.

He made me realize that all of American journalism needs something of Table Six that it now lacks—a sense of the whole community.

Daily newspapers go into the households of the more affluent top two-thirds of the population. Though not all of those readers have significant wealth, the contents of big-city papers are devoted more to the interests and needs of the most affluent. Advertisers and the financially well-off get most of the attention. Few dusty pick-ups or horseback riders are evident.

Broadcasting belongs to advertisers, lock, stock, and soul. Programs are as much designed for advertisers with the hope of attracting viewers as for viewers with a hope of attracting advertisers. It is common to show a pilot of a program first to advertisers to see if it is acceptable. Even "noncommercial" television is now so dependent on corporate sponsorship that over the years it has moved in the same direction, avoiding programs such as genuinely uninhibited and controversial public affairs documentaries because corporate sponsors have always been wary of any program that might alienate some customers. That's why "educational television" was created, but it is so poorly and so politically funded—unlike the BBC in England and NHK in Japan—that it has become, with all its good but shrinking programming, more and more a minor commercial network.

In the process, a voice for the needs and wants of the less affluent half of the American population becomes ever fainter in the country's mainstream news.

## CHAPTER 15

## Cardiac Therapy for Me (And the News?)

I n 1988, on a flight from New York, about two hours away from San Francisco I had a heart attack. My first reaction was puzzlement and then indignation: I do not have heart attacks. Then pain surpassed arrogance. "Marlene, I'm afraid I'm having chest pains."

When the plane landed, the ambulance was waiting on the tarmac.

That is when I discovered that lying on your back inside an ambulance wondrously clarifies your priorities. For that moment, I knew that when I was better—still arrogant, at no time did the thought occur to me that I might die—I would try to spend the rest of my life attending to what truly counts.

From then on, I would not shield my sensing of life by petty conceits and I would experience fully the human beings closest to my heart. Marlene was with me in the ambulance.

As we rode to the hospital, I somehow knew with greater clarity that almost all human beings are potentially decent and unselfish—if their society stresses those qualities as truly important. Perhaps the thought was also triggered when the ambulance stopped at a traffic light and a large woman driving a truck behind us blew me a kiss.

I spent the usual few days in darkened hospital rooms as an item in loops of wires and tubes feeding wavy yellow lines on electronic monitors. Then I was moved to a room that looked out over the beautiful Berkeley hills. The hillsides never looked more vibrant or the live oak trees more dramatic. I could see tiny figures moving rapidly, kids playing with leaps of exuberance. After the gloom of Intensive Care, the sun-drenched sight was like a blow to the senses. I felt that I would never again look at life around me with jaded eyes.

Inevitably, the intensity of that vision faded once I was out from under the hospital sheets and once more going up stairs two at a time. It turned out not to be a truly bad attack. But I have never forgotten what my heart attack gave me: unjaded eyes and a clear sense of my priorities in life.

I wish American journalism could share those ambulance perceptions. I do not wish it a heart attack, but I do wish it an attack of heart.

When I decided in the mid-1960s to write a book on the technical changes that would transform the media, including my own profession, it was not out of pessimism but hope for journalism. I think it was not coincidental that I wrote that in the 1960s, a decade full of both hope and change. For me, it was a liberating decade, the most creative one in my lifetime. Despite the darkening cloud of the Vietnam War, or perhaps because of it, the civil rights struggles created new ideas, new personal values, new aesthetics, new demands for racial equality, new examinations of how we educate the young, and new desires to find humanism in an overcommercialized national life.

In my tiny corner of the decade, it also accelerated changes in my life and in the directions of my journalism.

»

Leaving the *Springfield Morning Union* had been easy. The war had changed my perspective, and to return to the shallow, doctrinaire ways of Sherman Bowles's paper was out of the question. Besides, I aspired to become "a writer."

People leaving wartime services became eligible for the "52-20 Club," a subsidy of $20 a week for one year for re-entry to civilian life. That would not be enough to support my free-lance writing and a growing family in our Providence flat. So when my friend Elmer from the Air Corps said the flying magazine where he worked needed a writer-editor, I was off to New York.

Before long, I found myself the editor, shaping a new air travel magazine for a publisher full of "sky's-the-limit" promises for my budget. I discovered that "sky's the limit" is publishing's version of the lecher telling a woman, "Trust me." I quit when I discovered that the owner would agree with my pay requisitions to artists and writers, then send them half the agreed amount. To my protest, he said "You have to know how to deal with these bloodsuckers," so I bid goodbye to the bloodsucker.

In those first postwar years, trying to rent an advertised New York rental apartment usually required a white family and a stiff "fee" slipped under the counter to the building superintendent, money I couldn't afford, and I returned to Providence.

I spent sixteen years on the Providence papers, most of them happy ones. I liked doing fast stories and rewrites, but with time found myself doing longer series that were a better way for achieving fairness and balance in journalism than simply quoting the rhetoric of opposing politicians.

When John Kennedy won the election in November of 1960, I was assigned to be chief of the Washington bureau, but after a year I took a promised leave to use a Guggenheim Fellowship. I was lucky that the fellowship provided too little money to support my family. That made me eager to accept the invitation of an old friend, Don Oberdorfer, then working at a newly energized *Saturday Evening Post*, to take time from my fellowship research to do a handsomely paid story for the magazine.

The story was on the Student Non-Violent Coordinating Committee breaking the color line in Southern voting. My living and traveling with young, black students in Mississippi and Alabama made me realize that daily news reporting was no longer enough. More and more, I wanted to do stories and books in greater depth. Just as most of my years at the Providence papers had been happy ones, the five on a generous contract from the *Saturday Evening Post* in its liberal reincarnation were happier still, free to select the stories I wanted, and supported in as much time and research as I needed to get more than quick looks at national problems and the human beings caught up in them.

I didn't return to the Providence papers. Though the paper's parsimony made it easier, I was leaving mainly because the paper, under a new publisher and set of subeditors, was suffering from an affliction that periodically strikes newspapers like a rash: the desire of new editors to look like hard-boiled realists insisting that nobody is really interested in serious news, that readers want only to be entertained. The subtext usually is that most people are dumb. Nobody wants dull, badly written stories, but in the real world people are serious and undumb about the central concerns of their lives. But I liked and respected the Providence papers for what they had done in the past and I felt, correctly, they would resume when the rash disappeared. When I left, I told the top people what worried me about the paper.

» 

But the days of the three big, glossy, general-circulation magazines like the *Saturday Evening Post*, *Look*, and *Life* were numbered. By the late 1960s, most of the country's households had changed their old black-and-white TV for color sets, and the four-color, mass-sales advertisements that had been the economic lifeblood for the Big Three general-circulation magazines went to the new medium and, a century after their birth, big unspecialized magazines died.

I had written a "Letter from Washington" for every issue of the *Columbia Journalism Review* since its creation in 1961. In late 1967 before I left for Rand in California to do a book on the forthcoming electronic changes in the mass media, I wrote my last "Letter" about my morning paper, the *Washington Post*. I said it was the most irritating paper I knew because it was within "a lunge" of greatness but was not great. It had too much editorial policy evident in the news, it was inconsistent and loosely put together, yet it had all the raw ingredients I thought were needed to make a great paper.

In my last year at Rand, a call from Ben Bradlee at the *Post* led to a lunch with him and Managing Editor Gene Patterson. They asked if I would be interested in becoming an assistant managing editor to take over the National Staff. It was a put-up-or-shut-up challenge about the "lunge" and hard to decline. After I agreed, I had a meeting in a Beverly Hills hotel with Katharine Graham, who seemed to have an appealing mix of being both openly searching and firm, and the president of the Post Company at the time, Paul Ignatius, whom I also liked, not so much because of his Armenian background, but because he seemed more warm and open than most other news company executives I had met.

After my first year at the *Post*, Gene Patterson had called a meeting of subeditors to say that for the first time in an annual survey of Washington's two thousand most influential men and women, when asked which paper they would read if they could read only one, the *Post* had come out first. Since most movers and shakers in Washington are interested mainly in national news and every day read the *New York Times*, *Wall Street Journal*, and the *Post*, I felt progress had been made.

I liked my job and appreciated the newsroom's lack of bureaucracy. It was often lighthearted, even at the midafternoon news conference when editors bid for space and submitted summaries of stories for Page One. Once when the Foreign Editor nominated a profile of the new leader of Cambodia, Lon Nol, and Bradlee asked impatiently, "Why the hell should we have his profile on Page One on a big news day?" the Foreign Editor offered, hopefully, "Well, you have to admit, he's the only head of state in the world with a name that's a palindrome."

The Metropolitan Area Editor, Harry Rosenfeld, always jealous that National received the lion's share of space on Page One, and knowing Bradlee's weaknesses, always presented his stories with all the drama and gestures of a tireless ham actor. One day another editor, Larry Stern, and I hired a gypsy violinist from a Hungarian restaurant and as Harry began his one-man conference performance, at our signal, from just outside the conference room, the sound of schmaltzy gypsy laments came through to the conference. Bradlee was delighted, and Harry rose to the occasion, crying, "Play, gypsy, play!" But poor Harry's story still didn't make Page One.

Nevertheless, increasingly I missed reporting and writing. I had asked one of the most hard-nosed reporters on the National Staff, Bernard Nossiter, to begin a preliminary look to see if my hunch was correct that the country was about to see one of its periodic national crises from overcrowded, inhumane, and self-defeating prison conditions. Just as Nossiter was about to begin his national research, he was offered what he most wanted, the paper's London Bureau. I decided that after two years, it was time for me to stop running the National Desk and do some national reporting, and after the disastrous riot at Attica prison in New York, I began a prison series, in which, after months of research, I had myself secretly incarcerated in a maximum security prison in the Pennsylvania mountains to see what it was like on the other side of the bars.

My decision to leave the National Desk seemed more natural because other changes were occurring in my life. Moving to Washington was hard on the family. The war years and the ones in Providence were full of family adventures and the vicissitudes of growing boys. Now there was scattering, Chris to his own career and Eric to college.

In Providence a close circle of friends had made a difference for Betty during the usual family illnesses and adventures and my reporting trips. Life had much of the richness it had for both of us in wartime days. There were friends in Washington, but it is a city full of transients obsessed with fixed-agenda conversations on high-powered politics and journalism. Hours in the *Journal* bureau were often late, the office serving both the afternoon and the morning paper. Later, I was away traveling for the *Saturday Evening Post*. After two years of more normal family life during my research and writing in Santa Monica for the book at Rand, the return to Washington brought even more demanding hours at the *Washington Post*.

It was not an easy life at home with both children out of the nest and my being absorbed in a demanding job covering national news during two turbulent years of Richard Nixon's second term. After a year it led to a separation and then a divorce.

When I approached Bradlee about stepping down and doing the prison series, he agreed and said my successor would be Dick Harwood, the man I had succeeded but who would again take over national news. Bradlee said that after my prison stories, I should take over as the paper's second ombudsman. It was one of Bradlee's typical horizontal movements of editors, known in the newsroom as "Bradlee cushion shots."

Bradlee's appointments, reappointments, and creation of new chief assistant editors moved a newsroom satirist to post a notice on the bulletin board: "A meeting of all Washington Post Assistant Managing Editors will be held at 8 tonight in the Ballroom of the Mayflower Hotel."

With some reluctance I took the ombudsman's job but failed to convince him to drop my title as Assistant Managing Editor. I didn't think a critique of the paper was best done by someone with a title that implied some control over the content being criticized.

Tensions in the *Post* hierarchy were always high, perhaps natural on a paper full of talented and ambitious journalists led by a man who was quick-witted, unpredictable, and charming. The staff called him "the international jewel thief," a title I think he enjoyed. In the last months of my time at the *Post*, the newsroom adopted a policy that had a brief vogue in industry, "controlled tension," which pitched employees against each other. It caused a brief strike. The policy was renamed "creative tension," the whole idea silly because good reporting comes from good reporters who have confidence in sensitive and clear-headed editors. The plotting and rising unpleasantness did what it had been designed to do, make a man like Patterson resign. After a too-brief farewell gathering of newsroom people, I winced when Bradlee's sendoff was that Patterson had been the best Irish tenor in the newsroom. Gene smiled fixedly through it all, but at its end, as he dashed out the door, I heard him say passionately, "Let me get the hell out of this place."

By this time, I had met and married Betty Medsger, who had fled the grimy depression and religious rigidity of her hometown of Johnstown, Pennsylvania, by way of college, and then reporting, including a job on the *Philadelphia Evening Bulletin* and now the *Post*, where she edited the religion page.

The prison series seemed successful. But afterward, as ombudsman, I know some of my columns did not sit well. The *Post* was the first

paper in the country to have an in-house ombudsman-critic. I was enthusiastic because I had first called for such a person in a 1957 magazine article. I wanted experienced men and women to criticize newspapers and journalism the way papers criticized plays, music, and art.
But the *Post* had never carefully defined their place. I assumed that I
would write pretty much as I always had in journalism reviews. But
there was some bitterness after I did a column on a formal suit that the
paper's minority staff members had brought charging racial discrimi-
nation in the newsroom. I wrote that their lawsuit should have been
reported in the paper, as a similar suit by minorities within any other
well-known liberal organization in the city would have been.

There was also an incident from which my relations with Bradlee
never fully recovered. Invited to serve on a panel at Harvard on minorities and the news media, we panelists were supposed to respond to a
paper by the Congressional Black Caucus. I agreed with one point,
that there were far too few African-Americans hired and promoted in
the news media, for example, but I disputed one basic premise in the
Caucus's statement: "Mass communications in this country have been
used primarily for the purpose of oppressing non-whites."

I said if the Caucus wished to change the media, it had to understand the media better, and one thing it had to understand was that
whatever the racial policies of a news organization might be, the media's primary purpose was not to oppress blacks but to make money.
The argument became heated. I thought some of the black representatives were making bombastic defenses of the statement for the benefit
of the reporters covering the event. We argued heatedly. In growing
impatience, I posed to them what may have been an unwise hypothetical question: if they thought I was wrong, did they suppose that in cities with a majority black audience, like Washington, D.C., that blacks
would get a paper's attention more readily by calling it racist or threatening to boycott it?

When I returned to Washington, the newsroom was almost empty
but a note on my desk said to see Bradlee at once. He was alone in
his office.

He coldly handed me a torn sheet from the Associated Press wire machine. The AP had quoted one phrase of mine about the boycott but not its hypothetical context. Bradlee was pointing to that one quotation.

"Did you say those words?"

I said the quoted words were correct but had been said in a context that made it clear what I was getting at. But he couldn't wait to let out his anger:

"I can't believe it! My own lieutenant! Calling for a boycott of his own paper!"

I couldn't make him understand that I had not called for a boycott, that it was a hypothetical question about any newspaper. The word disloyalty began to enter the angry exchange. "That's more than I can take! You've been disloyal to the paper and you've been disloyal to me."

I said it sounded as though he wanted my resignation. His reply was noncommital.

I wrote out my resignation at my desk. When I had finished Bradlee had left the office and I put my sealed envelope on his desk. I also wrote a note to Kay Graham explaining my statement in Cambridge.

It was Friday and I spent the weekend thinking of what I would work at next. Very early Monday morning I received a phone call from Bradlee.

"Buddy, forget what I said. I need you. Come on back and let's talk."

I did go back, but it was never the same afterward and a year later, I resigned for good.

Somehow, even before I started cleaning out my desk, word had passed through the ever-present gossip circuits, and a story in *Time* magazine brought other job offers, to be dean of a journalism school or chair of a department, and even to teach political science.

Betty Medsger had become restless in her job, the office's "creative tension" had made work life less pleasant, and she left to spend time working on a book of photographs of unusual jobs now held by women. We traveled on our separate projects, she to places like coal mines in Kentucky and I on a book contract for a second book on prisons and jails.

We both had come to love Northern California. Washington's local industry of politics-journalism-and-lobbying and atmosphere of a specialized company town seemed to make Berkeley more attractive than ever. Berkeley looked beautiful, the San Francisco Bay Area had great university libraries, and the population was more lively and varied than the specialists who populated northwest Washington.

A few nights before our move, at a party in the home of a congressman, another guest, Sen. Gaylord Nelson, whom I had always liked, came toward me, booming (Senator Nelson always "boomed"), "What's this I hear about your going to Berkeley? You have to see my old A.A., Ed Bayley. He's dean of the journalism school out there. I'll call him tomorrow and tell him to speak to you. You've got to teach there."

Bayley, the former chief political reporter for the *Milwaukee Journal* (and later assistant to Governor Nelson) was on leave in New York from his deanship to write a book on how the press had dealt with Senator Joseph McCarthy. I went to New York and liked him at once, a man with a hesitant, almost bashful presence, but strong ideas. He asked me to teach a course and the next year was an enthusiastic supporter when I became a full professor in the Graduate School of Journalism. I stayed for more than fourteen happy years, but Betty and I decided to part amicably after a few years and took advantage of California's laws for uncontested divorces. We remain friends, probably encouraged by those civilized laws.

>>

One night I attended a Berkeley dinner party where the guest of honor was a well-known New York journalist and writer, a man I knew and admired. He charmed the dinner party in the standard role of a celebrity being lionized by folks in the provinces. I enjoyed watching, because, given the lecture circuit demands on best-seller authors, inevitably their dinner-party performances become as fixed as Chinese ritual drama. The man was playing it perfectly, with modestly murmured heroic war stories. As my eye strayed for a moment, I noticed a woman across from me at the dinner table, observing with exactly the same kind of smile the perfection of the performance. We caught each other at our similar inner thoughts and that is how I first met Marlene Griffith.

Like me, Marlene had been an immigrant. Members of her family had long been a part of prewar Vienna's intellectual and artistic life, but when Hitler marched into Austria, her family had escaped to the United States while Marlene was still a young girl. Marlene did her graduate work at Berkeley and was teaching English at Laney College in Oakland. We were married in a judge's chambers in San Francisco City Hall.

My years on the faculty of the University of California, somewhat to my surprise, gave me satisfaction comparable to that of reporting and writing, which the university leaves permitted me to continue for various national magazines. The Graduate School of Journalism was my kind of journalism education, a two-year graduate program for students who had completed four years of a liberal arts degree and had made mature decisions about their life work. We taught only print and broadcast journalism and public affairs documentary production— none of the advertising, public relations, or communications theory that too many college programs confuse with journalism. In my three years as dean I hoped to encourage teaching what American news most needed, which was skill and discipline, but also a sense of ethics and a social sensitivity often passed over lightly in quick news.

The school turned out the best hope for the future of American journalism and I gained some of our best young friends who now are journalists or produce public affairs documentaries. They do it, unfortunately, with some of the old familiar problems.

》

Not long ago, I had a sobering experience while taking part in a panel of journalists at Harvard's Center on Press, Politics, and Public Policy. My fellow panelists were among our best contemporary professionals. They were not the most famous and lavishly paid, but the most serious and thoughtful in mainstream American journalism. I read, watch, and listen to them regularly. The audience around the big square of the conference room in the Kennedy Center was a collection of other senior journalists, academics, and Harvard graduate students studying public policy.

After the session broke up, two youngish men, unknown to each other, asked to speak to me privately. Both, one of them a journalist, were experienced in their fields. Both had been there to find something closer to what, to them, was important in journalism, and both, independently, came away dismayed.

The two men were shocked because our panel, myself included, had spent all the time in a symposium entitled "Press and Politics" on how reporters should relate to public figures. It seemed to the two men like folklorists' stories about squabbles among the mythical Greek gods on top of Olympus and how the media gods and the political gods "relate" to each other. Nowhere in that discussion, the two men said, did we talk about whether how these parties "related" to each other had anything to do with the concerns of ordinary Americans whose household budgets, schooling, jobs, and culture are so profoundly shaped by the way the press treats politics and public issues. What difference did the relationship of these two elites make if not to the consequences for families across the country?

The two men were right.

Were we in a field that is mainly some legendary playground of the gods? So what if Paris kidnaps Helen, Zeus has a penchant for good-looking women, and Achilles is on the disabled list with heel problems?

Too much of our national reporting makes legends of political gods with endless detail on the speculations, warnings, encouragements, markings in the sand by pollsters and reading of entrails by soothsayers of Wall Street, the exchange rate killing made by King Midas, and the projected quarterly earnings of the builder who won the lumber contract for that odd-looking horse outside the wall of Troy. Like the Greek legends, our news concentrates on conflict and personalities but does not report much about what it means to the people who live at the bottom of Olympus. News as folklore of the deities is not enough.

A better central theme for our reporting is what politics and economics do to advance or defeat social justice. The conventions of our trade claim that social justice is in the eye of the beholder and therefore cannot be "objective" reporting. But in a democracy, is basic social justice really a matter of personal opinion?

As a principle in standard journalism, I prefer "fairness and balance" to "objectivity." And good reporting can go beyond personal opinion if it concentrates on the fundamentals of social justice in any democracy:

It is better to be fed than to starve, to be healthy than needlessly diseased, to be properly housed than live in decrepitude, to get a good education in a learning environment rather than be stuffed with irrelevance in a setting of squalor, to work rather than to be idle—to have a decent regard for the health of the whole community instead of a heedless race of every individual for personal gain alone.

Lapses and failures in the struggle for a better democracy deserve a commanding place in the national dialogue, which means in the news. That is what I mean when I say that I do not wish my profession to have a heart attack, but an attack of heart.

Our journalism needs to emphasize its own double vision. We need the cold-eyed reporting of the factual realities of the streets, the police station, the neighborhoods, the politics, the legislatures, the stock market and the nations of the world. But we need constantly to measure how this cold-eyed vision helps or hinders the achievement of true democracy and genuine social justice.

》

Producing truthful news has always been complicated because the news—presumably truthful information selected by news professionals—has to live under the same roof as advertising—a sales pitch to sell goods and services. The answer is to keep them in strictly separate quarters, but it has been a hard lesson for the media industry to learn.

When Harold Evans, once editor of *Times of London*, came to the United States, he said the challenge for American newspapers "is not to stay in business—it is to stay in journalism."

I found it easier to stay in journalism because there have been changes for the better. From the time of my first job on a newspaper,

I have seen both the public and journalists show heightened expectations for competent, honest news. The old "BOMs," Business Office Musts ordering reporters to write ads as news, are no longer acceptable and the pressure to make news the handmaiden of advertising and owners' private ambitions has had to take more subtle forms.

The battle continues. Scarcely a week goes by when I do not receive phone calls from reporters or editors in various parts of the country asking what can be done about clumsy attempts by their organization to twist the news to support an advertiser or the personal politics of the management. I tell them to do their homework in gathering convincing instances in their own newspaper or broadcast news, join likeminded colleagues in the newsroom, and arrange a civil meeting with their top editor. And I usually add, "Never underestimate the guilty conscience of an editor."

Executive editors are the crucial gateway to the news and too often have to choose between their independent professional judgment and pressures to make news more supportive of advertising and the corporate owner's concealed goals.

With each passing year more of our printed and broadcast news has become the property of large national and multinational corporations, with news staffs—and editors—shrinking in visibility within giant firms.

That is why I favor the election of the top editor for a fixed term by professional news staffs of large print and broadcast operations. For decades, some of the most distinguished papers in Britain, France, and Germany, among others *Le Monde* in Paris, have had their executive editors elected by the staff that reports the news.

Over the years, I have spoken to hundreds of local groups of journalists—city or county gatherings of reporters—and overwhelmingly, they are concerned with ethics and socially responsible reporting, and often dismayed at the needless inadequacies of their own newspaper or broadcast station. But they feel small and isolated in hundreds of cities. They need a single, large national voice that can let them speak collectively with more power than they have today.

There are national organizations of specialized reporters, in science, health, food, and other fields, but they are mainly concerned with technical problems and skills. Even so, most of them have been a useful influence on the ethics and skills of reporters within those specialties.

There has been a start for general bonding of all national reporters in the reporters' union, The Newspaper Guild, but it covers only a minority of newsrooms, and has had to struggle as automation has made it easier for newspapers to eliminate, weaken, or prevent all unions.

There are the beginnings of a larger general voice in The Society of Professional Journalists. But at present, it, too, has mostly small, scattered, local chapters with a total national membership of only thirteen thousand, half of them students. It could be the nucleus of a truly representative national association limited to working professionals in newsrooms. It could be analogous, perhaps, to the American Association of University Professors. I have seen too much seriousness and commitment among American journalists to think that their collective decisions on an editor would be frivolous or unable to improve the news.

》

I have called this book *Double Vision* for a combination of reasons. As middle-class immigrants in a traditional New England town in the 1920s, my family and I were both insiders and outsiders. We journalists are also both insiders and outsiders; we have access to the inner workings of society but have to remain detached observers. I have spent much of my career with another double vision. I have been a reporter and editor generating news but I have simultaneously been a critic and commentator on the news.

Perhaps those double visions have been the reason I can fill this book with criticism, without diminishing my love of the work. I value journalism's real accomplishments, and with all my complaints, I value the shrinking number of enlightened publishers and owners. Now that the bitterness has long passed, I think warmly of that old international jewel thief, Ben Bradlee.

Journalism is a profession in which I gladly spent my adult life. I found satisfactions in being an editor, a researcher, and an academic, but above everything else, I loved being a reporter.

With all its roller-coaster alternations of frustration and satisfaction, of the joy of working in a newsroom full of good ideas and enterprise, and grief when it falls into dull bureaucracy, for all the eternal office politics and conflicting ambitions within newsrooms, of breathless excitement followed by grinding tedium, of endemic underpayment because they know you like the work so much—it is still full of opportunity, excitement, individualism, and accomplishment.

Brushes with illness always heighten the sense of life. The wisdom of the Latin poet Horace two thousand years ago, *carpe diem*—capture the day, live the gift of each day of its fullest—has for years been the central principle of my life. "Capturing the day," it happens, is what journalism, in its own groping way, does every twenty-four hours.

I have never regretted the day many years ago when a chemical company interviewer was unexpectedly called to a meeting and permanently ended my planned entry to life as a chemist. It was that "accident" back in Springfield, Massachusetts, that led to my life as a journalist. It has given me an undeserved opportunity to see the life of my country with a variety of people, places, and circumstances I would never have chosen consciously. It has permitted me to learn about our society in ways that give me an endemic anger at continuing social injustice and the unnecessary weaknesses of my own profession. But it has also let me witness the decent instincts of ordinary men and women who despite all the unfair punishments of history confirm the resilience of the human psyche.

My years at Berkeley let me see a new generation of journalists ready, if given half a chance, to push their own small grain of sand onto a more benevolent shoreline. And when from time to time, some student asks if I were choosing my life work all over again, would I be a reporter, I always answer without hesitation, "You bet I would."